The Developing Labor Law

Fifth Edition

2007 Supplement

(covering 2006)

BNA Books Authored by the
ABA Section of Labor and Employment Law

Age Discrimination in Employment Law, 2006 Supplement

Covenants Not to Compete: A State-by-State Survey

The Developing Labor Law

Discipline and Discharge in Arbitration

Elkouri & Elkouri: How Arbitration Works

Employee Benefits Law

Employee Duty of Loyalty: A State-by-State Survey

Employment Discrimination Law

Employment Termination: Rights and Remedies, 2003 Supplement

Equal Employment Law Update

The Fair Labor Standards Act

The Family and Medical Leave Act

How ADR Works

How to Take a Case Before the NLRB

International Labor and Employment Laws

Labor Arbitration: A Practical Guide for Advocates

Labor Arbitration: Cases and Materials for Advocates

Labor Arbitrator Development: A Handbook

Labor Union Law and Regulation

Occupational Safety and Health Law

The Railway Labor Act

Tortious Interference in the Employment Context: A State-by-State Survey

Trade Secrets: A State-by-State Survey

Wage and Hour Laws: A State-by-State Survey

The Developing Labor Law

The Board, the Courts, and
the National Labor Relations Act

Fifth Edition

2007 Supplement

(covering 2006)

Editors-in-Chief

W.V. Bernie Siebert
Sherman & Howard LLC
Denver, CO

Paul Iversen
Williams & Iversen, PA
Roseville, MN

Barry J. Kearney
National Labor Relations Board
Washington, DC

Committee on the Development of the Law
Under the National Labor Relations Act
Section of Labor & Employment Law
American Bar Association

BNA Books, *A Division of BNA*, Arlington, VA

Library of Congress Cataloging-in-Publication Data

The developing labor law : the board, the courts, and the National Labor Relations Act / editor in chief, John E. Higgins, Jr. ... [et al.]. -- 5th ed.
    p. cm.
Includes index.
ISBN-13: 978-1-57018-572-4 (set)
ISBN-10: 1-57018-572-7 (set)
ISBN-13: 978-1-57018-584-7 (v.1)
ISBN-10: 1-57018-584-0 (v.1)
[etc.]
1. Labor laws and legislation--United States. 2. United States. National Labor Relations Act. 3. United States. National Labor Relations Board. I. Higgins, John E., 1939- II. American Bar Association. Committee on Development of the Law Under National Labor Relations Act. III. Title.

    KF3369.D48 2007
    344.7301--dc22

2006051672

Published by BNA Books, 1801 S. Bell Street, Arlington, VA 22202
bnabooks.com

ISBN 978-1-57018-629-5
Printed in Canada

BOARD OF EDITORS

Chapters 1–5—*(cont'd)*

Contributing Editors

GARY S. FEALK
Vercruysse Murray & Calzone
 PC
Bingham Farms, MI

DAVID E. KHOREY
KELLEY E. STOPPELS
Varnum, Riddering, Schmidt &
 Howlett LLP
Grand Rapids, MI

FREDERICK C. MINER
Ryley, Carlock & Applewhite
Phoenix, AZ

Chapter 6

Chapter Editors

ALLAN H. WEITZMAN
Proskauer Rose LLP
Boca Raton, FL

JEROME B. BUCKLEY, JR.
Carney, Buckley, Hays & Marsh
Portland, OR

Contributing Editors

MARIA ANASTAS
Davis Wright Tremaine LLP
San Francisco, CA

PAUL BOSANAC
National Labor Relations Board
Milwaukee, WI

LINDA BARGE-MILES
Tallahassee, FL

LOVIC A. BROOKS III
Ellzey & Brooks, LLC
Columbia, SC

DENISE BARTON WARD
Littler Mendelson P.C.
Melville, NY

RICHARD R. CARNEY
PING TOW-WORAM
Carney, Buckley, Hays & Marsh
Portland, OR

WILLIAM BEVAN III
Reed, Smith, Shaw & McClay
 LLP
Pittsburgh, PA

RICHARD L. CONNORS
Stinson, Morrison Hecker LLP
Overland Park, KS

STEPHANIE COTILLA
National Labor Relations
 Board
Baltimore, MD

JACOB H. BLACK
Robblee, Brennan & Detwiler
Seattle, WA

PEGGY DAVIS
Winston & Strawn LLP
Chicago, IL

JAMES R. DICKENS
Miller Nash LLP
Seattle, WA

JOHN R. DOLL
Logothetis, Pence & Doll
Dayton, OH

HENRY E. FARBER
Davis Wright Tremaine LLP
Bellevue, WA

THOMAS S. GIOTTO
Klett Rooney Lieber &
    Schorling
Pittsburgh, PA

ROBERT GUERRA
National Labor Relations
    Board
New York, NY

MEL R. KANG
ROBERT H. LAVIT
Schwerin, Campbell & Barnard,
    LLP
Seattle, WA

EBIN KRIM
KEVIN MANARA
DOUGLAS STRASNICK
Proskauer Rose LLP
Boca Raton, FL

NICOLE CUDA PEREZ
Spivak, Lipton, Watanabe,
    Spivak & Moss LLP
West Orange, NJ

Chapter 7

Chapter Editors

THOMAS ALLISON
Allison, Slutsky & Kennedy, PC
Chicago, IL

ARTHUR F. SILBERGELD
Proskauer Rose LLP
Los Angeles, CA

Contributing Editors

QUESIYAH S. ALI
Worcester, MA

KEITH R. BOLEK
O'Donoghue & O'Donoghue
    LLP
Washington, DC

ROBERT K. CARROL
JOSHUA M. HENDERSON
Nixon Peabody LLP
San Francisco, CA

ANDREA S. CHRISTENSEN
Kaye Scholer, LLP
New York, NY

JOSEF S. GLYNIAS
TERRY L. POTTER
Blackwell, Sanders, Peper,
    Martin LLP
St. Louis, MO

A. JOHN HARPER III
Baker & Hostetler LLP
Houston, TX

Chapter 7—*(cont'd)*

BERNARD P. JEWELER
RAFAEL MORELL
Ogletree, Deakins, Nash, Smoak
    & Stewart, PC
Washington, DC

JOLYNNE MILLER
National Labor Relations
    Board
Washington, DC

N. ELIZABETH REYNOLDS
Allison, Slutsky & Kennedy, PC
Chicago, IL

ARTHUR B. SMITH, JR.
Ogletree, Deakins, Nash, Smoak
    & Stewart, PC
Chicago, IL

PETER C. SWANSON
Minneapolis, MN

Chapter 8

Chapter Editors

MARC J. BLOCH
Duvin, Cahn & Hutton
Cleveland, OH

WARREN H. PYLE
Pyle, Rome, Lichten &
    Ehrenberg, PC
Boston, MA

Contributing Editors

DONALD C. CARROLL
Law Offices of Carroll & Scully,
    Inc.
San Francisco, CA

J. MICHAEL COLLOTON
Moss & Barnett
Minneapolis, MN

PETER REED CORBIN
Ford & Harrison LLP
Jacksonville, FL

ELLEN J. DANNIN
Pennsylvania State University
University Park, PA

NATALE V. DINATALE
Durant, Nichols, Houston,
    Hodgson & Cortese-Costa,
    PC
Bridgeport, CT

JEFFREY T. JOHNSON
Holland & Hart LLP
Denver, CO

MARY THERESA METZLER
Ballard Spahr Andrews &
    Ingersoll, LLP
Philadelphia, PA

KELLI A. WEBB
Littler Mendelson P.C.
Cleveland, OH

Chapter 9

Chapter Editors

G. ROGER KING
Jones Day
Columbus, OH

RICHARD M. RESNICK
Sherman, Dunn, Cohen, Liefer
& Yellig PC
Washington, DC

Contributing Editors

JOHN K. BAKER
White and Williams LLP
Allentown, PA

REBECCA BENNETT
Jones Day
San Diego, CA

JULIA LAPIS BLAKESLEE
Winston & Strawn LLP
Los Angeles, CA

RICHARD S. BROOK
PATRICIA E. PALMERI
Law Offices of Richard S. Brook
Mineola, NY

FRANCIS X. DEE
McElroy, Deutsch, Mulvaney, &
Carpenter, LLP
Newark, NJ

COLLEEN A. DEEP
E. MICHAEL ROSSMAN
TODD L. SARVER
Jones Day
Columbus, OH

JEFFREY S. DUBIN
Huntington, NY

BRIAN EASLEY
Jones Day
Chicago, IL

ROBERT EDMUND
Porter, Wright, Morris & Arthur
LLP
Columbus, OH

SCOTT FELDMAN
Troutman Sanders LLP
New York, NY

NICOLE A. FLYNN
Eastman & Smith Ltd.
Toledo, OH

DAVID M. GLANSTEIN
JOEL M. GLANSTEIN
O'Donnell, Schwartz, Glanstein
& Lilly, LLP
New York, NY

MELISSA GRIFFIN
Bechtel Corp.
San Francisco, CA

HARRY JOHNSON
Jones Day
Los Angeles, CA

Chapter 9—*(cont'd)*

MICHAEL J. MOBERG
Briggs & Morgan, PA
Minneapolis, MN

JAMES S. URBAN
Jones Day
Pittsburgh, PA

ALAN R. PETERMAN
Hiscock & Barclay, LLP
Syracuse, NY

FREDERICK W. VOGT
Mackall, Crounse & Moore, PLC
Minneapolis, MN

GLENN H. SCHLABS
Sherman & Howard LLC
Colorado Springs, CO

CHARLES F. WASKEVICH
Herold and Haines, PA
Warren, NJ

Chapter 10

Chapter Editors

GIL A. ABRAMSON
Hogan & Hartson, LLP
Baltimore, MD

PAUL IVERSEN
Williams & Iversen, PA
St. Paul, MN

Contributing Editors

WILLIAM D. CLASTER
JAMES N. KNIGHT
Gibson, Dunn & Crutcher LLP
Irvine, CA

BRYCE G. MURRAY
Taggart, Morton, Ogden, Staub
   & O'Brien LLC
New Orleans, LA

JOHN H. CURLEY
AT&T
Bedminster, NJ

DAVID R. HANSEN
Denver, CO

LETICIA PEÑA
National Labor Relations
   Board
Denver, CO

DANIEL J. HOYING
Taft, Stettinius & Hollister LLP
Cincinnati, OH

E. FREDERICK PREIS, JR.
McGlinchey Stafford PLLC
New Orleans, LA

JILL A. MAY
Taft, Stettinius & Hollister LLP
Dayton, OH

LOUIS ROSNER
Philadelphia, PA

ROSALIND ROWEN-ROSSI
National Labor Relations
    Board
Brooklyn, NY

RICHARD C. RYBICKI
Dickenson, Peatman &
    Fogarty
Napa, CA

Chapter 11

Chapter Editors

TODD A. LYON
Williams Zografos & Peck
Lake Oswego, OR

MARY L. KNOBLAUCH
Anthony Ostlund & Baer, P.A.
Minneapolis, MN

Contributing Editors

NATHAN P. BRENNA
Anthony Ostlund & Baer, P.A.
Minneapolis, MN

ERIC J. CU
State of California Public
    Employment Relations Board
Los Angeles, CA

ROBERT G. BRODY
CHRISTOPHER K. SMITH
Brody & Associates
Westport, CT

DAVID M. KIGHT
Spencer Fane Britt & Browne
    LLP
Kansas City, MO

MATTHEW COYLE
Lockheed Martin Corporation
Bethesda, MD

JASON J. VALTOS
Osborne Law Offices, PC
Washington, DC

Chapter 12

Chapter Editors

W.V. BERNIE SIEBERT
Sherman & Howard LLC
Denver, CO

LAURENCE GOODMAN
Willig, Williams & Davidson
Philadelphia, PA

Chapter 12—*(cont'd)*

Contributing Editors

MICHAEL F. DELANEY
JEFFREY M. PLACE
Spencer Fane Britt & Browne
  LLP
Overland Park, KS

ANDREW S. GOLDBERG
Laner Muchin Dombrow Becker
  Levin & Tominberg, Ltd.
Chicago, IL

FRANCIS A. MASTRO
Apruzzese, McDermott, Mastro
  & Murphy
Liberty Corner, NJ

STEPHEN C. MITCHELL
Fisher & Phillips LLP
Columbia, SC

AMY J. ZDRAVECKY
Neal, Gerber & Eisenberg LLP
Chicago, IL

Chapter 13

Chapter Editors

KENNETH R. DOLIN
Seyfarth Shaw LLP
Chicago, IL

GARY M. EBY
Manley Burke
Cincinnati, OH

Contributing Editors

JOEL ANDERSEN
MICHAEL IWAN
Dorsey & Whitney LLP
Minneapolis, MN

NED H. BASSEN
CHRISTINE M. FITZGERALD
Hughes Hubbard & Reed LLP
New York, NY

COLIN M. CONNOR
JOSHUA N. DALLEY
JOSHUA L. DITELBERG
SAM M. SCHWARTZ
BRIAN M. STOLZENBACH
DAVID L. STRECK
Seyfarth Shaw LLP
Chicago, IL

Martin J. Costello
Hughes & Costello
St. Paul, MN

Ross H. Friedman
Amanda Sonneborn
Morgan Lewis
Chicago, IL

Josiah A. Groff
Wesley G. S. Kennedy
Allison, Slutsky & Kennedy, PC
Chicago, IL

Joel I. Keiler
Law Offices of Joel Keiler
Reston, VA

Noah G. Lipschultz
Littler Mendelson P.C.
Minneapolis, MN

Thomas M. Lucas
Troutman Sanders LLP
Virginia Beach, VA

Thomas J. Marcoline
Law Office of Vincent Toomey
Lake Success, NY

James N. McCauley
Law Offices of James N. McCauley
Ithaca, NY

Darren M. Mungerson
Jenner & Block LLP
Chicago, IL

Michael D. Ray
Richard L. Samson
Ogletree, Deakins, Nash, Smoak & Stewart, PC
Chicago, IL

Michael L. Sullivan
Goldberg Kohn
Chicago, IL

William C. Tidwell III
Hand Arendall, LLC
Mobile, AL

Brian N. Wooley
Lathrop & Gage LC
Kansas City, MO

Chapter 14

Chapter Editor

A. John Harper II
Fulbright & Jaworski LLP
Houston, TX

Chapter 14—*(cont'd)*

Contributing Editors

MARK L. JUSTER
Laner Muchin Dombrow Becker
    Levin & Tominberg, Ltd.
Chicago, IL

D. JAMES PETROFF
Faulkner, Muskovitz & Phillips,
    LLP
Cleveland, OH

BRYCE G. MURRAY
Taggart, Morton, Ogden, Staub,
    Rougelot & O'Brien, LLC
New Orleans, LA

TODD W. SCHNELL
RBC Dain Rauscher Inc.
Minneapolis, MN

Chapter 15

Chapter Editors

NELSON D. ATKIN II
Barran Liebman LLP
Portland, OR

GWYNNE A. WILCOX
Levy, Ratner & Behroozi, PC
New York, NY

Contributing Editors

WILLIAM ("BILLY") C. BIRD IV
CHARLES W. REYNOLDS
Dover, Dixon & Horne PLLC
Little Rock, AR

THOMAS LENZ
Atkinson, Andelson, Loya, Rudd
    & Romo
Cerritos, CA

TODD A. HANCHETT
ANDREW SCHPAK
Barran Liebman LLP
Portland, OR

STEPHEN B. MAULE
McMahon, Berger, Hanna,
    Linihan, Cody & McCarthy
St. Louis, MO

DAVID L. HOSKINS
D. ("PAT") PATTON PELFREY
Frost Brown Todd LLC
Louisville, KY

DONA NUTINI
Law Office of Dona A.
    Nutini
Phoenix, AZ

GERALD L. PAULING II
BRIAN STOLZENBACH
Seyfarth Shaw LLP
Chicago, IL

TED R. SCOTT
Littler Mendelson P.C.
San Diego, CA

ANNE SENTER
Robblee, Brennan & Detwiler
Seattle, WA

STEPHEN J. STANFORD
Robison, Curphey &
   O'Connell
Toledo, OH

Chapter 16

Chapter Editors

MICHAEL R. BROWN
Seyfarth Shaw LLP
Boston, MA

HOWARD Z. ROSEN
Posner & Rosen
Los Angeles, CA

Contributing Editors

STACEY ASCHEMANN
Carterville, IL

NORMAN R. BUCHSBAUM
Law Offices of Norman R.
   Buchsbaum
Baltimore, MD

ADAM S. COLLIER
Bullard, Smith, Jernstedt,
   Wilson PC
Portland, OR

DOUGLAS A. DARCH
RICHARD B. LAPP
Seyfarth Shaw, LLP
Chicago, IL

CHRISTOPHER W. DEERING
Ogletree, Deakins, Nash, Smoak
   & Stewart, PC
Birmingham, AL

DIANA RICHARDS FRANCIS
Harris, Dowell, Fisher & Harris,
   LC
Chesterfield, MO

AMY MOOR GAYLORD
Franczek Sullivan PC
Chicago, IL

GERALD HATHAWAY
Littler Mendelson P.C.
New York, NY

LYNN F. JACOB
Williams Mullen
Richmond, VA

FRANK L. KOLLMAN
Kollman & Saucier, PA
Timonium, MD

Chapter 16—*(cont'd)*

ALAN S. LEVINS
Littler Mendelson P.C.
San Francisco, CA

BARRY W. MARR
Marr Hipp Jones & Pepper
Honolulu, HI

STEPHEN W. LYMAN
Hall, Render, Killian, Heath &
  Lyman, PC
Indianapolis, IN

TERENCE P. MCCOURT
Greenberg Traurig LLP
Boston, MA

PAUL V. LYONS
Foley Hoag, LLP
Boston, MA

RACHAEL SPLAINE ROLLINS
Seyfarth Shaw LLP
Boston, MA

JOSEPH MACK III
PPG Industries, Inc.
Pittsburgh, PA

MARK M. SCHORR
Erickson & Sederstrom, PC
Lincoln, NE

J. ROY WEATHERSBY
Wimberly & Lawson, PC
Atlanta, GA

Chapter 17

Chapter Editors

JOSEPH J. TORRES
Winston & Strawn LLP
Chicago, IL

IRA H. WEINSTOCK
Ira H. Weinstock, P.C.
Harrisburg, PA

Contributing Editors

RONALD S. ALLEN
NICHOLAS DIGIOVANNI, JR.
Morgan, Brown & Joy, LLP
Boston, MA

STEPHANIE K. BRINSON
Asher, Gittler, Greenfield &
  D'Alba, Ltd.
Chicago, IL

THOMAS J. BENDER
MICHELE A. MALLOY
CHRISTINA T. WINSTON
Littler Mendelson P.C.
Philadelphia, PA

KEVIN M. CLOUTIER
SHEILA P. FREDRICK
Winston & Strawn LLP
Chicago, IL

Robert W. Morgan
Berry Moorman, PC
Detroit, MI

Joseph J. Steflik, Jr.
Couglin & Gerhart, LLP
Binghamton, NY

Jon Zimring
Duane Morris LLP
Chicago, IL

Chapter 18

Chapter Editors

Armin J. Moeller, Jr.
Balch & Bingham LLP
Jackson, MS

Ira H. Weinstock
Ira H. Weinstock P.C.
Harrisburg, PA

Contributing Editors

H. David Kelly
Beins, Axelrod, Gleason &
  Gibson, PC
Washington, DC

Jeremy V. Kilburn
Paul L. Rosenthal
Preston & Malcom, PC
Monroe, GA

Clifford H. Nelson, Jr.
Leigh E. Tyson
Constangy, Brooks & Smith,
  LLC
Atlanta, GA

Stuart Newman
Erik S. Rodriguez
Seyfarth Shaw LLP
Atlanta, GA

Timothy F. Ryan
Morrison & Foerster
Los Angeles, CA

David M. Thomas II
Balch & Bingham LLP
Jackson, MS

Chapter 19

Chapter Editors

W. MELVIN HAAS III
Constangy, Brooks & Smith, LLC
Macon, GA

ERNEST B. ORSATTI
Jubelirer, Pass & Intieri
Pittsburgh, PA

Contributing Editors

JOHN COLWELL
National Labor Relations Board
Washington, DC

BECKY MCGINNIS
Lathrop & Gage, LC
Kansas City, MO

BRIAN KURTZ
Matkov, Salzman, Madoff &
Gunn
Chicago, IL

PETER M. PANKEN
Epstein, Becker & Green, PC
New York, NY

W. JONATHAN MARTIN II
Constangy, Brooks & Smith,
LLC
Macon, GA

W. JUDD PEAK
Frost Brown Todd LLC
Nashville, TN

JOHN T. MCCANN
Hancock & Estabrook, LLP
Syracuse, NY

VINCENT D. REESE
Lewis, Rice & Fingersh LLC
St. Louis, MO

LISA ANNE SABATINO
Pelino & Lentz, PC
Philadelphia, PA

Chapter 20

Chapter Editors

ROBERT M. STONE
Musick, Peeler & Garrett LLP
Los Angeles, CA

ERNEST B. ORSATTI
Jubelirer, Pass & Intrieri
Pittsburgh, PA

Contributing Editors

JOHN T. McCANN
Hancock & Estabrook, LLP
Syracuse, NY

RAYMOND D. NEUSCH
Frost Brown Todd LLC
Cincinnati, OH

LAURENCE E. STUART
Legge, Farrow, Kimmitt, McGrath & Brown LLP
Houston, TX

Chapter 21

Chapter Editors

TANJA L. THOMPSON
Kiesewetter Wise Kaplan
    Prather, PLC
Memphis, TN

ROBERT CLARK
United Steelworkers of
    America
Pittsburgh, PA

Contributing Editors

DEREK G. BARELLA
Winston & Strawn LLP
Chicago, IL

JOEL S. BARRAS
RYAN J. CASSIDY
Reed Smith LLP
Philadelphia, PA

JOHN J. KRIMM, JR.
Schottenstein Zox and Dunn
    Co., LPA
Columbus, OH

MATTHEW D. LAHEY
Schiff Hardin LLP
Chicago, IL

LAURA MAECHTLEN
Seyfarth Shaw LLP
San Francisco, CA

JEFFREY E. MYERS
Blank Rome LLP
Philadelphia, PA

TRACY S. PYLES
Littler Mendelson P.C.
Columbus, OH

SUSAN S. ROBFOGEL
Nixon Peabody LLP
Rochester, NY

JEFFREY K. ROSS
Seyfarth Shaw LLP
Chicago, IL

MATTHEW A. SIEBEL
Clifton Budd & DeMaria, LLP
New York, NY

CHRISTOPHER T. TERRELL
Balch & Bingham LLP
Birmingham, AL

Chapter 22

Chapter Editors

LEONARD SINGER
Interstate Brands Corporation
Kansas City, MO

CHRISTOPHER T. HEXTER
Schuchat, Cook & Werner
St. Louis, MO

Contributing Editors

GREGORY D. BALLEW
Fisher & Phillips, LLP
Kansas City, MO

NORMAN R. BUCHSBAUM
Law Offices of Norman R.
  Buchsbaum
Baltimore, MD

KRISTINA DETWILER
Robblee, Brennan &
  Detwiler
Seattle, WA

MERRITT J. GREEN
McLean, VA

STANLEY M. SAUNIER, JR.
Lexington, KY

MARK W. SCHNEIDER
Littler Mendelson P.C.
Minneapolis, MN

JENNIFER SCHUBERT
Davis Wright Tremaine LLP
Seattle, WA

STEPHEN J. SCHULTZ
Marks, Golin & Finch, LLP
San Diego, CA

Chapter 23

Chapter Editors

DAVID S. ADELSTEIN
Bush Quinonez Gottlieb Singer
  Lopez Kohanski Adelstein &
  Dickinson
Burbank, CA

MATTHEW LEE WIENER
Dechert LLP
Philadelphia, PA

Contributing Editors

MARK T. BENNETT
Marks, Golia & Finch, LLP
San Diego, CA

KEITH R. JEWELL
Beverly Enterprises
Fort Smith, AR

WILLIAM J. EMANUEL
Littler Mendelson P.C.
Los Angeles, CA

BRIAN E. LEWIS
Hinckley, Allen & Snyder LLP
Boston, MA

LETICIA PEÑA
National Labor Relations Board
Denver, CO

Chapter 24

Chapter Editors

JOHN S. IRVING
Kirkland & Ellis LLP
Washington, DC

RICHARD WILLIAMS
Williams & Iversen, PA
Roseville, MN

Contributing Editors

NICHOLE G. BRIGHTBILL
Kirkland & Ellis LLP
Washington, DC

BENJAMIN GIPSON
Seyfarth Shaw LLP
Los Angeles, CA

PATRICK E. DEADY
Hogan Marren, Ltd.
Chicago, IL

DAVID J. WOOLF
Drinker Biddle & Reath
  LLP
Philadelphia, PA

Chapter 25

Chapter Editors

PAUL IVERSEN
Williams & Iversen, PA
Roseville, MN

ELIZABETH WELCH LYKINS
Lykins Law, PC
Grand Rapids, MN

Contributing Editors

BROOKS R. AMIOT
DLA Piper US LLP
Baltimore, MD

RICHARD HARDICK
National Labor Relations Board
Washington, DC

ELLIOT STEPHEN AZOFF
Baker & Hostetler LLP
Cleveland, OH

JAY J. LEVIT
Levit, Mann & Halligan, PC
Richmond, VA

HOLLACE J. ENOCH
National Labor Relations Board
Washington, DC

STEPHAN JAN MARCULEWICZ
Miles & Stockbridge
Baltimore, MD

DEBORAH E. GODWIN
Godwin Morris Laurenzi &
  Bloomfield, P.C.
Memphis, TN

KATHLEEN MCKINNEY
National Labor Relations
  Board
New Orleans, LA

KELLY GOING
CYNTHIA JACKSON
Baker & McKenzie
Palo Alto, CA

JEFFERY W. PAGANO
King, Pagano & Harrison
New York, NY

ALBERT W. PALEWICZ
National Labor Relations Board
Baltimore, MD

Chapter 26

Chapter Editors

SCOTT T. SILVERMAN
Zinober & McCrea, P.A.
Tampa, FL

GUERINO (JODY) CALEMINE III
Committee on Education and
  Labor
U.S. House of Representatives
Washington, DC

Contributing Editors

MARC GUILFORD
HOWARD M. KASTRINSKY
King & Ballow
Nashville, TN

ANNE MARIE LOFASO
WVU College of Law
Morgantown, WV

NICHOLE MILLER
Steptoe & Johnson, LLP
Phoenix, AZ

DANIEL B. PASTERNAK
Greenberg Traurig, PA
Phoenix, AZ

BERTRAND B. POGREBIN
New York, NY

LUIS RAMIREZ
Phoenix, AZ

JEANNE E. TENG
Littler Mendelson P.C.
New York, NY

ROBERT P. TINNIN, JR.
Tinnin Law Firm
Albuquerque, NM

STACY ZIMMERMAN
National Labor Relations Board
Washington, DC

Chapter 27

Chapter Editors

SAMUEL H. HELDMAN
The Gardner Firm, PC
Washington, DC

WENDY NUTT
Mandalay Resort Group
Las Vegas, NV

Chapter 27—*(cont'd)*

Contributing Editors

MICHAEL J. DiMATTIA
RICHARD D. SUTTON
McGuire Woods LLP
New York, NY

RICHARD J. HAFETS
AMY BETH LEASURE
DLA Piper US LLP
Baltimore, MD

BENJAMIN E. GEHRT
SANG-YUL LEE
Seyfarth Shaw LLP
Chicago, IL

THOMAS R. TRACHSEL
Felhaber, Larson, Fenlon &
Vogt, PA
Minneapolis, MN

NANCY A. WALKER
McNeill & Walker
Philadelphia, PA

Chapter 28

Chapter Editors

KENNETH L. WAGNER
Blitman & King LLP
Syracuse, NY

REID CARRON
Faegre & Benson LLP
Minneapolis, MN

Contributing Editors

DANIEL ALTCHEK
Proskauer Rose LLP
New York, NY

FLOYD A. CLUTTER
Cohen & Grigsby, PC
Pittsburgh, PA

JASON ASCHENBRAND
STEPHEN L. SHEINFELD
Winston & Strawn LLP
New York, NY

EDWIN S. HOPSON
MICHAEL K. KIRK
Wyatt, Tarrant & Combs LLP
Louisville, KY

DANIEL R. BRICE
STEPHANIE A. MINER
Blitman & King LLP
Syracuse, NY

ROBERT E. PAUL
Zwerdling, Paul, Leibig, Kahn,
Thompson & Driesen PC
Washington, DC

JEFFREY M. PLACE
Spencer Fane Britt & Browne
 LLP
Kansas City, MO

PETER D. POST
Reed, Smith, Shaw & McClay
 LLP
Pittsburgh, PA

ANN MARIE SCARPINO
National Labor Relations Board
Washington, DC

MICHAEL J. TEDESCO
Law Office of MJ Tedesco
Beaverton, OR

NORMAN I. WHITE
McNees, Wallace & Nurick
 LLC
Harrisburg, PA

BRENT L. WILSON
Elarbee, Thompson, Sapp &
 Wilson, LLP
Atlanta, GA

LAWRENCE T. ZIMMERMAN
Law Offices of Lawrence T. Zimmerman
Washington, DC

Chapter 29

Chapter Editor

MARGARET ANGELUCCI
Asher, Gittler, Greenfield & D'Alba, Ltd.
Chicago, IL

Contributing Editors

JEFFREY BOSLEY
MEREDITH LOM
Winston & Strawn LLP
New York, NY

JONATHAN C. FRITTS
Morgan Lewis
Washington, DC

L. ANTHONY GEORGE
Jackson Kelly PLLC
Denver, CO

JAY W. KIESEWETTER
R. BRADLEY MOKROS (Research
 Specialist)
Kiesewetter Wise Kaplan
 Prather, PLC
Memphis, TN

JOSEPH MCCOIN
Miller & Martin PLLC
Chattanooga, TN

Chapter 29—*(cont'd)*

PAUL M. OSTROFF   SUELLEN OSWALD
Lane, Powell PC   Littler Mendelson P.C.
Portland, OR   Cleveland, OH

LAWRENCE J. SONG
Epstein, Turner & Song, PC
Los Angeles, CA

Chapter 30

Chapter Editor

ROBIN K. LUCE
Butzel Long
Detroit, MI

Contributing Editors

GEORGE N. DAVIES   BENJAMIN STEFFANS
Nakamura, Quinn & Walls, LLP   Butzel Long
Birmingham, AL   Detroit, MI

Chapter 31

Chapter Editors

GEORGE D. ADAMS   CHRISTOPHER N. GRANT
Greenebaum Doll & Mcdonald,   Schuchat, Cook & Werner
  PLLC   St. Louis, MO
Louisville, KY

Contributing Editors

KEITH E. EASTLAND   KATHLEEN JORGENSON
NATHAN D. PLANTINGA   DeCarlo, Connor & Shanely
Miller, Johnson, Snell &   Los Angeles, CA
  Cummiskey, PLC
Grand Rapids, MI

WILLIAM MORRIS (BILL)
LAMOREAUX
Dallas, TX

AMANDA C. SOMMERFELD
Winston & Strawn LLP
Los Angeles, CA

LETICIA PEÑA
National Labor Relations
Board
Denver, CO

DAVID S. TIMMS
The Mason Law Firm Co., LPA
Dublin, OH

Chapter 32

Chapter Editors

JUDITH BATSON SADLER
Sadler & Sykes, LLP
Houston, TX

KAREN NEILSEN
National Labor Relations Board
Cleveland, OH

Contributing Editors

WILLIAM BRADY
ELLEN GRACHEK
MARILYN L. WIDMAN
Alotta, Farley & Widman Co.,
LPA
Toledo, OH

LYLE B. BROWN
N. VICTOR GOODMAN
Benesch, Friedlander, Coplan &
Aranoff, LLP
Columbus, OH

LORI BUPP
DAVID MIKLAS
J. DAVID RICHESON
Richeson & Coke, PA
Ft. Pierce, FL

KERRY LIN DAVIDSON
ANNELISE (ANNA) WERMUTH
Meckler Bulger & Tilson
Chicago, IL

MICHAEL C. HARRINGTON
Murtha Cullina LLP
Hartford, CT

MARK P. HUDSON
KELLI LIEURANCE
SCOTT S. MOORE
Baird Holm LLP
Omaha, NE

LISA LOVERDI
Sadler & Sykes, LLP
Houston, TX

Chapter 32—*(cont'd)*

ALBERT W. PALEWICZ
National Labor Relations Board
Baltimore, MD

Chapter 33

Chapter Editors

KURT M. GRAHAM
Varnum, Riddering, Schmidt &
  Howlett LLP
Grand Rapids, MI

STANLEY D. WILLIAMS
National Labor Relations
  Board
Overland Park, KS

Contributing Editors

GARY S. FEALK
Vercruysse Murray & Calzone
  PC
Bingham Farms, MI

DAVID E. KHOREY
KELLEY E. STOPPELS
Varnum, Riddering, Schmidt &
  Howlett LLP
Grand Rapids, MI

FREDERICK C. MINER
Ryley, Carlock & Applewhite
Phoenix, AZ

FOREWORD

Since 1945 the ABA Section of Labor and Employment Law has expanded its stated purposes in response to the evolution of the field. Currently, they include the following: (a) to study and report upon continuing developments in the field of labor and employment law; (b) to provide a forum for members of the Association interested in the field of labor and employment law to meet and confer; (c) to assist the professional growth and development of practitioners in the field of labor and employment law; (d) to establish and maintain working liaison with state, federal, and, where applicable, multinational agencies having jurisdiction over matters affecting labor and employment law toward achieving procedural reform and administrative due process; (e) to study and report upon proposed and necessary legislation and rule making within the field encompassed by the jurisdiction of this Section; (f) to promote justice, human welfare, industrial peace, and the recognition of the supremacy of law in labor-management relations and the employment relationship; and (g) to establish, moderate, and sponsor seminars, workshops, forums, and other programs promoting the advancement of knowledge and practice in the field of labor and employment law.

Through the publication of books such as *The Developing Labor Law* and through annual and committee meeting programs designed to provide a forum for the exchange of ideas, the Section has pursued these stated goals. Gradually, the Section has built a library of comprehensive legal works intended for the use of the Section membership as well as the bar generally.

The Section of Labor and Employment Law is pleased to provide this first supplement to the Fifth Edition to its classic treatise on the National Labor Relations Act as part of its library of books published by BNA Books, A Division of BNA. The combined efforts of many individual authors recruited by the Committee on the Development of the Law Under the National Labor Relations Act of the Section are reflected in this work.

The Section wishes to express its appreciation to the Committee members, and in particular to the editors-in-chief, W.V. Bernie Siebert, Paul Iversen, and Barry J. Kearney, and the associate editors and chapter editors. This group has tried to accomplish two primary objectives: (1) to be equally balanced and nonpartisan in its viewpoints, and (2) to ensure the book is of significant value to the practitioner, student, and sophisticated nonlawyer.

The views expressed herein do not necessarily represent the views of the American Bar Association, or its Section of Labor and Employment Law, or the National Labor Relations Board, United States government, or any other organization, but are simply the collective, but not necessarily the individual, views of the authors. Information on the affiliation of government employees who contributed to this work is for informational purposes only and does not constitute any official endorsement of the information provided herein.

JAMES R. LAVAUTE
Chair

BARBARA BERISH BROWN
Chair-Elect

Section of Labor
and Employment Law
American Bar Association

September 2007

PREFACE

This first supplement to the Fifth Edition follows the organization of the Fifth Edition exactly. It updates the Fifth Edition through 2006. This supplement does not contain headings where there have been no significant developments under that heading since publication of the Fifth Edition.

The efforts of all the members of the Committee toward publication of this supplement are deeply appreciated. This is truly a working and producing Committee. In addition, we wish to express our appreciation for the support and assistance of the staff of BNA Books who have spent many hours editing and proofing the manuscript and otherwise working with us on this supplement. Special thanks are also given to the Section of Labor and Employment Law and its governing Council for their valuable support and encouragement in this endeavor.

We believe that the final product is ample justification for the efforts of all involved.

W.V. BERNIE SIEBERT
PAUL IVERSEN
BARRY J. KEARNEY

September 2007

SUMMARY TABLE OF CONTENTS

PART II

PROTECTED EMPLOYEE ACTIVITY

PART III

THE REPRESENTATION PROCESS AND UNION RECOGNITION

PART IV

THE COLLECTIVE BARGAINING PROCESS

Part VII

RELATIONS BETWEEN EMPLOYEE AND UNION

PART VIII

ADMINISTRATION OF THE ACT

DETAILED TABLE OF CONTENTS

PART II

PROTECTED EMPLOYEE ACTIVITY

PART V

ARBITRATION AND THE ACT

PART VI

ECONOMIC ACTION

Part I

HISTORY OF THE NATIONAL LABOR RELATIONS ACT

HISTORICAL DEVELOPMENTS

There have been no new changes or developments in the law since publication of the Main Edition.

PROTECTED EMPLOYEE ACTIVITY

Chapter 6

INTERFERENCE WITH PROTECTED RIGHTS

I. Overview

C. Employer Interference With Section 7 Rights: Section 8(a)(1)

3. Motive Not an Essential Element of Section 8(a) (1) Violations

While motive is not an essential element of a Section 8(a) (1) violation, in *Meijer, Inc. v. NLRB*, the Sixth Circuit found that employer knowledge of the protected nature of the conduct is an essential and requisite element of a Section 8(a) (1) violation.[1]

---

[1]463 F.3d 534, 180 LRRM 2289, *aff'g in part, vacating in part* Meijer, Inc., 344 NLRB No. 115, 177 LRRM 1253 (2005) (6th Cir. 2006).

D. Union Restraint and Coercion—Section 8(b)(1)(A)

2. Nature of the Violation

In *Randell Warehouse of Arizona, Inc.*,[2] the Board overruled its initial disposition of this case,[3] which itself had overruled prior precedent, and returned to the standard that in the absence of a valid explanation conveyed to employees in a timely manner, photographing employees engaged in Section 7 activity constitutes objectionable conduct whether engaged in by a union or an employer.

Prior to an election, union representatives took photographs of the distribution of union literature outside the employer's facility. The photographs included both employees who accepted and rejected proffered literature. In *Randell I*, the Board overruled its decision in *Pepsi-Cola Bottling Co.*[4] and held that union photographing or videotaping of employees engaged in protected activities during an election campaign, without more, did not necessarily interfere with employees' Section 7 rights. The *Randell I* Board justified treating union surveillance differently from employer surveillance because "photographing employees during an organizing campaign is one means by which unions can determine the identity and leanings of employees and carry out their legitimate objective of obtaining majority support," whereas greater coercive potential attached to photographing by employers, which control employees' terms and condition of employment.[5] The District of Columbia Circuit declined to enforce the Board's order, holding that it failed to explain why it departed not only from its holding in *Pepsi-Cola Bottling Co.*, but also from its holding in *Mike Yurosek & Sons, Inc.*,[6] where union representatives' threats toward employees, concurrent with union photography of employee activity, were found to be unlawful.[7]

In *Randell II*, the Board established a single standard—applicable to both employers and unions—to determine whether there is objectionable conduct where employees are photographed while engaged in Section 7 activity. The new standard balances the protection of

---

[2]347 NLRB No. 56, 180 LRRM 1017 (2006) (*Randell II*).
[3]Randell Warehouse of Ariz., Inc., 328 NLRB 1034, 161 LRRM 1265 (1999) (*Randell I*).
[4]289 NLRB 736, 128 LRRM 1275 (1988).
[5]328 NLRB at 1036–37.
[6]292 NLRB 1074, 130 LRRM 1308 (1989).
[7]252 F.3d 445, 167 LRRM 2340 (D.C. Cir. 2001), *remanding* 328 NLRB 1034, 161 LRRM 1265 (1999).

employee free choice with the legitimate interests of employers and unions in requiring a "legitimate justification" for photographing.[8] Furthermore, except in cases where the justification is self-evident (e.g., violence or mass picketing, etc.), the justification must be communicated to employees in a timely manner.[9] The Board's rationale in overruling the lower standard for evaluating union photographing was that employees subject to union photographing of Section 7 activity prior to an election could reasonably fear reprisal from unions, which have the capacity to affect them. "The opportunities for and means of reprisal available to unions may differ from those available to employers, but they are no less real or intimidating."[10]

E. "Freedom of Speech"—Section 8(c) in General

1. Threat or Prophecy?

The courts continue to examine surrounding conduct.[11]

II. ORGANIZATIONAL AND PREELECTION ACTIVITY

A. In General: Relation of Unfair Labor Practices to "Laboratory Conditions" Required for Elections

The Board continues to conclude that the maintenance of overbroad confidentiality rules will not overturn an election if they could not reasonably have affected the results of the election. In *Longs Drug Stores California, Inc.*,[12] the Board found unlawful a confidentiality provision in the employer's employee handbook that prohibited employees from discussing their wages with one another. However, the Board found that the employer's conduct was so minimal and isolated that it was virtually impossible to conclude that the misconduct could have affected the election results. The Board reached this

---

[8]Randell Warehouse of Ariz., Inc., 347 NLRB No. 56, slip op. at 11 (2006) (*Randell II*).

[9]*Id.*

[10]*Id.*, slip op. at 7.

[11]Food & Commercial Workers Local 204 v. NLRB, 447 F.3d 821, 179 LRRM 2708 (D.C. Cir. 2006).

[12]347 NLRB No. 45, 180 LRRM 1001 (2006). *But see* S.T.A.R. Inc., 347 NLRB No. 8, 179 LRRM 1387 (2006) (union's objectionable fee-waiver policy, disseminated by the employer, sufficient to set aside election despite employer's articulation of nonobjectionable policy).

conclusion because the confidentiality provisions were not adopted in response to the union's organizing drive, the more recent provisions were not widely disbursed, and there was no evidence that the provisions were enforced.

B. Unlawful Employer Conduct

1. Employer's Restrictions on Union and Employee Activity on Employer's Property

a. Basic Presumptions

The Board recently further clarified the meaning of "solicitation" in *Scripps Health*.[13] There, the Board found a hospital violated Section 8(a)(1) when a supervisor told on-duty nurses that they could not talk about the union at a semi-walled-off nurses' station. Evidence also demonstrated that nonwork-related discussions during working time were otherwise permitted by the hospital at this nurses' station. In *Scripps*, the union-represented nurse mentioned that there was an upcoming union meeting before she was silenced by the supervisor. The Board found that mentioning an upcoming union meeting did not constitute "solicitation," rather, it was "simply engaging in talk about the union."[14]

Bans on solicitation during "company time," or during "business hours," or "working hours" remain presumptively invalid. In *Parkwood Developmental Center, Inc.*,[15] the Board determined the employer violated Section 8(a)(1) when a supervisor told an employee that employees could not talk about union business during "company time."

b. Rights of Employees Over Nonemployees

The Board continues to scrutinize cases involving shopping center access rights. In *Salmon Run Shopping Center, LLC*,[16] the Board

---

[13]347 NLRB No. 4, 179 LRRM 1253 (2006).
[14]*Id.* at 1254.
[15]347 NLRB No. 95, 180 LRRM 1178 (2006), *see also* Moeller Aerospace Tech., Inc., 347 NLRB No. 76, 180 LRRM 1056 (2006) (Board found a supervisor's statement unlawful because it prohibited an employee from soliciting signatures for a union petition on "company time" and during "working hours," but allowed such solicitation during the employee's lunch break); Consolidated Biscuit Co., 346 NLRB No. 101, 180 LRRM 1243 (2006) (Board found the employer unlawfully instructed employees not to talk about the union on "company time").
[16]348 NLRB No. 31, 180 LRRM 1395 (2006).

found that a shopping mall violated Section 8(a)(1) by discriminatorily excluding the union from its premises for purpose of distributing union literature. The Board concluded that the mall's action was discriminatory in light of the fact that it failed to respond to the union's numerous requests for access to the mall to distribute the literature and that the mall offered only pretextual rationales for denying access in it response.

c. No-Solicitation and No-Distribution Rules Generally

The Board has recently brought telephone calls into the realm of working and nonworking time. In *St. Mary's Hospital of Blue Springs*,[17] the Board found an employer lawfully reprimanded an off-duty employee for telephoning an on-duty employee to discuss labor-management issues.

(2) Facial Validity of Rule

It remains the rule that employers may not require employees to obtain permission before engaging in solicitation at the workplace.[18] The Board continues to hold that where an employer's no-solicitation/no-distribution rule is ambiguous, the ambiguity is resolved against the employer as promulgator of the rule.[19]

Employers' no-solicitation/no-distribution rules continue to be scrutinized by the Board, especially if utilized in a nonwork area. In *Meijer, Inc. v. NLRB*,[20] the Sixth Circuit enforced the Board's order prohibiting the employer from banning union solicitation in its parking lots and from promulgating or publishing any similar policy. The court, however, vacated the Board's holding to the extent it found the employee was unlawfully ejected from the parking lot, stating that the supervisor did not know the employee was distributing union literature because the employee did not so state.

Confirming its rulings regarding working time and working areas, the Board found an employer unlawfully disciplined employees for distributing union literature during "company time" and

---

[17]346 NLRB No. 76, 179 LRRM 1221 (2006).

[18]Ivy Steel & Wire, Inc., 346 NLRB No. 41, 179 LRRM 1060 (2006). *See also* North Am. Pipe Corp., 347 NLRB No. 78, 180 LRRM 1125 (2006) (citing MTD Prods., Inc., 310 NLRB 733, 144 LRRM 1230 (1993)).

[19]Supervalu Holdings, Inc. dba Bigg's Foods, 347 NLRB No. 39, 180 LRRM 1534 (2006) (retail employer's orally-amended no-distribution rule ambiguously overbroad as to where handbilling to customers was prohibited).

[20]463 F.3d 534, 180 LRRM 2289 (6th Cir. 2006), *aff'g in part, vacating in part* Meijer, Inc., 344 NLRB No. 115, 177 LRRM 1253 (2005).

unlawfully directed off-duty employees to stop distributing union leaflets in a nonworking area in *North Hills Office Services*.[21] However, in *Children's Center for Behavioral Development*,[22] the Board found that a no-solicitation policy prohibiting specific staff conduct in all of the employer's buildings and surrounding grounds was lawful because it expressly targeted personal commercial business rather than concerted protected activity.

(3) Unlawful Promulgation or Enforcement

The Board continues to find that no-solicitation rules need to be uniformly enforced to retain their validity.[23] In *SNE Enterprises, Inc.*,[24] an employer unlawfully selectively enforced an otherwise valid no-solicitation policy by allowing employees to engage in working time solicitations, but terminating an employee for soliciting on behalf of the union during working time. The Board also found that the employer unlawfully maintained an overbroad rule prohibiting employees from discussing disciplinary action taken against them with their co-workers.

In *St. Francis Medical Center*,[25] however, the Board concluded that the employer did not disparately enforce its no-solicitation, no-distribution rule with respect to posting materials in the workplace, even though the employer violated Section 8(a)(1) by refusing to remove from work areas flyers that disparaged an employee because of her union activities. Although a supervisor condoned the posting of offensive flyers by refusing to remove them, there was no evidence that the employer enforced its rule against union-related solicitations and distributions but not against nonunion solicitations and distributions.

New rules developed in response to organization continue to be scrutinized by the Board. In *Invista*,[26] an employer unlawfully created a new work rule requiring employees to stay in their own work areas

---

[21]346 NLRB No. 96, 180 LRRM 1118 (2006).

[22]347 NLRB No. 3, 179 LRRM 1321 (2006) (the employer's no-solicitation policy stated that, "staff should not be permitted to solicit, obtain, accept or retain services, merchandise, commodities, etc. for personal gain/profit during working hours. This conduct is prohibited in all buildings and on surrounding grounds").

[23]Publix Super Mkts., Inc., 347 NLRB No. 124, 180 LRRM 1480 (2006) (employer violated §8(a)(1) of the Act by its disparate enforcement of the no-distribution rule against pro-union postings while permitting postings for the sale of various items such as automobiles, dinner tickets, etc.).

[24]347 NLRB No. 43, 180 LRRM 1431 (2006).

[25]347 NLRB No. 35, 179 LRRM 1345 (2006).

[26]346 NLRB No. 107, 179 LRRM 1328 (2006).

during their breaks and prohibiting them from going to other break areas. The new rule was promulgated after a union organizing drive began. The Board found that the rule was discriminatorily motivated with the intent to undermine organizational activities.

Employee use of e-mail for solicitation may be resolved in forthcoming Board decisions. In March 2007, the Board heard oral argument in *The Register-Guard*.[27] There, the Board will consider whether employees have the right to use their employer's e-mail system to communicate about the union or any other concerted, protected matters with other employees.

d. Implementation of Rules: Timing as an Element of Legality

The Board continues to consider the timing of the implementation of a no-solicitation or no-distribution rule as an important factor in determining the rule's validity.[28]

An overly broad no-solicitation/no-distribution rule posted outside the employer's parking lot violated Section 8(a)(1), notwithstanding a lawful rule published in the employee handbook.[29] An employer's e-mail message to employees that only bars union literature is facially invalid.[30] A no-distribution rule, orally amended in response to off-duty employees' union handbilling of customers, was ambiguously overbroad.[31]

e. Union Buttons and Insignia

The Board continues to adhere to its position that an employer may lawfully promulgate and enforce a rule prohibiting the wearing of union buttons and insignia only if "special circumstances" justify the restriction.[32] Even though a hospital's ban on wearing

---

[27]Cases 36-CA-8743-1.

[28]Invista, 346 NLRB No. 107, 179 LRRM 1328 (2006) (employees prohibited from using break rooms outside their work areas after union campaign).

[29]Food & Commercial Workers Local 204 v. NLRB, 447 F.3d 821, 179 LRRM 2708 (D.C. Cir. 2006).

[30]Enloe Med. Ctr., 348 NLRB No. 63, 181 LRRM 1055 (2006), *supplementing* 345 NLRB No. 54, 178 LRRM 1123, and 346 NLRB No. 82, 179 LRRM 1369.

[31]Supervalu Holdings, Inc. dba Bigg's Foods, 347 NLRB No. 39, 180 LRRM 1534 (2006). *See also* Airport 2000 Concessions LLC, 346 NLRB No. 86, 179 LRRM 1337 (2006) (supervisor's statement prohibiting employees from talking to organizers in dining area where employees spend their breaks was an overbroad interpretation of no-solicitation rule).

[32]Jupiter Med. Ctr. Pavilion, 346 NLRB No. 61, 179 LRRM 1161 (2006) (nursing home operator lawfully directed a certified nursing assistant to remove a union pin from his uniform, out of concern the pin could tear a patient's fragile skin); North Hills Office Servs., Inc., 346 NLRB No. 96, 180 LRRM 1118 (2006);

union buttons outside immediate patient care areas is presumptively invalid, the Board concluded that a hospital had lawfully prohibited the wearing of a new union button stating: "RNs Demand Safe Staffing."[33] There, the hospital allowed other union buttons and only restricted this button in locations where patients or families could see it because of the concern that patients or their families might conclude that the hospital maintained unsafe staffing levels. The Board also has concluded that employees were lawfully told to wash off temporary pro-union tattoos to prevent contamination of a food manufacturer's products.[34]

In *W San Diego*,[35] a majority of the Board held that a hotel did not violate Section 8(a)(1) when it prohibited an employee from wearing a union button in public areas of the hotel, based on well defined uniform requirements aimed at achieving the hotel's desired image and ambiance. A different majority of the Board, however, held that the hotel did violate the Act when it prohibited the same employee from wearing the button in nonpublic areas where no guests were present. The Board also unanimously reversed an administrative law judge's (ALJ's) finding that the hotel had acted unlawfully in prohibiting another employee from wearing union stickers on her uniform in the hotel kitchen, a nonpublic area. This aspect of the Board's decision was based on the employer's reasonable concern that the stickers might fall into the food or onto food preparation surfaces.

g. No-Access Rules

In defining the right of off-duty employees to enter or remain on plant premises for the purpose of engaging in union activities, the Board continues to apply the principles of *Tri-County Medical Center*.[36]

BellSouth Telecomms., Inc. 346 NLRB No. 59, 179 LRRM 1134, *supplementing* 335 NLRB 1066, 168 LRRM 1049) (2001), *see also Airport 2000*, 346 NLRB No. 86, 179 LRRM 1337 (employer failed to establish "special circumstances" to justify allowing other kinds of pins and buttons, while prohibiting union pins and buttons, when employer allowed employees to wear pro-union buttons during a rally but prohibited these buttons during working time).

[33]Sacred Heart Med. Ctr., 347 NLRB No. 48, 179 LRRM 1377 (2006).

[34]Consolidated Biscuit Co., 346 NLRB No. 101, 180 LRRM 1243 (2006).

[35]348 NLRB No. 24, 180 LRRM 1321 (2006).

[36]222 NLRB 1089, 91 LRRM 1323 (1976), *see* Central Valley Meat Co., 346 NLRB No. 94, 179 LRRM 1281 (2006) (employer violated the Act by prohibiting an off-duty union supporter from waiting for a ride in its parking lot, while allowing other employees to wait in the parking lot).

h. Prohibiting Protected Activity on Private Property Open to the Public

In *NLRB v. Babcock & Wilcox Co.*[37] the Supreme Court held that an employer's property rights would prevail against nonemployees seeking access on private property open to the public, unless the employer discriminatorily applied its policy of exclusion. The discriminatory exception applies where the Board determines that an employer's reasons for prohibiting union agents from communicating with customers is pretextual.[38]

2. *Specific Conduct That Violates Section 8(a)(1)*

a. Threats to Withdraw, and Withdrawals of, Benefits

(1) Permissible Predictions and Prohibited Threats

In its efforts to find a consistent line separating permissible predictions of adverse consequences resulting from unionization from prohibited threats of reprisal, the Board continues to distinguish between slight differences in language, such as use of the word "could" versus "would."[39]

However, statements to employees that convey a threat of loss of existing or proposed benefits remain unlawful if they reasonably "leave the employees with the impression that what they may ultimately receive depends upon what the union can induce the employer to restore."[40] In *Promedica Health Systems, Inc.*,[41] the Board found that an employer violated Section 8(a)(1) by telling employees that the implementation of an approved wage increase might be in doubt due to the obligation to engage in collective bargaining with a union, should the union prevail in the upcoming election.

---

[37]351 U.S. 105, 38 LRRM 2001 (1956).

[38]Salmon Run Shopping Ctr., LLC, 348 NLRB No. 31, 180 LRRM 1395 (2006).

[39]George L. Mee Mem'l Hosp., 348 NLRB No. 15, 181 LRRM 1320 (2006) (employer's statement to employees that benefits "*could* go down" as a result of unionization found to be lawful, in comparison to hypothetical statement that "benefits and wages *would* go down") (emphasis added).

[40]Promedica Health Sys. Inc., 343 NLRB 1351, 1354, 177 LRRM 1037 (2004), *enforced in part* NLRB v. Promedica Health Sys., Inc., 180 LRRM 2789, 2006 Fed. Appx. 0737N (6th Cir. 2006) (quoting Earthgrains Co., 336 NLRB 1119, 1119–20, 172 LRRM 1185 (2001), *enforced sub nom.* Sara Lee Bakery Group, Inc. v. NLRB, 61 Fed. Appx. 1 (4th Cir. 2003) (unpublished)).

[41]343 NLRB 1351, 177 LRRM 1037 (2004), *enforcement denied in relevant part* NLRB v. Promedica, 180 LRRM 2789, 2006 Fed. Appx. 0737N.

The employer first informed employees that they would soon receive a wage increase.[42] Then, after the filing of an election petition, the employer told employees that the wage increase would be implemented if the union lost the election, but the wage increase would be made part of the collective-bargaining process if the union won the election. The Board concluded that the employer's statements left employees with "the clear impression that a wage increase for the [employees] was going to occur, but that a union victory might jeopardize that occurrence by virtue of it being subject to the collective-bargaining process."[43]

Upon the Board's petition for enforcement and Promedica's cross-petition for review, the Sixth Circuit denied enforcement as to the above portion of the Board's decision.[44] The court concluded that the Board's findings lacked substantial evidentiary support, and held that the employer's statements, when viewed in context, could not have improperly influenced a reasonable employee because these statements made clear the employer's desire to raise wages regardless of the electoral outcome. As a result, the Sixth Circuit concluded that the employer's statements regarding the delayed wage increase did not violate the Act.

The Board has also reaffirmed that expressions of personal opinion concerning the effects of unionization on employees are protected by the free speech provisions of Section 8(c).[45]

---

[42] *Id.*

[43] *Id.*, 343 NLRB at 1354.

[44] *NLRB v. Promedica*, 180 LRRM 2789, 2006 Fed. Appx. 0737N (6th Cir. 2006).

[45] Int'l Baking Co. & Earthgrains, 348 NLRB No. 76, 181 LRRM 1229 (2006) (finding no violation where supervisor told employee that "the Union wasn't a good thing. That it wasn't right. That [he] was one of the most senior drivers there," that he was making decent money, that the union would harm him, and that it would be better for him not to sign a union card. The Board held that the supervisor was "merely expressing her lawful opinion concerning the effects of unionization on the employees."); George L. Mee Mem'l Hosp., 348 NLRB No. 15, 181 LRRM 1320 (2006) (finding no violation where supervisor told employees that unions just want employees' money and that employees would have to pay union dues without a guarantee of receiving benefits in return); Children's Ctr. for Behavioral Dev., 347 NLRB No. 3, 179 LRRM 1321 (2006) (employer's memo conveying nothing more than employer's negative opinion of the union, its position, and its actions protected by §8(c)).

(2) Futility of Organizing

In *Weldon, Williams & Lick, Inc.*,[46] the Board further clarified the distinction between threats of futility and lawful comments protected by Section 8(c) of the Act. After an employee e-mailed management and notified it that he had contacted a union, he went to his supervisor's cubicle, as he did every morning, and asked the supervisor what he thought about the e-mail. The supervisor responded, "They are not going to let that happen. No way."[47] The supervisor then said he did not pretend to understand anything about unions and that he was not going to talk to the employee about it. The Board reversed the ALJ and concluded that the supervisor's statement did not unlawfully threaten that union representation would be futile.[48] The Board looked at the "episode as a whole" and noted the supervisor's low-level position, as well as the fact that he had not initiated the subject of unionization. The Board noted that the supervisor had "only expressed his opinion that 'they' [meaning upper management] would not let that happen" in response to the employee's solicitation of his opinion.[49] It further noted that the supervisor had immediately changed the topic of conversation, and had dispelled any inference of coercion by offering to place the employee on a policy implementation committee.[50]

(3) Inevitability of Strikes or Violence

Notwithstanding the foregoing, an employer may lawfully inform employees that they would be permanently replaced if they went on strike.[51]

---

[46]348 NLRB No. 45, 181 LRRM 1008 (2006).

[47]*Id.*, slip op. at 5.

[48]*Id.*

[49]*Id.*

[50]*See also* Winkle Bus Co., Inc., 347 NLRB No. 108, 180 LRRM 1369 (2006) (A manager asked an employee, "do you want to wait for years for a raise like those people?" This statement was made in reference to a newspaper article describing a labor situation at an unrelated employer. In finding the comment lawful, the Board viewed the comment as simply and accurately indicating that wage increases could be delayed because of the uncertainties of the collective bargaining process).

[51]George L. Mee Mem'l Hosp., 348 NLRB No. 15, 181 LRRM 1320 (2006) (finding no violation where employer told employees that if they went on strike they would be permanently replaced).

(4) Assessing Recurrent Phrases and Themes

(a) "Serious Harm." Employer statements that a contract with a client prohibits unions is unlawful, unless supported by objective facts.[52]

(b) "Bargaining Will Start From Scratch." The Board continues to find that such statements are unlawful and constitute objectionable conduct.[53]

(c) Statements Regarding Plant Closings. Courts continue to enforce the Board's findings on this point,[54] including that such statements are usually not lawful.[55]

b. Promises and Grants of Benefits

Employer knowledge of an organizing campaign is essential to finding that a grant or promise of benefits is unlawful under Section 8(a)(1). In *Hampton Inn NY-JFK Airport*,[56] the employer's promised wage increase was not unlawful because it was announced while the employer was unaware of the ongoing organizing campaign. Despite the employer's admission that it announced the wage increase in response to "concerns about a potential union organizing campaign," the Board found that an employer's knowledge of ongoing union activity "is an essential element of [an] 8(a) (1) violation." In these cases, the Board focuses its analysis "on whether the [employer] intended to interfere with actual union organizational

---

[52]The Wackenhut Corp., 348 NLRB No. 93, 181 LRRM 1186 (2006) (employer's statement that it had an agreement with client that it would not "formulate a union" unlawful).

[53]Exelon Generation Co., LLC, 347 NLRB No. 77, 180 LRRM 1551 (2006) (objection to election sustained based on employer's statements that union selection would result in loss of rotating schedules, flextime, and ability to accept or reject overtime); Consolidated Biscuit Co., 346 NLRB No. 101, 180 LRRM 1243 (2006) (preelection statements by employer's president that bargaining would start "from zero," "with a clean slate" and that employees would "probably lose" certain benefits violated §8(a)(1)).

[54]*See* Amptech, Inc. v. NLRB, 165 Fed. Appx. 435 (6th Cir. 2006); Atlantic Veal & Lamb, Inc. v. NLRB, 156 Fed. Appx. 330 (D.C. Cir. 2005).

[55]Smithfield Foods, Inc., 347 NLRB No. 109, 181 LRRM 1069 (2006) (employer's constant reminders that three union-represented companies at its location had closed were not unlawful threats but protected "relevant, factual information about the Union's history at the facility" where the employer expressly disclaimed any certainty about the connection between the previous closures and the union, and the employer never predicted that it would close the facility if the employees voted for the union).

[56]348 NLRB No. 2, 181 LRRM 1034 (2006).

activity among its employees, rather than whether the [employer] wanted to stay 'one step ahead' of the union by diminishing the appeal of unionization."[57] The Board has also continued to use the promise or grant of benefits during an organizing campaign, along with evidence of other serious unfair labor practices, to support the issuance of a *Gissel*[58] remedial bargaining order.[59]

(2) Soliciting or Remedying Employee Grievances

The Board continues to follow the rule that an employer's solicitation of grievances is permissible, so long as there is no promise to remedy the grievances. In *Airport 2000 Concessions*,[60] the Board found the employer's conduct—which consisted of a manager meeting with two employees who expressed their dissatisfaction with various aspects of the company in response to his prompting—lawful. The Board reiterated that "[t]he essence of a solicitation of grievances/implied promise of benefit violation is the promise of remedying the grievance, not the mere solicitation."[61] It found that, despite soliciting the grievances, the employer did not promise or assure the employees that it would remedy those grievances, and thus did not act unlawfully. The Board reached this conclusion despite the employer's statements, in response to the employees' complaints, that "maybe [it] could provide better benefits later."[62] This statement was not problematic according to the Board, however, because it was a conditional statement and, therefore, insufficient to constitute a promise.[63] The Board cautioned that it was not abandoning any of the well-established principles concerning implied promises to remedy grievances, recognizing that an employer's solicitation of grievances "raises a rebuttable presumption of an implied promise

---

[57]*Id.* (quoting NLRB v. Gotham Indus., Inc., 406 F.2d 1306, 1310 (1st Cir. 1969)).

[58]NLRB v. Gissel Packing Co., 395 U.S. 575, 71 LRRM 2481 (1969).

[59]*See* Evergreen Am. Corp., 348 NLRB No. 12, 181 LRRM 1288 (2006); Concrete Form Walls, Inc., 346 NLRB No. 80, 179 LRRM 1193 (2006).

[60]346 NLRB No. 86, 179 LRRM 1337 (2006).

[61]*Id.*, slip op. at 5 (citing Ryder Transp. Servs., 341 NLRB 761, 769 (2004), *enforced* 401 F.3d 815 (7th Cir. 2005)).

[62]*Id.*, slip op. at 5.

[63]*See id.* (citing Curwood, Inc., 339 NLRB 1137 (2003)), *enforced in relevant part* 397 F.3d 548 (7th Cir. 2005).

to remedy those grievances."[64] In this instance, it simply found that the employer had rebutted that presumption.[65]

Conversely, in *Register Guard*,[66] the Board concluded that the employer had violated Section 8(a)(1) by improperly soliciting employee grievances and promising to remedy them. There, the Board determined that the employer had failed to rebut the presumption that the solicited grievances would be remedied, where it not only solicited employee concerns and promised to look into them, but also affirmatively informed the employees that it would address two of the concerns and created additional positions in response to one of them. The Board further noted that the solicitation occurred in the context of an "emergency" meeting—a practice that was atypical and inconsistent with past practice.

(3) Withholding Benefits During an Election Campaign

It continues to be the case that an employer may delay a wage increase under certain circumstances, but that both the Board and the courts will closely scrutinize the employer's reasoning and explanation accompanying that delay. In *NLRB v. Promedica Health Systems*,[67] the Sixth Circuit denied the Board's petition for enforcement because it found that the employer's statements regarding a delayed wage increase were proper. The Board had concluded that the employer's comments—that the wage increase was "on hold" until after the election and that "upon completion of the organizing campaign, irrespective of whether the Union was accepted or rejected, the raise could be brought up again either to be implemented or to be part of the collective bargaining process" —could cause an employee to believe that the wage increase would not occur if the employees selected union representation.[68] The Sixth Circuit disagreed, finding that the employer's comments evidenced a clear intent to implement the raise after the election "one way or another."

---

[64]*Id.*, 346 NLRB No. 86, slip op. at 5.

[65]*Id. See also* American Red Cross Mo., 347 NLRB No. 33, 181 LRRM 1013 (2006) (no violation of §8(a)(1) where employer distributed survey to employees asking about working conditions that they felt needed to be improved, where such actions were consistent with the employer's past practice of soliciting employee feedback).

[66]344 NLRB No. 150, 177 LRRM 1382 (2005).

[67]2006 Fed. Appx. 0737N, 180 LRRM 2789 (6th Cir. 2006).

[68]Promedica Health Sys., Inc., 343 NLRB 1351, 1354, 177 LRRM 1037 (2004).

c. Interrogation and Polling

(1) Systematic Polling

In *Unifirst Corp.*[69] the Board, in a 2–1 decision, reversed the ALJ and affirmed as lawful an employer's poll conducted to confirm whether the employees desired continued representation. There, while a decertification petition was blocked pending completion of the investigation of certain unfair labor practice charges, the employer was presented with a petition with 40 employee signatures asking for an election to determine whether employees desired continued representation. In light of the petition, the employer conducted a poll and learned that the majority opposed continued representation. Armed with this knowledge, the employer withdrew recognition of the union. The Board found the employer's conduct lawful and consistent with Board precedent, as well as with the Supreme Court's decision in *Allentown Mack.*[70] It noted that the employer could have withdrawn recognition of the union under established precedent by virtue of the 40-employee petition it received, which evidenced the union's actual loss of majority support. But it also recognized that the employer properly polled the employees to confirm their actual loss of support for the union so as to avoid a violation of Section 8(a)(5). Thus, the Board reiterated the principle that "an employer [who] makes the choice not to continue recognition, and wishes to make sure that a withdrawal of recognition would be lawful...may lawfully poll its employees to make sure that the Union in fact no longer enjoys majority status."[71]

In her dissent, Member Liebman disagreed with the majority that the poll was lawful, contending that the majority's conclusions are contrary to the Board's *Struksnes* decision.[72] In particular, Member Liebman viewed the *Struksnes* decision as unequivocally rendering a poll unlawful when it is taken while a petition for a Board election is pending and she would place no significance on the fact that a decertification petition—as opposed to a representation petition—was pending.[73] Her dissent concluded that "the *Struksnes* prohibition against polling employees while a petition is pending remains the law." In addition, as for withdrawing recognition of a union, her dis-

---

[69]346 NLRB No. 52, 179 LRRM 1116 (2006).
[70]Allentown Mack Sales & Serv. v. NLRB, 522 U.S. 359 (1998).
[71]*Unifirst Corp.*, slip op. at 5, 179 LRRM 1116.
[72]*Id.* at 1126–27.
[73]*Id.* at 1126 (citing S.M.S. Auto. Prods., 282 NLRB 36, 125 LRRM 1125 (1986)).

sent urged a wait-and-see approach, concluding that "contrary to the majority's claim, an employer has no need to poll employees as a safeguard before unilaterally withdrawing recognition... [the employer] may safely continue to recognize the Union while awaiting the results of the Board's election."

(2) Individual or Isolated Questioning

Although the criteria for determining the validity of interrogation by means other than polling remains unclear, the *Bourne* test[74] continues to gain acceptance. The factors considered in the *Bourne* test include: (1) the background, (2) the nature of the information sought, (3) the identity of the questioner, (4) the place and method of interrogation, and (5) the truthfulness of the reply.[75]

In *Holiday Inn-JFK Airport,*[76] the Board affirmed its adherence to the *Bourne* test and applied the *Bourne* factors to hold that an unlawful interrogation occurred where a supervisor called a probationary employee into her office to ask "how she felt about the union." In determining that a violation of Section 8(a)(1) occurred, the Board relied on the fact that the employee was a probationary employee and had not yet been offered a permanent position, coupled with the supervisor's ambiguous remark that "we're all family," which could reasonably be interpreted, against a background of employer hostility and discrimination arising out of other unfair labor practices found in this case, to imply that employees who supported the union threatened the "family atmosphere."

The Board also continues to find violations of Section 8(a)(1) when management directly interrogates employees during union organizing campaigns.[77]

---

[74]Bourne v. NLRB, 332 F.2d 47, 56 LRRM 2241 (2d Cir. 1964), *enforcing as modified* 144 NLRB 805, 54 LRRM 1158 (1963). *See* Section II.B.2.c., *supra.*
[75]Holiday Inn-JFK Airport, 348 NLRB No. 1, 181 LRRM 1040 (2006).
[76]*Id.*
[77]*See* Smithfield Foods, Inc., 347 NLRB No. 109, 181 LRRM 1069 (2006) (employer violated §8(a)(1) where supervisor asked employee if she supported the union and whether she had signed an authorization card); Food & Commercial Workers Local 204 v. NLRB, 447 F.3d 821, 179 LRRM 2708 (D.C. Cir. 2006) (employer violated §8(a)(1) where, in addition to a coercive atmosphere, a supervisor approached known union supporters and asked "Why do you... guys want a Union, the Union can't do anything for you but cause trouble between the workers and the Company."); Children's Servs. Int'l, Inc., 347 NLRB No. 7, 179 LRRM 1273 (2006) (interim director engaged in coercive interrogation where she accused an employee of authoring a union flier, which was highly critical of the director, after the employee refused to accept a copy of the flier at a meeting organized to discuss the flier). *But see* U-Haul Co. of Cal., 347 NLRB No. 34, 180 LRRM 1093 (2006) (shop

(3) Preparation of Defense for Trial of Unfair Labor Practice Case

The Board recently applied the safeguards set forth in *Johnnie's Poultry*[78] to an employer letter inquiring about whether its employees intended to strike.[79] Immediately following service upon the employer of the union's strike notice, the employer in *Washoe Medical Center* sent a letter and preprinted response card to unit employees informing them that it had received the strike notice and stating in part:

> [W]e need to know whether you intend to work or not. Please indicate your decision. If you do not complete and submit the enclosed response card by this date, we must assume you intend not to work on June 26.

The letter also stated: "[N]o one can require you to strike if you do not want to do. Regardless of your decision, no reprisal can or will be take against you."

The Board majority concluded the pre-strike letter was not unlawful interrogation because it satisfied the safeguards set forth in *Johnnie's Poultry*. The Board found (1) the letter was a straightforward, factual explanation of the employer's legitimate purpose for ascertaining employees' intentions during the strike, was tailored to serve only that legitimate purpose, and described the means of collecting the needed information and time frame for the submission; (2) the letter acknowledged the voluntary nature of the employer's request for information by explaining what it would do in the event of nonsubmission; and (3) the letter unambiguously and even-handedly assured employees that no reprisal can or would be taken against them as a result of their decisions regarding strike participation. Member Liebman dissenting on this part, viewed the letter as unlawfully coercive because the letter could be read to promise protection only for employees who chose not to strike.

---

manager's questioning at a meeting of 30 employees directed at a single employee was not found to be coercive where the manager did not reprimand the employee for supporting the union, employee was not asked about his union sentiments, and where the questioning was posed in response to the employee's public distribution of union literature concerning a different union campaign) and Washoe Med. Ctr., 348 NLRB No. 22 (2006) (employer did not unlawfully interrogate employees about a potential strike because it satisfied the *Johnnie's Poultry* standards).

[78] 146 NLRB 770 (1964), *enforcement denied*, 344 F.2d 617 (8th Cir. 1965).

[79] *See* Washoe Med. Ctr., 348 NLRB No. 22, 180 LRRM 1502 (2006).

d. Surveillance and Photographing

Surveillance of employees by an employer, regardless of whether the employees know of it, is unlawful.[80] Additionally, the Board has consistently held that an employer violates Section 8(a)(1) if it creates the impression of surveillance among its employees.[81]

The Board continues to permit employer observation of employee activity, such as picketing and handbilling, that has occurred on or near employer property. However, the employer's observation must be consistent with the protection of legitimate employer interests in good order and productivity.[82]

The random or isolated viewing of a union gathering by an employer agent is not prohibited surveillance. The Board has adhered to its decision in *Aladdin Gaming, LLC*,[83] in which it found no violation where two supervisors watched employees solicit others to sign union cards for 2 minutes. In *Airport 2000 Concessions, LLC*,[84] the Board relied on its decision in *Aladdin Gaming, LLC*, in holding that the employer did not violate Section 8(a)(1) where a supervisor intruded into an employee's conversation with a union organizer, because the supervisor's presence in the area was not "out of the ordinary" and therefore not coercive.

---

[80]*See* Ivy Steel & Wire, Inc., 346 NLRB No. 41, 179 LRRM 1060 (2006) (employer engaged in unlawful surveillance where the general manager was seated at a window in the bar across from the union hall during a union meeting). *But see* Consolidated Biscuit Co., 346 NLRB No. 101, 180 LRRM 1243 (2006) (employer did not violate §8(a)(1) by erecting ten "no trespassing" signs and four signs notifying onlookers that their activities were being monitored by a video camera, where employees knew the cameras were in place for over a year).

[81]*See* Classic Sofa, Inc., 346 NLRB No. 25, 179 LRRM 1049 (2006) (employer created an impression of surveillance where company president called employee into his office and said "Congratulations... [y]ou joined the Union" and further stated that it was "no big deal" and if the employee had informed him that the employee wanted a union, he "could have helped you get a union"); Rogers Elec., Inc., 346 NLRB No. 53, 179 LRRM 1113 (2006) (employer created an unlawful impression of surveillance in violation of §8(a)(1) where company president held up a telephone bill on which he had highlighted calls made to the state Department of Labor and Industry and told employees that he knew the calls had been made from the jobsite).

[82]Smithfield Foods, Inc., 347 NLRB No. 109, 181 LRRM 1069 (2006) (employer did not engage in unlawful surveillance by redirecting a security camera to the area where employee handbilling had taken place, where the employees engaged in handbilling had previously trespassed onto employer's property; employer's concern about further trespassing was reasonable).

[83]345 NLRB No. 41, 178 LRRM 1288 (2005).

[84]346 NLRB No. 86, 179 LRRM 1337 (2006).

f. Employer Violence

While an employer's use of threats or violence against employees because of protected activities violates Section 8(a)(1), the Board in *Children's Services International, Inc.*,[85] held that the employer did not violate Section 8(a)(1) when the interim director stated that a union flier that was critical of her made her want "to hit something." The Board reasoned that no threat of reprisal had occurred because it would be unreasonable to infer that the director actually intended to hit the employees.

g. Discipline and Discharge of Supervisors

An employer does not violate Section 8(a)(1) when it interrogates a supervisor regarding his or her union activity, as supervisors are excluded from the protections of the Act.[86]

3. Other Unlawful Employer Interference

b. Requests for Employee Statements to the NLRB

The Board will find unlawful statements or inquiries designed to elicit information concerning the extent of an employee's involvement in the Board's investigation of unfair labor practice charges, as well as statements or inquiries made to discourage such participation.[87]

c. Employer Conduct Relating to Authorization Cards

The Board continues to hold that an employer may not offer assistance to employees to withdraw membership in the union in the context of contemporaneous unfair labor practices. In *North Hills Office Services, Inc.*,[88] the Board found an employer's offer to help an employee "get out of" the union constituted unlawful assistance. In so holding, the Board reiterated that, "[a]n employer may lawfully inform employees of their right to revoke their authorization cards, even where employees have not solicited such information, as long

---

[85]347 NLRB No. 7, 179 LRRM 1273 (2006).
[86]Concrete Form Walls, Inc., 346 NLRB No. 80, 179 LRRM 1193 (2006) (employer did not violate §8(a)(1) where, after finding union literature in its supervisors' trucks, the employer questioned supervisors about their union activity).
[87]Management Consulting, Inc., 349 NLRB No. 27, 181 LRRM 1433 (2007) (supervisor's statement to employee that employee "did not want to get involved" in the processing of unfair labor practice charges constituted a direct admonition to her not to get involved in protected activities and thus violated §8(a)(1)).
[88]346 NLRB No. 96, 180 LRRM 1118 (2006).

as the employer makes no attempt to ascertain whether employees will avail themselves of this right nor offers any assistance, or otherwise creates a situation where employees would tend to feel peril in refraining from such revocation."[89]

d. Suits and Threats of Suits Against Employees

In a memorandum opinion,[90] the Ninth Circuit partially denied enforcement of the Board's decision in *Champion Home Builders Co.*,[91] previously cited at footnote 578 in the Main Edition. The court remanded to the Board the issue of whether a restraining order prohibiting a former employee from entering or coming within 50 yards of the employer's premises was preempted by the Board's previous order.[92]

III. OTHER CONCERTED ACTIVITY

A. Protected Concerted Activity: In General

1. *Individual Versus Concerted Activity: Employee Claim of Right Under a Collective Agreement*

The Board continues to apply its *Interboro* doctrine to protect an individual employee who presents group concerns under a collective bargaining agreement. The Board will not, however, extend this protection to an individual employee acting solely on his or her own behalf.[93]

Similarly, a sole employee picketing for recognition of herself, and no others, will not gain the Act's protections. In *International Transportation Service v. NLRB*,[94] the District of Columbia Circuit found that an employee who picketed for recognition of a union as her personal bargaining representative did not engage in protected activity and that her employer did not unlawfully discharge her in

---

[89]*Id.* (quoting R. L. White Co., 262 NLRB 575, 576, 111 LRRM 1079 (1982) (footnote omitted)).

[90]Carpenters Local 1109 v. NLRB, Nos. 04-76138, 05-71904, 05-72762, 2006 WL 3487113 (9th Cir. Dec. 4, 2006).

[91]343 NLRB 671, 176 LRRM 1557 (2004).

[92]Carpenters Local 1109 v. NLRB.

[93]Tampa Tribune, 346 NLRB No. 38, 179 LRRM 1001 (2006) (shop steward's use of profanity towards his supervisor found unprotected where he was acting based on his individual interests and not in his capacity as a steward).

[94]449 F.3d 160, 179 LRRM 2897 (D.C. Cir. 2006).

violation of the Act. The Board had found that the employer violated the Act because, inter alia, the individual picketing was protected union activity. The court, however, reasoned that the employee sought to have the union represent only herself, and that her actions were not on behalf of other employees. Accordingly, she could not have been engaged in a concerted activity protected by Section 7.

2. *Individual Versus Concerted Activity: Employee Claim of Right Under Employment, Safety, and Other Laws*

The Board continues to protect employees who express group concerns related to safety and other laws. However, in *Five Star Transportation, Inc.,*[95] the Board scrutinized particular statements made by employees to determine whether their individualized expressions of concern in fact call for the protection of fellow employees. In *Five Star*, the Board found that the employer, which entered into a new contract to provide school bus transportation services to a school district, violated Section 8(a)(1) by refusing to hire six of 11 bus drivers who worked for its predecessor and who sent individual letters to a school committee urging the committee to retain the previous contractor.

The Board held that all 11 drivers engaged in concerted activity by preparing and submitting individual letters to the school committee. However, the Board also found that only six of the drivers had engaged in protected activity because their letters primarily raised common employment-related concerns. The remaining five drivers did not engage in protected activity because two of the drivers' concerns were limited to a discussion of generalized safety concerns, as opposed to common employment-related concerns, and the other three drivers disparaged the employer's business reputation.

In *Asheville School, Inc.,*[96] the Board refused to extend protection to a payroll accountant who divulged confidential wage and salary information to other employees. The Board held that the employer's legitimate concern in protecting confidential personnel records in the custody of its payroll accountant outweighed the employee's Section 7 interest in disclosing the information. The Board further held that the employee had no agenda for group action and that mere "griping" was unprotected by the Act.[97]

---

[95] 349 NLRB No. 8, 181 LRRM 1137 (2007).
[96] 347 NLRB No. 84, 180 LRRM 1544 (2006).
[97] *Id.*, slip op. at 9.

3. Employee Activity for "Other Mutual Aid or Protection"

In *NLRB v. Hotel Employees & Restaurant Employees Local 26*,[98] the First Circuit upheld the Board's determination that an employee of the union had engaged in protected concerted activity. As part of a leafletting campaign to publicize its dispute with a hotel employer, the union required its employees to distribute leaflets on the picket line 7 days per week. The employee was terminated after she made several proposals to modify the leaflet distribution schedule. The court held that this was concerted activity, rejecting the union's argument that the employee's scheduling complaints were self-motivated. The employee had polled her co-workers to determine their scheduling preferences, presented scheduling ideas to the union president that would benefit all employees, and there was evidence that some employees supported her ideas.

In *North Carolina License Plate Agency #18*,[99] the Board found that three employees were engaged in protected concerted activity during a meeting with a manager where they complained about favoritism, wages, and bonuses and threatened to file a complaint with the state Department of Motor Vehicles (DMV), for which the employer was a contractor. The Board rejected the employer's argument that a complaint to the DMV would not be protected because the DMV lacked control over the labor relations of its contractors, as evidence showed that the DMV received and investigated customer complaints about its contractors' employees and could intervene in personnel matters where there was a serious problem with an employee. Moreover, the employer admitted that the employees were discharged based on their complaints, and the discharge occurred immediately after their threat to complain to the DMV, which the Board construed as evidence of animus toward the employees' protected activity.[100]

---

[98]446 F.3d 200, 179 LRRM 2641 (1st Cir. 2006), *enforcing* 344 NLRB No. 70, 177 LRRM 1089 (2005).

[99]346 NLRB No. 30, 179 LRRM 1033 (2006). *See also* Sunrise Senior Living, Inc., 344 NLRB No. 151, 177 LRRM 1316 (2005) (employees signing and presenting group petition that complained about facility care and contemplated work stoppage engaged in protected concerted activity), *enforced*, 183 Fed. Appx. 326, 179 LRRM 2920 (4th Cir. 2006).

[100]Champion Home Builders Co., 343 NLRB 671, 176 LRRM 1557 (2004), previously cited at footnote 650 in the Main Edition, was subsequently enforced in part and denied enforcement in part by Carpenters Local 1109 v. NLRB, Nos. 04-76138, 05-71904, 05-72762, 2006 WL 3487113 (9th Cir. 2006). The Ninth Circuit enforced the Board's order with respect to its finding that the employer violated the Act.

4. Limits on Protection of Concerted Activity[101]

In *Ellison Media Co.*,[102] the Board distinguished *Holling Press, Inc.*[103] in finding that a discussion between two employees of alleged sexual harassment constituted protected activity. The employee in *Ellison Media* told his co-worker that he believed he had overheard a supervisor make an offensive sexual comment. The co-worker, who had previously complained to management about offensive remarks made by the same supervisor, urged the employee to report the incident. The supervisor threatened to discharge both employees if they continued to gossip, and the Board found that this violated the employees' right to discuss sexual harassment complaints with other employees. The Board distinguished *Holling Press*, which held that an employee's efforts to enlist a co-worker's help to pursue her individual sexual harassment complaint was for her benefit alone. In contrast, the co-worker in *Ellison* supported the harassment complaint and had herself reported similar offensive remarks in the past.

In *Ogihara America Corp.*,[104] three employees sent an anonymous letter to the employer complaining about a supervisor's substandard work performance. Concerned about retaliation by the employer, the employee who sent the letter wrote an uninvolved co-worker's name in the return address. Reversing the ALJ, the Board upheld the employee's discharge for deliberately falsifying the name of the sender of the letter. The Board assumed that the complaints in the letter were protected, but found the employee's conduct was sufficiently egregious such that he lost protection under the Act. The unauthorized use of his co-worker's name on the letter was a "deliberate falsity" that posed a substantial risk to his co-worker's reputation and employment status.

In *Slusher v. NLRB*,[105] the Seventh Circuit reversed the Board's decision in *Exxon Mobil*.[106] The Board had held that the employer's termination of a union steward was justified where the steward circulated copies of another employee's DUI records among his co-workers in violation of the employer's antiharassment policy. The Board, reversing the ALJ, found that the steward's motive was to harass the employee whose records he distributed and that that conduct was

---

[101] *See also* Section III.C., *infra.*
[102] 344 NLRB No. 136, 177 LRRM 1285 (2005).
[103] 343 NLRB 301, 175 LRRM 1449 (2004).
[104] 347 NLRB No. 10, 180 LRRM 1009 (2006).
[105] 432 F.3d 715, 178 LRRM 2705 (7th Cir. 2005).
[106] 343 NLRB 287, 175 LRRM 1425 (2004).

unprotected. The Seventh Circuit, however, found that the Board improperly rejected the ALJ's credibility findings, and reinstated the ALJ's decision. The ALJ had concluded that the steward's actions were protected because he distributed the records to demonstrate to union members, in advance of an upcoming union decertification election, that the employer was not applying its drug and alcohol policy consistently.

B. Protected Concerted Activity: Specific Conduct

1. Work Stoppages

The Board in *QSI, Inc.*,[107] found that a walkout to protest the employer's discharge of certain managers and supervisors was protected concerted activity. The Board noted that although several federal circuit courts have considered the reasonableness of the means of protesting a supervisor's termination,[108] the Board will continue its practice of not imposing a "reasonable means" requirement on concerted activity, consistent with the Supreme Court's decision in *NLRB v. Washington Aluminum Co.*[109] Even if that requirement were to apply, the Board found that the walkout was reasonable because the employees concluded that further discussion with the employer would be ineffective, they had no bargaining representative to present their grievances to the employer, and the walkout posed no immediate threat to the safety or health of others.[110]

In *Phoenix Processor Limited Partnership*,[111] the Board held that a shipboard work stoppage was unprotected because the employees were seamen and thus their actions amounted to mutiny in violation of maritime law. There, the employer's facility was a floating fish-processing factory at sea and the employees were fish processors. Dissatisfied with the length of their shifts, the employees sat in the ship's library and refused the captain's order to return to work. The Board concluded that the employer did not violate the Act when it subse-

---

[107]346 NLRB No. 97, 180 LRRM 1037 (2006).

[108]*Id.* (citing Yesterday's Children, Inc. v. NLRB, 115 F.3d 36, 155 LRRM 2385 (1st Cir. 1997)); NLRB v. Oakes Mach. Corp., 897 F.2d 84, 133 LRRM 2753 (2d Cir. 1990); Dobbs Houses, Inc. v. NLRB, 325 F.2d 531, 54 LRRM 2726 (5th Cir. 1963); Bob Evans Farms, Inc. v. NLRB, 163 F.3d 1012, 160 LRRM 2024 (7th Cir. 1998).

[109]370 U.S. 9, 50 LRRM 2235 (1962).

[110]Vencare Ancillary Servs., 334 NLRB 965, 168 LRRM 1029 (2001), previously cited at footnote 690 in the Main Edition, was subsequently denied enforcement in Vencare Ancillary Servs. v. NLRB, 352 F.3d 318, 173 LRRM 2865 (6th Cir. 2003).

[111]348 NLRB No. 4, 180 LRRM 1401 (2006).

quently terminated the employees who engaged in the work stoppage because, as seamen, their failure to obey the captain's order was a violation of maritime law.[112]

3. Filing or Processing of Grievances

In *OPW Fueling Components v. NLRB*,[113] the Sixth Circuit upheld the Board's decision that a union steward who was terminated for signing two employees' names to a grievance was engaged in protected activity. The union steward wrote the names and signatures of two employees affected by the grievance without first seeking their permission, and subsequently was suspended and terminated for violating the employer's policy on falsification of records. Applying *Roadmaster v. NLRB*,[114] the court held that the union steward's concerted activity did not lose its protection under the Act. In signing the employees' names to the grievance, the union steward was acting in good faith and for a legitimate reason, and without intent to deceive the employer.

4. Weingarten: *Employee Request or Demand for Union Representation During Investigation*

a. Covered Interviews and Meetings

Titanium Metals Corp.,[115] previously cited at footnote 723 in the Main Edition, was subsequently enforced in part and denied enforcement in part in *Titanium Metals Corp. v. NLRB*.[116] The court enforced the Board's order insofar as it found that the employer wrongfully questioned a certain employee in the absence of a union representative.

b. Rights of Unrepresented Employees

The Board continues to follow the holding in *IBM Corp.*,[117] that unrepresented employees are not entitled to a co-worker representative during investigatory interviews.[118] On the other hand, the Board

---

[112]*Id.* See also Southern S.S. Co. v. NLRB, 316 U.S. 31, 10 LRRM 544 (1942).

[113]443 F.3d 490, 179 LRRM 2449 (6th Cir. 2006), *enforcing* 343 NLRB 1034, 176 LRRM 1390 (2004).

[114]874 F.2d 448, 131 LRRM 2483 (7th Cir. 1989), *enforcing* 288 NLRB 1195, 129 LRRM 1008 (1988).

[115]340 NLRB 766, 173 LRRM 1402 (2003).

[116]392 F.3d 439, 176 LRRM 2073 (D.C. Cir. 2004).

[117]341 NLRB 1288, 174 LRRM 1537 (2004).

[118]Publix Super Mkts., Inc., 347 NLRB No. 124, 180 LRRM 1480 (2006).

also continues to hold that the *Weingarten* rights of employees are still applicable where an employer unlawfully refuses to bargain with a majority union.[119]

d. Role of Union Representative

The Board continues to hold that a union representative at an investigatory interview cannot be restricted to the role of a mere observer but must be afforded the opportunity to provide "advice and active assistance" to a represented employee.[120]

7. Appeals to Agencies and Filing of Court Actions

The Board recently held that an employer violated Sections 8(a)(4) and (1) by maintaining a mandatory arbitration policy as a condition of employment. In *U-Haul of California,*[121] the Board majority concluded that the mandatory arbitration policy was unlawful under the test set forth in *Lutheran Heritage Village-Livonia,*[122] because it would reasonably be read by employees to prohibit the filing of unfair labor practice charges and require employees to resort to the employer's arbitration procedures instead of filing charges with the Board. Chairman Battista dissented. He found the policy not unlawful because there was no evidence the rule had been applied to the protected activity of invoking Board processes, there was no evidence that it was intended to apply to such activity, and the policy did not explicitly bar any Section 7 activity.

C. Limits on Protection of Concerted Activities[123]

3. Other Unprotected Activity

The Board continues to hold that otherwise protected concerted activity may lose the protection of the Act where the activity is disloyal to the employer and its business. In *Elko General Hospital,*[124] the Board found that an employer was justified in terminating an employee who, during a captive audience preelection meeting, stated that her husband had a bad experience at the employer's hospital facility,

---

[119]Five Star Mfg., Inc., 348 NLRB No. 94 (2006).
[120]Washoe Med. Ctr., Inc., 348 NLRB No. 22, 180 LRRM 1502 (2006).
[121]347 NLRB No. 34, 180 LRRM 1093 (2006).
[122]343 NLRB No. 75, 176 LRRM 1044 (2004).
[123]*See also* Section III.A.4., *supra.*
[124]347 NLRB No. 123, 180 LRRM 1326 (2006).

and that she wished the employer were still run by the county. The employee also attempted to end the meeting by calling on her co-workers to leave the meeting and return to work. The Board held that an employer "need not tolerate" such "disloyal" actions of an employee.[125]

a. Breach of Confidentiality

The Board continues to rely on the test it set forth in *Lutheran Heritage Village-Livonia*[126] in evaluating the legality of confidentiality provisions.[127] Thus, in *Longs Drug Stores California*, the Board[128] found that the employer violated Section 8(a)(1) by maintaining overbroad confidentiality provisions in employee handbooks.

However, the Board in *Asheville School, Inc.*,[129] while acknowledging its longstanding policy that employee discussions of wage and benefit information deemed confidential by the employer is protected activity, found an employee's publication of wage information of other employees to be unprotected where the employee was a payroll accountant whose job provided confidential access to this payroll information not otherwise available to any employee.

b. False Allegations or Affidavits Concerning the Employer

The Board continues to find that an employee loses the protection of the Act when the employee deliberately makes statements the employee knows to be false or with reckless disregard for their truth. The Board, in *TNT Logistics North America, Inc.*,[130] found that the employer was justified in terminating three employees who stated in a letter to the employer's corporate management and to the employer's primary customer, that management had asked employees to "fix" or falsify logbooks.[131]

---

[125]*Id. But see* North Carolina License Plate Agency #18, 346 NLRB No. 30, 179 LRRM 1033 (2006) (employer not justified in terminating three employees for inquiring about opening a competing business where employer knew of alleged disloyalty and did nothing about it until employees engaged in protected concerted activity).

[126]343 NLRB No. 75 (2004).

[127]343 NLRB 646 (2004).

[128]347 NLRB No. 45 (2006).

[129]347 NLRB No. 84, 180 LRRM 1544 (2006).

[130]347 NLRB No. 55, 180 LRRM 1041 (2006).

[131]*See also* Kvaerner Phila. Shipyard, Inc., 347 NLRB No. 36, 180 LRRM 1147 (2006) (Board affirmed ALJ's deferral to arbitrator's decision upholding discharge of employee who falsely suggested in a letter to fellow employees that the employer was wrongfully withholding money from employee paychecks).

c. Disparagement of the Employer or Its Business Activities

In *Endicott Interconnect Technologies, Inc. v. NLRB*,[132] the District of Columbia Circuit, applying *Jefferson Standard*[133] and denying enforcement of a Board ruling, held that an employee lost the protection of the Act by making disloyal, disparaging, and injurious statements about the employer's recent layoffs to a newspaper reporter and on the newspaper's online message board.[134]

d. Disruptive, Profane, or Vulgar Behavior

In *Corrections Corp. of America*,[135] the Board, balancing an employee's right to engage in concerted activity with the employer's right to maintain order and control, found that an employee's limited use of profanity did not cause him to lose the protection of the Act where use of profanity was common at the facility and the incident in question involved only a single profane statement spoken in the employee's role as a union leader. In contrast, however, the Board found that a shop steward's use of profanity towards his supervisor was unprotected where he was acting based on his individual interests and not in his capacity as a steward.[136]

In *Airo Die Casting, Inc*,[137] the Board adopted the ALJ's conclusion that an employee's use of a racially derogatory term, absent any threats or violence, did not rise to a level where he forfeited the protection of the Act. A majority of the Board noted, however, that in an appropriate case, the use of such a term may be so incendiary as to render the use unprotected.[138]

---

[132]453 F.3d 532, 179 LRRM 3276 (D.C. Cir. 2006), *denying enforcement to* 345 NLRB No. 28, 178 LRRM 1169 (2005).

[133]NLRB v. Electrical Workers (IBEW) Local 1229 (Jefferson Standard Broad. Co.), 346 U.S. 464, 33 LRRM 2183 (1953).

[134]*But see* Noble Metal Processing, Inc., 346 NLRB No. 78, 179 LRRM 1333 (2006) (employee's conduct in challenging his manager at departmental meeting was protected activity and not deliberately false or malicious).

[135]347 NLRB No. 62, 180 LRRM 1330 (2006).

[136]Tampa Tribune, 346 NLRB No. 38, 179 LRRM 1001 (2006).

[137]347 NLRB No. 75, 180 LRRM 1056 (2006).

[138]*Id.*, slip op. at 1 n.3, 180 LRRM at 1056.

IV. UNION RESTRAINT AND COERCION

A. Section 8(b)(1)(A): Restraint and Coercion of Employees

2. Fines and Discipline of Union Members

The Board continues to hold that unions may impose reasonable fines on their members as long as the circumstances surrounding the discipline conform to the four requirements set forth in *Scofield v. NLRB*.[139] In *Electrical Workers (IBEW) (Verizon New England)*,[140] the Board reaffirmed that a union can fine its members for declining to participate in a concerted refusal to work voluntary overtime, as distinguished from mandatory assignments.

The Board, however, need not wait until a union actually imposes discipline to find a violation. Filing and processing charges against an employee who has resigned from the union can still have a "restraining and coercive effect" sufficient to violate the Act.[141]

a. Discipline for Activity That Contravenes a Policy of the NLRA, Including the Filing of NLRB Petitions and Charges

The Board still finds a violation of Section 8(b)(1)(A) when a union threatens its members with retaliation for filing a charge with the Board. A union official's statement to an employee that "we're going to sue you" constituted such retaliation when the employee had filed unfair labor practice charges.[142]

b. Impact of Discipline on Employment Relationship

A union's duty to inform employees of their obligations before seeking discharge includes information for *Beck*[143] objectors about the allocation of dues. In *Teamsters Local 492 (United Parcel Service)*,[144] the Board found that although the union correctly informed several employees who had filed *Beck* objections the percentage of their dues that were to be reduced, the union violated Section 8(b)(1)(A)

---

[139]394 U.S. 423, 70 LRRM 3105 (1969).

[140]348 NLRB No. 50, 181 LRRM 1212 (2006).

[141]Teamsters Local 492 (United Parcel Serv.), 346 NLRB No. 37, 179 LRRM 1062 (2006).

[142]Ironworkers Local 340 (Consumers Energy Co.), 347 NLRB No. 57, 180 LRRM 1166 (2006).

[143]487 U.S. 735 (1988).

[144]346 NLRB No. 37, 179 LRRM 1062 (2006).

when it failed to inform these employees the basis for the calculations used to determine their dues, that the employees had a right to challenge the union's calculations, and that the information provided was independently verified. However, when not sought by any party, the Board chose not to alter present Board law that a union need not provide a breakdown of representational and nonrepresentational expenses when giving the *Beck* and *General Motors* notice to employees.[145]

The Board continues to find that internal discipline by unions may not prevent the reemployment of an employee[146] or impose adverse working conditions on employees.[147]

c. The Effect of Resignation on Legality of Discipline

The Board has held that a union must honor the resignation of any employee promptly. A resignation that is mailed is effective at 12:01 a.m. local time the day after mailing.[148] Accordingly, no discipline may be imposed after that time.

e. Discipline for Intraunion Activity

In *Food & Commercial Workers Local 7R*,[149] the Board held that a union organizer's comment was not intraunion discipline, but rather was coercive and threatening in violation of Section 8(b)(1)(A). The union organizer indicated that he would grab a union member by "her hair and take her out" if she came to another union meeting. Reversing the decision of the ALJ, the Board concluded that this statement constituted a threat of physical violence that went beyond internal union disciplinary action and thus violated the Act. While the Board does not proscribe union conduct that is purely

---

[145] Food & Commercial Workers Local 648 (Safeway, Inc.), 347 NLRB No. 83, 180 LRRM 1230 (2006).

[146] Plumbers & Pipe Fitters Local 420 (Carrier Corp.), 347 NLRB No. 53, 180 LRRM 1015 (2006).

[147] Electrical Workers (IBEW) Local 429, 347 NLRB No. 46, 180 LRRM 1048 (2006). *Compare* Roadway Express, Inc., 347 NLRB No. 122, 180 LRRM 1543 (2006) (union did not act unlawfully when it caused the employer to discipline an employee who was a *Beck* objector because, among other things, the union had a pattern of raising drivers' logs to the attention of the employer, the employee incurred several complaints about his logs from co-workers, other drivers were disciplined for log entries similar to the employee, and the union's complaints about the employee's logs were "arguably" valid).

[148] *Teamsters Local 492 (United Parcel Serv.)*, 346 NLRB No. 37 (citing Pattern Makers (Michigan Model Mfrs. Ass'n), 310 NLRB 929, 930, 142 LRRM 1345 (1993)).

[149] 347 NLRB No. 97, 180 LRRM 1466 (2006).

intraunion discipline, it does proscribe threats by unions against employees for exercising their protected rights to be involved in intraunion activities.

The Board continues to recognize that a union may not impose internal union discipline against a member after they have resigned from the union. Processing such charges may have the effect of unlawfully restricting union members from exercising their right to resign.[150]

3. Violence and Threats

In *NLRB v. Precision Indoor Comfort Inc.*,[151] the Sixth Circuit upheld the Board's longstanding principle that an isolated comment made by a union supporter to a fellow employee during the course of a representation election campaign was not serious enough to set aside the results of the election. The court reasoned that a fellow employee's comment that "the guys are going to want to" do the employee physical harm if he did not vote for union representation did not create a general atmosphere of fear and coercion and thus did not violate Section 8(b)(1)(A) of the Act.

---

[150] *Teamsters Local 492 (United Parcel Serv.)*, 346 NLRB No. 37, 179 LRRM 1062.
[151] 456 F.3d 636, 180 LRRM 2080 (6th Cir. 2006), *enforcing* 344 NLRB No. 24, 176 LRRM 1416 (2005).

CHAPTER 7

DISCRIMINATION IN EMPLOYMENT

II. Employer Discrimination

A. Persons Within the Protection of Section 8(a)(3)

The Board and the courts continue to follow the rule enunciated by the Supreme Court in *NLRB v. Town & Country Electric*,[1] that the definition of "employee" in Section 2(3) of the Act includes paid union organizers who obtain employment for the purpose of organizing the employer's workplace.[2]

"It is axiomatic" that supervisors are excluded from Section 8(a) (3) such that their union activities are not protected.[3] However, the Board also continues to hold that a supervisor's discharge does violate Section 8(a)(1) if it results from that supervisor's unfavorable testimony at a Board hearing,[4] or the supervisor's refusal to commit unfair labor practices.[5]

While the Supreme Court in *Hoffman Plastic Compounds, Inc. v NLRB*[6] barred back pay to employees not legally authorized to work in the United States, this holding does not prevent undocumented aliens from being considered "employees" under Section 2(3) of the Act.[7]

To that end, the Board rejected an employer's contention that it could legally discharge employees under the Act because they were

---

[1]516 U.S. 85, 150 LRRM 2897 (1995).

[2]C&K Insulation, Inc., 347 NLRB No. 71, 180 LRRM 1397 (2006); Progressive Elec., Inc. v. NLRB, 453 F.3d 538, 179 LRRM 3265 (D.C. Cir. 2006).

[3]Concrete Form Walls, Inc, 346 NLRB No. 80, 179 LRRM 1193 (2006) ("In fact, an employer may lawfully discharge a supervisor for engaging in pro-union conduct even though such a discharge could cause employees to reconsider or abandon their own protected concerted activity.").

[4]SNE Enters., Inc., 347 NLRB No. 43, 180 LRRM 1431 (2006).

[5]Bon Harbor Nursing, 348 NLRB No. 70, 180 LRRM 1521 (2006).

[6]535 U.S. 137, 169 LRRM 2769 (2002).

[7]Agri Processor Co., Inc., 347 NLRB No. 107, 180 LRRM 1222 (2006).

undocumented aliens.[8] The Board also held that these employees were eligible voters in a Board election.[9] Evidence offered by the employer to show that the employee's Social Security numbers did not match those in the Social Security database was not sufficient to show they were working illegally in the United States.[10]

B. Purpose of the Discrimination

1. Conduct Requiring Proof of Union Animus: The Wright Line Rule

In *Planned Building Services,*[11] the five-member Board unanimously held that where it is alleged that a putative successor employer has unlawfully refused to hire its predecessor's employees to avoid a bargaining obligation, the proper analytical framework is the traditional *Wright Line*[12] analysis and not the "modified *Wright Line* analysis"[13] set forth in *FES,*[14] which otherwise "generally applies in cases involving a discriminatory failure to hire or refusal to consider for hire."[15]

The Board stated that it had decided "to clarify the applicable standard in successorship-avoidance cases"[16] given the "mixed treatment of the question in our post-*FES* precedent."[17] The Board observed that in some post-*FES* cases in the successorship context it had applied the "modified *Wright Line* analysis" of *FES,* which defined the general counsel's burden as one to show not only unlawful motivation but also that the employer was actually hiring at the time of the alleged unlawful conduct and that the applicant had the relevant experience or training for the position, while in other successorship cases both before and after *FES* it had applied a traditional *Wright Line* analysis in which the existence of a job opening and sufficiency of the employee's qualifications are presumed for purposes of the general counsel's burden. Finding "no purpose to require the Gen-

---

[8] *Concrete Form Walls,* 346 NLRB No. 80, 179 LRRM 1193.
[9] *Id.*
[10] *Id.*
[11] 347 NLRB No. 64, 180 LRRM 1081 (2006).
[12] Wright Line, Wright Line Div., 251 NLRB 1083 (1980), 105 LRRM 1169, *enforced,* 662 F.2d 899, 108 LRRM 2513 (1st Cir. 1981), *cert. denied,* 455 U.S. 989, 109 LRRM 2779 (1982).
[13] *Id.,* 251 NLRB at 1086.
[14] 331 NLRB 9, 164 LRRM 1065 (2000).
[15] *Planned Bldg. Servs.,* 180 LRRM at 1083.
[16] *Id.* at 1085.
[17] *Id.* at 1086.

eral Counsel to demonstrate, in each successorship case, that the employees have relevant experience or training for essentially the same jobs in the successor's work force that they performed in the predecessor's work force,"[18] and that "it is similarly of little use"[19] to require the general counsel to demonstrate that the employer was hiring or had concrete plans to hire when it is plain and obvious that "a successor employer must fill vacant positions in starting up its business,"[20] the Board concluded that "these additional elements that the Board added to the General Counsel's initial burden in *FES* are not appropriately part of the General Counsel's burden in establishing refusal-to-hire allegations in a successorship setting."[21]

2. Conduct Inherently Destructive of Section 7 Rights

In *Bud Antle, Inc.*,[22] the employer entered into an agreement with two unions providing for an end to a 14-year-long lockout of employees. Pursuant to the terms of the agreement, the employer offered reinstatement to the locked out employees and afforded each of them 30 days in which to accept the offer. The agreement also provided that the employer would staff its workforce with the most senior of: (1) its replacement employees; and (2) the locked out employees who accepted reinstatement, dating their seniority from their original date of hire to the date of commencement of the lockout. The locked out employees accepted the reinstatement offer prior to the expiration of the 30-day period.

The employer, however, delayed the reinstatement of the formerly locked out employees for approximately 60 days from the date of its letters offering reinstatement. A divided Board, applying *Great Dane Trailers*[23] and *International Paper*,[24] found that the employer's initial delay while it waited for the 30-day deadline to accept reinstatement to expire was not inherently destructive of employee rights and the impact was only "comparatively slight." The employer also had a legitimate and substantial business justification "based on the need to determine the identity and the number of returning employees and to dovetail their seniority with the seniority of the replacement work-

---

[18] *Id.* at 1086.
[19] *Id.*
[20] *Id.*
[21] *Id.*
[22] 347 NLRB No. 9, 180 LRRM 1507 (2006).
[23] 338 U.S. 26, 65 LRRM 2465 (1967).
[24] 319 NLRB 1523, 151 LRRM 1033 (1995), *enforcement denied*, 115 F.3d 1045, 155 LRRM 2641 (D.C. Cir. 1997).

ers; and the efficiencies created by starting and training a potentially large number of returning workers all at once."[25] The Board concluded that "because no party submitted independent evidence that the Respondent's actions were motivated by an antiunion motive," there was no violation of Section 8(a)(3) in this initial period of delay.[26] However, the Board found that the second 30 days of delay was not justified by legitimate and substantial business reasons and therefore violated Section 8(a)(3).

In addition, following reinstatement of the locked out employees the employer limited their overtime opportunities for a period of 4 weeks. The employer had a policy of limiting the overtime opportunities of newly hired employees for 4 weeks, which it deemed a training period. The Board found that the employer's limiting of overtime of the locked out employees was not inherently destructive of employee rights but had only a "comparatively slight" impact "in the circumstances of this case" and that the employer had articulated a legitimate and substantial business justification for its actions. It relied principally on the "unprecedented" 14-year length of the lockout, during which the employer had instituted operational changes to its business that it could reasonably determine required retraining of the reinstated employees to be able to perform their work assignments quickly and efficiently.

In *Roosevelt Memorial Medical Center*,[27] a divided Board held that the employer's reduction of hours of employees who had announced a strike that was later postponed was not "inherently destructive" of employees' rights. The Board majority held that the actual effect on employees' hours was "comparatively slight," and that most of the affected employees actually worked their full work week. Further, the employer had a business justification for its actions in that it had already committed to pay agency-supplied temporary employees who were to work during the strike.

Member Liebman dissented, arguing that reducing the hours of only those employees who had stated their intention to strike, and leaving the hours of other employees unaffected, was "inherently destructive" without regard to the number of hours of pay; and, even if the adverse effect were found to be "comparatively slight." Additionally, the employer's claimed business justifications were

---

[25] *Bud Antle*, 180 LRRM at 1511.
[26] *Id.* at 1512.
[27] 348 NLRB No. 64 (2006).

unsubstantiated and implausible and the employer's action could be explained only by its hostility toward the intended strikers.

C. Specific Conduct

1. Discharge or Discipline for Union Activity

a. Elements of an Unlawful Discharge

The Board continues to adhere to the two-part *Wright Line*[28] standard in unlawful discharge cases where an employer asserts an allegedly proper business reason for the discharge.[29] Under this standard, the general counsel has the burden of proving that an employee's union membership or protected activities were a motivating factor for the employer's discharge. Thereafter, the burden of proof shifts to the employer to prove that it would have taken the same action even in the absence of an employee's union membership or protected activities.[30] The Board continues to hold that when an employer admits to discharging an employee because of his or her protected activities, the *Wright Line* standard is inapplicable.[31]

b. Constructive Discharge

The Board continues to adhere to the theory that an employer may constructively discharge an employee if the employer deliberately made working conditions unbearable to force the employee to resign; however, in such a case, there must be a change in working conditions that was intended to force the employee to quit or would have that foreseeable outcome.[32]

c. Employer's Knowledge of Employee's Union Activity

The Board continues to require that the general counsel prove that the employer had knowledge of an employee's union membership or protected activities before or at the time the employer under-

---

[28]Wright Line, Wright Line Div., 251 NLRB 1083, 105 LRRM 1169 (1980), *enforced*, 662 F.2d 899, 108 LRRM 2513 (1st Cir. 1982), *cert. denied*, 455 U.S. 989, 109 LRRM 2779 (1982).

[29]*See, e.g.*, Weldon, Williams & Lick, Inc., 348 NLRB No. 45, 181 LRRM 1008 (2006).

[30]Alan Ritchey, Inc., 346 NLRB No. 26, 178 LRRM 1421 (2006).

[31]Allied Aviation Fueling of Dallas, LP, 347 NLRB No. 22, 180 LRRM 1255 (2006).

[32]Smithfield Foods, Inc., 347 NLRB No. 110, 181 LRRM 1132 (2006).

takes the allegedly unlawful discharge.[33] In addition, the Board continues to require the general counsel to show that the employer knew of the employee's union membership or protected activities at the time of the discharge.[34] However, the Board also continues to infer an employer's knowledge of an employee's union activities from the small size of the employer's facility.[35]

d. Inferential Proof of Employer's Animus

The Board continues to find an employer's asserted justification for a discharge to be pretextual based on any number of factors. For example, the Board continues to infer that an employer's asserted justifications for discharging an employee are pretextual when the discharge occurs shortly after the employee engages in protected activity.[36] The Board also continues to find asserted justifications to be pretextual where there are changes in the employer's reason for termination,[37] the reason is false,[38] the employer has previously tolerated the type of conduct in which the employee alleged engaged,[39] or the employer treats the employee differently than other employees who engaged in the same conduct.[40] The opposite also continues to hold true. An employer's warnings for specific conduct may suggest that a discharge based upon similar conduct is not discriminatorily motivated.[41] Similarly, evidence that an employer has meted out

---

[33]Construction Prods., Inc., 346 NLRB No. 60, 179 LRRM 1108 (2006).

[34]Conley Trucking, 349 NLRB No. 30 (2007) (general counsel established employer's direct knowledge with statement by owner that he heard employee and two others "were trying to get union in here"); Septix Waste, Inc., 346 NLRB No. 50, 179 LRRM 1073 (2006) (presence of supervisor at union meeting attended by employee, as well as employer's receipt of employee's dues checkoff card, provided evidence of employer knowledge). *But see* Caribe Ford, 348 NLRB No. 74, 180 LRRM 1479 (2006) (general counsel failed to establish employer knowledge).

[35]Five Star Mfg., 348 NLRB No. 94 (2006).

[36]Weldon, Williams & Lick, Inc., 348 NLRB No. 45, 181 LRRM 1008 (2006). *See also* Healthcare Employees Local 299 v. NLRB, 463 F.3d 909, 180 LRRM 2533 (9th Cir. 2006) (employer subcontracted entire department less than month after representation petition filed and 2 weeks before election, resulting in disenfranchisement of one quarter of eligible employees).

[37]*Conley Trucking*, 349 NLRB No. 30.

[38]U-Haul Co. of Cal., 347 NLRB No. 34, 180 LRRM 1093 (2006).

[39]T. Steele Constr., Inc., 348 NLRB No. 79 (2006); *Septix Waste*, 346 NLRB No. 50, 179 LRRM 1073.

[40]*Conley Trucking*, 349 NLRB No. 30 (employer tolerated employees with worse attendance records than discharged employee); *T. Steel Constr.*, 348 NLRB No. 79 (employer kept employees with worse attendance records than discharged employee).

[41]Alan Ritchey, Inc., 346 NLRB No. 26, 178 LRRM 1421 (2006).

discipline for certain conduct on a consistent basis may continue to rebut charges of pretext.[42]

2. Lockouts

The purpose or motive underlying the lockout continues to be the critical factor in determining whether the lockout violates the Act.

In *Steelworkers v. NLRB*,[43] the union petitioned for review of a Board decision which held that the employer did not commit an unfair labor practice by partially locking out union members and not probationary employees who were not members of the union after reaching impasse in negotiations. Thereafter, the employer withdrew recognition based on a decertification petition signed by a majority of the employees. The administrative law judge (ALJ) had rejected the company's contention that the employees had gone on strike but determined that the lockout was lawful nonetheless because it was in furtherance of the employer's legitimate business purpose: to pressure the union to accept its bargaining proposals. The Board affirmed the ALJ's decision.[44]

The District of Columbia Circuit stated that "[a]lthough we give deference to Board decisions, we cannot uphold a decision that is inconsistent with controlling precedent."[45] The court noted that the union showed a perfect correlation between union membership and the employees who were locked out, thus demonstrating discriminatory conduct. The court pointed out that the burden was on the employer to present evidence that the lockout had been motivated by legitimate business objectives and the employer had not presented evidence on this point. The case was remanded to the Board to determine if the decertification petition had been tainted by the illegal lockout.

The Supreme Court recently denied review of a Seventh Circuit decision where the Court of Appeals found that the employer had

---

[42]West Irving Die Casting of Ky., Inc., 346 NLRB No. 35, 179 LRRM 1045 (2006).

[43]179 Fed. Appx. 61, 179 LRRM 2896 (D.C. Cir. 2006), *remanding* 343 NLRB No. 479 (2004).

[44]343 NLRB 479, 175 LRRM 1513 (2004)

[45]*Steelworkers*, 179 Fed. Appx. at 62 (referring to NLRB v. Great Dane Trailers, Inc., 388 U.S. 26 (1967)).

failed to carry its burden of showing a business justification for its partial lockout.[46]

Finally when an employer has lawfully locked out employees and hired temporary replacements, the manner in which locked out employees are reinstated will depend on the nature of the employer's operations.[47] In *Bud Antle, Inc.*,[48] the Board found that the employer did not violate the Act when it initially waited 30 days to reinstate locked out employees and treated those employees as new employees for the purpose of assigning overtime. However, the employer did violate the Act when it further delayed the reinstatement for another 30 days.

3. Plant Closings

b. Partial Closings

A medical center's implementation of a decision to subcontract the work of its respiratory care department 3 weeks after a union filed an election petition led the Ninth Circuit to conclude that the employer closed a part of its operations and discharged its employees for antiunion reasons, in violation of Section 8(a)(3).[49] Disagreeing with the Board,[50] the court concluded that a strong inference of antiunion animus as a motivating factor for the subcontracting had been established by the medical center's commencement of planning for subcontracting in the same month it became aware of organizing, by the medical center's knowledge that the respiratory care department employees were the core of the union's support and by its implementation of the decision to subcontract within a few weeks after the filing of the election petition. The court also found that the medical center's proffered business reasons for subcontracting the work were shifting, unreliable and pretextual, and appeared to be a fabrication, thus negating the Board's conclusion that the medical center had established that it would have subcontracted the work even in the absence of union activity.

---

[46]Midwest Generation, EME, LLC v. Electrical Workers (IBEW) Local 15, 127 S. Ct. 42, 180 LRRM 2832 (2006), *denying petition for certiorari in* 429 F.3d 651 (7th Cir. 2005).

[47]*Bud Antle, Inc.*, 347 NLRB No. 9, 180 LRRM 1507 (2006).

[48]*Id.*

[49]Healthcare Employees Local 399 v. NLRB, 463 F.3d 909, 180 LRRM 2533 (9th Cir. 2006).

[50]St. Vincent Med. Ctr., 338 NLRB 888, 172 LRRM 1025 (2003).

In another case,[51] a divided Board found that the employer harbored antiunion animus when it subcontracted maintenance and food service work but had satisfied its *Wright Line* burden of proving that it would have subcontracted work for legitimate reasons even in the absence of union activity by its showing of financial adversity and anticipated cost savings from subcontracting maintenance work and by its inability to find adequate replacements for two kitchen employees who had quit.

5. Replacement and Reinstatement of Economic Strikers

a. Development of the Law

The Board continues to be guided by the principles set forth in *NLRB v. Fleetwood Trailer Co.*,[52] *NLRB v. Great Dane Trailers, Inc.*,[53] and *Laidlaw Corp.*[54] governing the reinstatement and replacement of former economic strikers.

b. Nature of the Duty to Reinstate

Consistent with precedent, the Board follows the rule that former economic strikers have the right to return to their prestrike jobs or to substantially equivalent positions, if and when such jobs are available.

In *L.B.&B. Associates, Inc. dba North Fork Services Joint Venture*,[55] the Board found that a laborer/escort position was not substantially equivalent to the prestrike helper/laborer position and that the employer lawfully refused to reinstate the former striker. The Board explained that in order to trigger reinstatement rights the post-strike job must be substantially equivalent to the prestrike job *and* the former striker must be qualified to perform the post-strike job. The Board found that the laborer/escort position was not substantially equivalent because it required a limited background investigation clearance (LBI) and had the added duty of escorting visitors and other workers in and out of secure areas. Because there was no record evidence that the former striker possessed an LBI, the Board found it questionable whether the former striker was qualified for the laborer/escort position. The Board found, however, that

---

[51]Yeshiva Ohr Torah Cmty. Sch., Inc. dba Manhattan Day Sch., 346 NLRB No. 89, 179 LRRM 1241 (2006).

[52]389 U.S. 375, 66 LRRM 2737 (1967).

[53]388 U.S. 26, 65 LRRM 2465 (1967).

[54]171 NLRB 1366, 68 LRRM 1252 (1968), *enforced*, 414 F.2d 99, 71 LRRM 3054 (7th Cir. 1969), *cert. denied*, 397 U.S. 920, 73 LRRM 2537 (1970).

[55]346 NLRB No. 92, 180 LRRM 1059 (2006).

the employer unlawfully failed to reinstate an economic striker to an "ordinary seaman" position even though he was an "ablebodied" seaman before the strike, where the employer's ordinary and ablebodied seaman positions were substantially equivalent, with the same duties and requiring the same skills, the pay differential was not a result of difference in skills and duties, and the employer recalled three other ablebodied seamen to ordinary seaman positions.

The same employer was found to have violated the Act by conditioning its offer of reinstatement to a ferry worker who was a former economic striker on the employee's willingness to report for work at a dock in New York.[56] The Board found that the fact that the employer lawfully changed the ferry starting point from Connecticut to New York during the strike did not relieve the employer of its obligation to offer the ferry worker reinstatement. The Board noted that ferry workers had been allowed to start work at the Connecticut dock before the strike, four co-workers still started their day in Connecticut, and the employer advertised the vacancy as being in both states. The employer presented no justification or explanation for its refusal to allow this ferry worker to start work in Connecticut.

The Board continues to hold that vacancies arising from the departure of replacement workers may not be preferentially offered to currently working personnel.[57]

c. Defenses and Limitations

The Board continues to place the burden on the employer to demonstrate that it is justified in refusing reinstatement to strikers who seek to return to work.

An employer who refuses to reinstate a former striker on the ground that the striker has been permanently replaced has the burden of proving that the replacement is permanently employed.[58]

An employer is not required to offer reinstatement to a striker who has abandoned his employment; however, the employer must

---

[56] *Id.*

[57] *Id.* (finding that employer violated Section 8(a)(3) by failing to reinstate a former striker to the vacant chef position she held prior to the strike, rejecting, as a matter of law, the employer's asserted justification that it preferred to promote from within).

[58] Supervalu, Inc., 347 NLRB No. 37, 180 LRRM 142 (2006) (although employer established that 33 of 36 economic strikers had been permanently replaced before they made unconditional offers to return to work, employer unlawfully refused to reinstate three part-time warehouse employees who participated in economic strike, when 39 part-time positions had not yet been filled with permanent replacements at the time the three employees made unconditional offers to return).

present "unequivocal evidence of the striker's intent to permanently sever employment relationship."[59] The Board found that an employer violated Section 8(a)(3) by failing to reinstate a former economic striker, despite the contention that he resigned during the strike when he received accrued vacation pay, where the striker never informed the employer that he had resigned, told the employer's agent that he had not resigned, and had not obtained employment elsewhere.

In *Sutter Health Center dba Sutter Roseville Medical Center*,[60] the Board ruled that an employer failed to establish a substantial and legitimate business justification for delaying the reinstatement of economic strikers for 4 days and closing its cafeteria and thereby delaying reinstatement of the strikers employed there. In rejecting the employer's contention that the 5-day grace period for reinstating unfair labor practice strikers should be extended to economic strikers,[61] the Board observed that there was no showing of a need for further time where, among other things, the union gave the employer 2 weeks' notice of the 1-day strike and accompanied that notice with an unconditional offer to return to work at the end of the strike. Moreover, the Board found that the history of such strikes between the parties lessened the possibility that the employer would be faced with uncertainties as to the strikers' return to work.

In *New England Health Care Employees v. NLRB*,[62] the Second Circuit reversed the Board, and held that the employer had an "independent unlawful purpose" in hiring permanent replacements, and therefore violated Section 8(a)(3) when it refused to reinstate the replaced economic strikers upon their unconditional offer to return to work. The ALJ had found that the employer acted with "the independent and unlawful purpose of punishing the strikers and breaking the union's solidarity," relying on the employer's conscious concealment of the hiring of permanent replacements so that it could hire as many replacements as possible before the union learned of it and made an unconditional offer to return to work. The court found that the employer's decision to hire permanent replacements could have a legitimate business purpose, but its conscious concealment of that

---

[59]L.B.&B. Assocs., Inc. dba North Fork Servs. Joint Venture, 346 NLRB No. 92, 180 LRRM 1049 (2006).

[60]348 NLRB No. 29, 180 LRRM 1393 (2006).

[61]Drug Package Co., 228 NLRB 108, 94 LRRM 1570 (1977), *modified on other grounds in* 570 F.2d 1340, 97 LRRM 2851 (8th Cir. 1978).

[62]448 F.3d 189, 179 LRRM 2577 (2d Cir. 2006), *denying enforcement to* 343 NLRB 1301, 176 LRRM (2004).

action was based solely on a desire to break the union. The court remanded the matter to the Board for further consideration. The court declined to consider the union's argument that the employer bore the burden of establishing that its hiring of replacements was itself motivated by a legitimate and substantial business necessity, finding that the general counsel had not made that argument before the Board.

7. Discrimination Against Union Organizers and "Salts"

Both the Board and courts continue to hold that union appli-cants retain their status as protected employees.[63]

The Board continues to require the general counsel in refusal-to-hire cases to prove the elements set forth in *FES*.[64] If the general counsel meets this burden, the employer can rebut the presump-tion of an unfair practice by showing the applicant would have been rejected even in the absence of union affiliation.[65]

Starcon International Inc.[66] addressed the burden of proof to require instatement in refusal-to-hire cases. After the Board awarded relief to all of the union salts who applied and were denied employ-ment, the Seventh Circuit held that the Board may not automati-cally order the employer to offer all of the applicants jobs or give them back pay.[67] Only those applicants who *actually* would have been hired and taken the job if not for the employer's antiunion animus are entitled to such relief.[68] On remand, the Board placed the bur-den of proving the applicants would have accepted a job offer on

---

[63]Progressive Elec., Inc. v. NLRB, 453 F.3d 538, 179 LRRM 3265 (D.C. Cir. 2006), *enforcing* 344 NLRB No. 52, 177 LRRM 1054 (2005) (holding that eight union electricians wearing clothing showing their union affiliation and "equipped with a video camera and tape recorder" were employees entitled to protection).

[64]331 NLRB 9, 164 LRRM 1065 (2000). *See* Oasis Mech., Inc., 346 NLRB No. 91, 179 LRRM 1254 (2006) (the general counsel must show (1) the employer was hiring or had plans to hire at the time of the conduct, (2) the applicants had the required experience or training for the position, and (3) antiunion animus con-tributed to the decision not to hire).

[65]Wye Elec. Co., Inc., 348 NLRB No. 8 (2006) (the employer met its burden of proof by showing it did not hire the union applicant because the employer reason-ably believed he "smelled strongly of alcohol" when submitting his application).

[66]323 NLRB 977, 158 LRRM 1063 (1997), *enforcement granted in part and denied in part*, 176 F.3d 948, 161 LRRM 2233 (7th Cir. 1999), *on remand* 344 NLRB No. 127, 177 LRRM 1248 (2005), *enforced*, 450 F.3d 276, 179 LRRM 2962 (7th Cir. 2006).

[67]*Starcon Int'l*, 176 F.3d at 951–52.

[68]*Id.*

the union instead of the employer.[69] More recently, the Seventh Circuit enforced that order, but pointed out that the Board could have adopted a different position with respect to that burden of proof.[70]

9. Discrimination Based on Terms of Collective Bargaining Agreement

a. Enforcement of Union-Security Provision

The Board continues to hold that a union violates Sections 8(b) (1) (A) and (2) of the Act if it causes an employer to discharge an employee without informing the employee of the employee's *Beck* rights.[71]

III. Union Inducement of Employer to Discriminate

A. Union Inducements as Unfair Labor Practice Prohibited by Section 8(b)(2)

The Board continues to find that a union violates Section 8(b) (2) by attempting to cause or causing an employer to discriminate by refusing to hire a member who incurs in disfavor with the union's leadership.[72]

1. Union Liability Requires Showing of Agency

The Board continues to hold that an agency relationship exists where a union official or committee acts under the express authority of a collective bargaining agreement.[73]

---

[69] *Starcon Int'l*, 344 NLRB No. 127, slip op. at 2, *enforced*, 450 F.3d 276 (stating "[t]he burden of proving an entitlement to relief is usually placed on the person seeking the relief, and we are given no reason for departing from that presumption in salting cases, especially since the departure would place on the employer the burden of proving a negative").

[70] 450 F.3d 276, 179 LRRM 2962 (7th Cir. 2006).

[71] Food & Commercial Workers Local 648 (Safeway, Inc.), 347 NLRB No. 83, 180 LRRM 1230 (2006).

[72] Plumbers & Pipe Fitters Local 420 (Carrier Corp.), 347 NLRB No. 53, 180 LRRM 1015 (2006) (forcing signatory employer to refuse to hire a union member who had been working for a nonsignatory employer); Ironworkers Local 340 (Consumers Energy Co.), 347 NLRB No. 57, 180 LRRM 1166 (2006) (forcing employers to sign letters precluding union dissident from further employment opportunities).

[73] Electrical Workers (IBEW) Local 429, 347 NLRB No. 46, 180 LRRM 1048 (2006) (joint apprenticeship training committee found to be union agent where the parties' agreement expressly authorized it with collective bargaining duties;

IV. DISCRIMINATION BECAUSE OF INVOLVEMENT WITH NLRB PROCEDURES: SECTION 8(a)(4)

B. Actual Filing of Charge Not Required

The Board continues to hold that Section 8(a)(4)'s protection is not limited to employees who file a charge or give testimony. An employer violates Section 8(a)(4) by discharging an employee because it believes, rightly or wrongly, that the employee assisted a former employee who filed unfair labor practice charges against it.[74]

C. Release From Normal Work Schedule

An employer violates Section 8(a)(4) by requiring employees who have been subpoenaed by the union for a representation hearing to use vacation time, where the employer has a past practice of permitting the use of unpaid leave for that purpose and the employer's action is motivated by antiunion animus.[75] However, in finding a violation the Board majority expressly declined to rely on its earlier decision in *Western Clinical Laboratory*[76] that required subpoenaed employees to use vacation time rather than unpaid leave violated Section 8(a)(4) even without a showing of discriminatory treatment.[77]

D. Proof Scheme for Section 8(a)(4) Charges Follows Section 8(a)(3) Charges

Proximity in timing between the protected activity and the adverse action does not necessarily establish a causal nexus. In *Ogihara America Corp.*,[78] the Board found that the employee's testimony in an unfair labor practice preceeding was not a motivating factor in his dismissal despite closeness in time, where the employee was

---

committee violated §8(b)(2) by adversely affecting an employee's employment because of his dues delinquency and antiunion views).

[74]Operating Engineers Local 39, 346 NLRB No. 34, 179 LRRM 1041 (2006).

[75]Exelon Generation Co., 347 NLRB No. 77 (2006).

[76]225 NLRB 725, 93 LRRM 1292 (1976), *enforcement granted in part and denied in part,* 571 F.2d 457, 97 LRRM 3162 (9th Cir. 1978).

[77]*Exelon,* 347 NLRB No. 77. The dissent in *Exelon Generation Co.* would have relied on *Western Clinical Laboratory* in finding a violation.

[78]347 NLRB No. 10, 180 LRRM 1009 (2006).

fired promptly after the employer discovered that he had engaged in deceptive conduct. In *W. E. Carlson Corp.*,[79] the denial of a wage increase shortly after an employee testified did not violate Section 8(a)(4) where the decision to deny the increase had been made before the employee's testimony, and placing the same employee on probation and then discharging him was not a violation despite proximity in timing where the employee had a history of performance and conduct problems.

In *International Baking Co. & Earthgrains*,[80] the employer did not violate Section 8(a)(4) by terminating an employee who was involved in Board proceedings for having an improper work permit, where the employee's undocumented status was discovered in the regular course of the employer's system for reviewing work permits that were about to expire. By contrast, in *Concrete Form Walls, Inc.*,[81] the employer violated Section 8(a)(4) by discharging four undocumented employees who voted in a representation election, where the employer was already suspicious of their immigration status before the election but did not investigate until after they voted, and the employer made no attempt to verify the work eligibility of employees who did not vote. The Board rejected the employer's defense based on the Immigration Reform and Control Act (IRCA) on the ground that the discharges were not actually motivated by compliance with the IRCA, stating that "an employer cannot use compliance with another statute as a smokescreen for its true purpose of retaliating against employees for exercising their Section 7 rights."[82]

Even where an employer's adverse action is found to be in retaliation for other protected concerted activity in violation of Section 8(a)(3), a Section 8(a)(4) violation will not be found absent evidence connecting the adverse action to the employee's participation in Board proceedings.[83]

F. Types of Section 8(a)(4) Misconduct

The Board continues to hold that Section 8(a)(4) is violated by various retaliatory acts short of discharge, such as reassigning an employee to a more physically difficult job and taking away his pri-

---

[79] 346 NLRB No. 43, 179 LRRM 1137 (2006).
[80] 348 NLRB No. 76 (2006).
[81] 346 NLRB No. 80, 179 LRRM 1193 (2006).
[82] *Id.*
[83] Success Vill. Apartments, Inc. (*Success Village I*), 347 NLRB No. 100 (2006); Dish Network Serv. Corp., 347 NLRB No. 69 (2006).

vate work area,[84] increasing an employee's workload,[85] implementing a new conflict of interest policy that prevented an employee from pursuing her longstanding real estate business,[86] and requiring employees to sign a mandatory arbitration policy that would effectively preclude the filing of unfair labor practice charges.[87]

[84]Five Star Mfg., 348 NLRB No. 94 (2006).
[85]Chinese Daily News, 346 NLRB No. 81, 179 LRRM 1182 (2006).
[86]Success Vill. Apartments, Inc. (*Success Village II*), 348 NLRB No. 28 (2006).
[87]U-Haul Co. of Cal., 347 NLRB No. 34, 180 LRRM 1093 (2006).

Chapter 8

EMPLOYER DOMINATION OF AND ASSISTANCE TO LABOR ORGANIZATIONS

II. LABOR ORGANIZATION DEFINED

A. Requirement of Participation by "Employees"

Public employees are not deemed "employees" under Section 2(5) and therefore groups composed entirely of such individuals are not labor organizations.[1]

B. Requirement of "Dealing with" Employers

The Board continues to broadly construe the themes of several key cases, including *Cabat Carbon Co., Crown Cork & Seal Co., Electromation, Inc.,* and *Georgia Power Co.*[2] in deciding whether "dealing with" does or does not exist in particular circumstances.

For example, in *Ead Motors Eastern Air Devices, Inc.,*[3] the Board affirmed the administrative law judge's (ALJ's) conclusion that the employer violated Section 8(a)(2). The evidence showed that the employer, at the request of an employee, set up a "Have your say" committee to try and establish consistent policies after the employer had withdrawn recognition of the union. The employer established the committee, named it, solicited employee committee members, chose the members to serve from those who volunteered, encouraged other employees to tell members of the committee about their concerns or recommendations, paid employees to attend committee meetings and held committee meetings during work time. The employer's human resource director chaired the committee meetings and set committee expectations. The committee discussed issues such as vacation policy, sick/personal pay days, benefits, flex care, breaks and make up policy. Management representatives were leaders of subcommittee groups. The employer changed some policies based on committee recommendations. The Board agreed with the

---

[1]American Fed'n of Teachers v. Federacion de Maestros de P.R., 381 F. Supp. 2d 65 (D. P.R. 2005); Hadley v. Haw. Gov't Employees' Ass'n, No. 05-00660, 2006 WL 695036, 180 LRRM 2956 (D. Haw. Mar. 13, 2006); Simpson v. Auto Workers Local 6000, 394 F. Supp. 2d 991, 178 LRRM 2358 (E.D. Mich. 2006).

[2]Cabot Carbon Co., 117 NLRB 1633, 40 LRRM 1058 (1957), *enforcement denied,* 256 F.2d 281, 42 LRRM 2272 (5th Cir. 1958), *rev'd and remanded,* 360 U.S. 203, 44 LRRM 2204 (1959) (dealing found); Crown Cork & Seal Co., 334 NLRB 699, 167 LRRM 1257 (2001) (no dealing found); Electromation, Inc., 309 NLRB 990, 142 LRRM 1001 (1992), *enforced,* 35 F.3d 1148, 147 LRRM 2257 (7th Cir. 1994) (dealing found); Georgia Power Co., 342 NLRB 192, 175 LRRM 1130 (2004), *review denied, enforcement granted,* 427 F.3d 1354, 178 LRRM 2257 (2005) (no dealing found).

[3]346 NLRB No. 93, 180 LRRM 1192 (2006).

ALJ that the committee was a "labor organization" and the employer dealt with the committee and, in fact, assisted and dominated it. However, the court in *Mayhew v. Longshoremen Local 1771*[4] found that a joint seniority board made up of employee representatives and representatives of a multi-employer bargaining group did not constitute a labor organization and did not exist for the purpose of dealing with the employer of its members because its purpose was to make final decisions in accordance with a negotiated seniority plan, and employees did not participate in the board; only local union representatives and representatives of the employer multi-employer unit.

III. EMPLOYER DOMINATION

Prohibited domination of a labor organization exists when the organization is controlled or directed by the employer, rather than by the employees. The Board and the courts continue to apply the standards set forth in *Electromation, Inc.*[5] and *E.I. DuPont de Nemours*[6] for determining when a labor organization is "dominated." Domination exists where the employer plays a significant role in the creation of an employee committee and the selection of members for the committee.[7]

IV. EMPLOYER INTERFERENCE

A. Unlawful Recognition or Other Assistance

While the Board and court decisions note the distinction between unlawful domination and unlawful interference or assistance, certain conduct by an employer can constitute violations of both aspects of Section 8(a)(2). For example, in *EAD Motors Eastern Air Devices, Inc.*,[8] the Board found both unlawful domination and assistance by the employer when, after withdrawing recognition of the union, the

---

[4]No. C.A. 2-05-01558-PMD, 2005 WL 3055597 (D.S.C. Nov. 15, 2005).

[5]309 NLRB 990, 142 LRRM 1001 (1992), *enforced*, 35 F.3d 1148, 147 LRRM (7th Cir. 1994).

[6]311 NLRB 893, 143 LRRM 1121 and 1268 (1993).

[7]Ead Motors E. Air Devices, Inc., 346 NLRB No. 93, 180 LRRM 1192 (2006) ("Have Your Say" committee found to violate §8(a)(2) where the employer decided the structure of the committee, selected its members, and the committee met during working time).

[8]*Id.*

employer established an employee committee to discuss terms and conditions of employment, held the committee meetings on company time and paid employees when attending the meetings.

The Board continues to hold that an employer violates Section 8(a)(2) by recognizing and bargaining with a union if the union's majority status is tainted by unlawful coercion or assistance. In *Dairyland USA Corp.*,[9] the Board found that the employer violated Section 8(a)(2) when it recognized a union that did not represent an uncoerced majority of employees due to the employer's unlawful assistance, which included directing employees to sign authorization cards, having a supervisor present when employees signed authorization cards, threatening an employee with discharge if he did not sign an authorization card, and promising increased benefits to employees if they supported the union.

Although a successor employer provides unlawful assistance by prematurely recognizing and executing a collective bargaining agreement with a union, the Board recently held that a "perfectly clear" successor employer did not violate Section 8(a)(2) by recognizing the union and entering into a collective bargaining agreement with the union prior to hiring its workforce and commencing operations when the successor informed the union that it would hire the predecessor's employees and would not unilaterally establish initial terms and conditions of employment.[10]

The Board continues to hold that an employer provides unlawful assistance and interference when it continues bargaining or executes a collective bargaining agreement with a union with knowledge that the union has lost majority status.[11]

B. Employer Preference Among Contending Unions

Although the Board has found that an employer provides unlawful assistance by granting more aid and access to a preferred union than that provided to the unfavored union, the Board recently held that the employer did not provide unlawful assistance to its pre-

---

[9]347 NLRB No. 30, 180 LRRM 1074 (2006).
[10]Road & Rail Servs., Inc., 348 NLRB No. 77, 181 LRRM 1057 (2006).
[11]Regency Grande Nursing & Rehab. Ctr., 347 NLRB No. 106, 181 LRRM 1157 (2006) (employer violated Act when it extended recognition to a union at a time when the union represented a minority of the employees in the unit); Dura Art Stone, Inc., 346 NLRB No. 14, 179 LRRM 1127 (2005) (employer had knowledge of employee disaffection petition establishing the union had lost majority status).

ferred union by allowing employees to utilize store facilities, equipment and time to conduct union organizing activities on behalf of the favored union because there was no evidence that it restricted employees supporting the competing union from such activities and there was little evidence that management was contemporaneously aware of any such activity.[12]

C. Conduct of Supervisors

The Board continues to hold that an employer violates Section 8(a)(2) when its supervisors provide authorization cards to employees and instruct employees to sign those cards.[13]

VI. Employer Support Versus Cooperation

The Board recently affirmed that employers are not required to give a union's nonemployee supporters the same degree of campaign access which is provided to employees who support one union or another.[14] Thus, an employer did not illegally assist one union when it removed nonemployee supporters of a second union from the premises.[15] Additionally, where local managers could not continuously monitor all of the stores in their area for activities to garner support for a local union and local managers did not immediately become aware of the supporters' presence, the employer did not give inappropriate support to the union.[16] Finally, the Board found that where an employer has a general policy allowing employees to use store equipment for personal use unless the privilege is "abused," there was no evidence that the employer was aware of any "abusive" use of the equipment by supporters of any particular union, and supporters of two rival unions were each allowed the same access, the employer did not provide illegal support.[17]

---

[12]Independent Drug Clerks Ass'n (Raley's), 348 NLRB No. 25 (2006).
[13]Planned Bldg. Servs., Inc., 347 NLRB No. 64, 180 LRRM 1081 (2006).
[14]See Raley's, 348 NLRB No. 25.
[15]Id.
[16]Id.
[17]Id.

VII. THE UNION AS PARTY TO THE EMPLOYER'S DOMINATION, ASSISTANCE, OR SUPPORT

When an employer provides unlawful assistance, the union that has accepted the unlawful support or assistance violates Section 8(b)(1)(A).[18] The Board continues to hold that it is a violation of the Act for an unlawfully assisted union to threaten to have employees fired if they refuse to sign a union membership application and a dues checkoff authorization card.

A union will also violate Section 8(b)(2) when it enters into a contract with an employer containing a union-security clause at a time when it is not the majority representative.[19] A union that represents a majority of bargaining-unit employees will also violate Sections 8(b)(1)(A) and 8(b)(2) by accepting recognition and extending the terms of a contract to a group of employees who have not been properly accreted into the unit.[20] Specifically, the Act prohibits a union from extending a contract to a unit of previously unrepresented employees who have historically been excluded from the bargaining unit at a time when the employees have not designated the union as their exclusive representative.[21]

Even where a union is the valid majority representative of a group of employees, it may still violate Sections 8(b)(1)(A) and 8(b)(2) of the Act when it enters into a contract that contains provisions that interfere with employees' rights under the Act. For example,

---

[18]Dairyland USA Corp., 347 NLRB No. 30, 180 LRRM 1074 (2006) (union violated § 8(b)(1)(A) after it gained access to the employer's facility pursuant to a neutrality agreement, by accepting unlawful assistance from the employer, which included a supervisor's order to employees to sign union authorization cards, a threat of termination if an employee did not sign a card, promises of improved medical benefits if an employee supported the union and threats of loss of work should a rival union organize the facility).

[19]Id.; NLRB v. Retail Clerks Local 588 (Raley's Inc.), 587 F.2d 984, 100 LRRM 2299 (9th Cir. 1978), enforcing 227 NLRB 670, 94 LRRM 1443 (1976). Cf., Raley's and Independent Drug Clerks Ass'n, 348 NLRB No. 25 (2006) (no §8(b)(1)(A) or 8(b)(2) violation where Board found union did not receive unlawful assistance, that subsequent recognition of union and execution of contract was lawful, and that union's imposition of late fee on members who were in arrears in their dues was in accord with a valid union-security clause).

[20]Teamsters UPS Nat'l Negotiating Comm. (United Parcel Serv.), 346 NLRB No. 49, 179 LRRM 1035 (2006).

[21]Id.

in *Lee v. NLRB (BellSouth Telecommunications, Inc.)*,[22] the Fourth Circuit remanded a Board decision that had upheld a provision in a collective bargaining agreement requiring employees to wear employer-provided uniforms that bore both the employer and union logos. The Fourth Circuit held that the uniform requirement unlawfully restrained employees in their right to refrain from union activity encompassed in the Act. The union violated Sections 8(b)(1)(A) and 8(b)(2) by: (1) proposing the agreement that required employees wear the union logo on their uniforms, (2) agreeing to the proposal, and (3) accepting the employer's financial support in supplying the uniforms. Similarly, the employer violated Sections 8(a)(1), (2) and (3) by paying to place the logo of the union on the uniforms and making the wearing of the uniform a condition of employment.

VIII. REMEDIES

The Board continues to order disestablishment in cases of company unions or unlawfully dominated employee committees, even where the complaint has alleged only unlawful employer assistance.[23] Similarly, the NLRB orders continue to provide that the order "shall not be construed to authorize or require the Respondent employer to withdraw or eliminate any wage increase or other benefits... established pursuant to the agreement."[24]

The Board continues to issue broad cease-and-desist orders not limited to the violations found where the respondent has shown a proclivity to violate the Act or where the violations are egregious.[25]

In a supplemental decision following *Human Development Ass'n v. NLRB*,[26] the Board refused to recognize the defense of laches to a delay of 13 years in the issuance of a compliance specification to

---

[22]393 F.3d 491, 176 LRRM 2321 (4th Cir. 2005), *vacating and remanding* BellSouth Telecomms., Inc., 335 NLRB 1066 (2001), *on remand*, BellSouth Telecomms., Inc., 346 NLRB No. 59, 179 LRRM 1134 (2006) (accepting Fourth Circuit's decision as the law of the case).

[23]*See Dairyland*, 347 NLRB No. 30, 180 LRRM 1074.

[24]*Id.*

[25]*See* Planned Bldg. Servs., Inc., 347 NLRB No. 64, 180 LRRM 1081 (2006) (ordering a broad and corporate-wide remedy).

[26]937 F.2d 657, 137 LRRM 2761 (D.C. Cir. 1991), *enforcing* 293 NLRB 1228, 132 LRRM 1068 (1989), *cert. denied*, 503 U.S. 950, 139 LRRM 2808 (1992).

a Board order to reimburse unit employees, with interest, for moneys paid by or withheld from them for dues, fees and obligations of membership in the union.[27]

---

[27] *See* Human Dev. Ass'n, 348 NLRB No. 35, 181 LRRM 1135 (2006).

Part III

THE REPRESENTATION PROCESS
AND UNION RECOGNITION

CHAPTER 9

RESTRICTIONS ON PREELECTION ACTIVITY: "LABORATORY CONDITIONS"

I. Introduction

C. Considerations in Assessing Objection Allegations [Amended Heading Title]

1. Substantive [New Topic]

A number of factors are considered by the Board in determining whether alleged conduct interferes with an election. Often the conduct may also be alleged as an unfair labor practice. The factors considered include whether the conduct is de minimis or isolated, the dissemination of the conduct among the employees, the size of the unit and the narrowness of the election results.

a. De Minimis or Isolated Conduct [New Topic]

The Board applies the standard set forth in *Cambridge Tool & Mfg. Co.*,[1] in determining whether to set aside an election, viz., whether the misconduct, taken as a whole, warrants a new election because it has "the tendency to interfere with the employees' freedom of choice" and "could well have affected the outcome of the election."[2]

In *Bon Appetit Management Co.*,[3] the Board described the test for determining whether conduct is de minimis.[4] In *Double J Services*,[5] the Board found several work-rules changes, including changes in eating

---

[1]316 NLRB 716, 148 LRRM 1261 (1995).

[2]*See also* Metaldyne Corp., 339 NLRB 443, 172 LRRM 1418 (2003); Waste Automation & Waste Mgmt. of Penn., 314 NLRB 376, 146 LRRM 1264 (1994); Mercy General Hosp., 334 NLRB 100, 168 LRRM 1438 (2001).

[3]334 NLRB 1042, 169 LRRM 1068 (2001).

[4]*See* Sir Francis Drake Hotel, 330 NLRB 638, 163 LRRM 1173 (2000) (margin of results can be a factor). *See also* Chicagoland Television News, 330 NLRB 630, 163 LRRM 1297 (2000).

[5]347 NLRB No. 58, 180 LRRM 1156 (2006).

practices and break procedures, to be more than de minimis and therefore set aside the election.

b. Dissemination [New Topic]

In *Crown Bolt, Inc.*,[6] a divided full Board reversed *Spring Industries*[7] and "all other decisions in which the Board has presumed dissemination of plant-closure threats or other kinds of coercive statements." The Board stated that such threats are "very severe" but that

> [S]everity of a threat is one factor, among several, to be considered in deciding whether to set aside an election. See *Caron International*, 246 NLRB 1120 (1979) (noting the factors the Board considers in resolving the question whether misconduct affected the results of an election; factors include the number of violations, their severity, the extent of dissemination, and the size of the unit).[8]

In an interesting twist to the dissemination issue, the Board, in a 2–1 decision, set aside an election won by the union based on an objectionable election fee waiver statement, even though the union had disseminated a brochure found to be coercive to only one employee.[9] In turn, that employee gave the brochure to a supervisor and ultimately the employer copied that last page of the brochure containing a promise to waive initiation fees only to union card signers and disseminated it to the entire voting unit a few weeks before the election. Thereafter, the union met with approximately 19 voting unit employees and articulated a nonobjectionable fee waiver policy to such unit employees. The Board concluded, however, that

---

[6]343 NLRB 776, 176 LRRM 1065 (2004).

[7]332 NLRB 40, 165 LRRM 1161 (2000).

[8]*Crown Bolt*, 343 NLRB at 779. *See also* Delta Brands, Inc., 344 NLRB No. 10, 176 LRRM 1305 (2005) (while it may be axiomatic that an overly broad no-solicitation rule violates the Act, it is not axiomatic that such a rule warrants setting aside an election without additional evidence as to the effect such rule had on the election. Further, the Board will not presume that such an overly broad rule has been disseminated to the voting unit); Werthan Packaging, Inc., 345 NLRB No. 30, 178 LRRM 1107 (2005) (single threat and at most of five interrogations, where at most a total of five employees out of approximately 200 employees were directly affected, insufficient to overturn election that union lost by 21 votes, where the record did not establish the threat and interrogations were disseminated to the other unit employees); Hollingsworth Mgmt. Serv., 342 NLRB 556, 176 LRRM 1059 (2004); Erie Brush & Mfg. Corp., 340 NLRB 1386, 174 LRRM 1047 (2003); MB Consultants, Ltd., 328 NLRB 1089, 162 LRRM 1111 (1999).

[9]S.T.A.R., Inc., 347 NLRB No. 8, 179 LRRM 1387 (2006) Member Liebman dissented, stating that "[s]etting aside the election here is inequitable" given the fact that the union disseminated the brochure to only one employee.

it would not "presume dissemination of a union's clarification of an ambiguous offer to waive fees to all, or a substantial majority, of the 136 unit employees."[10] Further, the Board stated that it would not "preclude the Employer from relying on its own dissemination of the brochure to show that the Petitioner's objectionable conduct affected all 136 unit employees."[11] "Consequently, the brochure was the sole source of information about initiation fees for as many as 117 employees."[12]

In *Longs Drug Stores of California*,[13] the Board found that otherwise objectionable "confidentiality" provisions in an employee handbook did not affect the election results because the handbook was distributed to only 5 of 285 voters.

c. Narrowness of Election Results [New Topic]

The narrowness of the vote in an election is a relevant consideration.[14] It is not, however, dispositive and as the Board noted in *Accubuilt, Inc.*,[15] it will assess the general atmosphere at the location, "rather than comparing the number of employees subject to any sort of threats against the vote margin."[16]

II. GROUNDS FOR SETTING ASIDE ELECTIONS

A. Employer and/or Union Conduct

4. Appeals to Racial Prejudice

The Board follows the same standard for appeals to religious or other protected-class prejudices as it does for appeals to racial prejudice. In *Honeyville Grain, Inc.*,[17] for example, the Board held that union agents' statements that the employer was "run by Mormons" and "giving its money to the Mormon Church"—and that "Mormons are missionaries, and missionaries speak good Spanish"— were not sufficient grounds for setting aside the union's election

---

[10] *Id.*, slip op. at 1–2.
[11] *Id.*, slip op. at 3.
[12] *Id.*
[13] 347 NLRB No. 45, 180 LRRM 1001 (2006).
[14] Robert Orr-Sysco Food Servs., 338 NLRB 614, 171 LRRM 1457 (2002).
[15] 340 NLRB 1337, 173 LRRM 1545 (2003).
[16] *See also* Lamar Adver. of Jamesville, 340 NLRB 979, 173 LRRM 1377 (2003).
[17] 342 NLRB No. 61, 175 LRRM 1384 (2004) (not published in Board volume), *enforced*, 444 F.3d 1269, 179 LRRM 2656 (10th Cir. 2006).

victory. Enforcing the Board's decision, the Tenth Circuit upheld the Board's application of the *Sewell* burden-shifting test to cases involving appeals to religious prejudice.[18] Significantly, the Tenth Circuit rejected the employer's request for a "per se rule that, in a representative election, the party making use of the religious message bears the initial burden to show that the message was germane to the issue[.]" Instead, the court held that "a party challenging an election bears the preliminary burden to prove that the remarks at issue were inflammatory or formed the theme of the campaign." Only if this burden is met will "the party who allegedly made the remarks [have to] prove that they were germane." Applying this test, the court noted that the union's comments were "wholly inappropriate" but nonetheless held that substantial evidence supported the Board's determination that the remarks were not inflammatory or a central theme of the union's campaign.

B. Employer Conduct

7. Pro-Union Conduct of a Supervisor

Consistent with its *Harborside*[19] decision, the Board set aside an election finding that the solicitation of cards by two leadpersons constituted objectionable coercive conduct that materially affected the outcome of the election. In *SNE Enterprises, Inc.*,[20] the Board found "nothing in the leads' conduct that would assure employees that they could vote how they wish or otherwise relieve the solicitation of its inherently coercive nature," satisfying the first *Harborside* prong. The Board also determined that the number of employees who signed cards solicited by the leadpersons was "more than enough to affect the outcome of the election," satisfying the second *Harborside* prong and requiring that a second election be held. The Board has continued to apply its *Harborside* doctrine in subsequent cases.[21]

---

[18]444 F.3d at 1274.
[19]343 NLRB 906, 176 LRRM 1113 (2004).
[20]348 NLRB No. 69, 180 LRRM 1449 (2006).
[21]*See* Millard Refrigerated Servs., Inc., 345 NLRB No. 95, 178 LRRM 1434 (2005); Chinese Daily News, 344 NLRB No. 132, 177 LRRM 1225 (2005); *compare* Northeast Iowa Tel. Co., 346 NLRB No. 47, 179 LRRM 1057 (2006) (conduct of supervisor not sufficient to set aside election).

C. Union Conduct

3. Waiver of Initiation Fees

The specific language used by the union in waiving initiation fees is often of critical importance. The offer must be unconditional and unambiguous.

In *S.T.A.R., Inc.*,[22] a divided Board set the election aside, finding interference where the union communicated to employees in a brochure that it would waive initiation fees for only those employees who actively supported the union. The brochure did not make clear that those employees who sat silent or advocated against unionization during the campaign would also be exempt. Further, the Board reached this conclusion since only a fraction of the employees later learned that the union would, contrary to a reasonable reading of the brochure, waive the initiation fees for all employees hired before a first contract was achieved and a majority of the voting unit employees had seen the improper conditioned waiver through employer dissemination.

The Seventh Circuit, in *NLRB v. River City Elevator*,[23] held that the union did not significantly interfere with the election when it offered to reduce initiation fees for all employees unconditionally without regard to whether the employee joined the union before or after the election. The offer operated to remove the artificial obstacle to employees joining the union, rather than as an effort to influence voting.

4. Other Union Conduct

c. Videotaping

Unexplained photographing or videotaping of employees by unions during the preelection period, unlike preelection polling, may constitute grounds for setting aside the results of a representation election unless a valid explanation is conveyed to employees in a timely manner.[24] In *Pepsi-Cola Bottling Co.*, the Board held that "absent any legitimate explanation from the Union, we find that employees could reasonably believe that the Union was contemplating some

---

[22]347 NLRB No. 8, 179 LRRM 1387 (2006).
[23]289 F.3d 1029, 170 LRRM 2001 (7th Cir. 2002).
[24]Randell Warehouse of Ariz., 347 NLRB No. 56, 180 LRRM 1017 (2006).

future reprisals against them."[25] In *Randell Warehouse of Arizona, Inc.*,[26] (*Randell I*) the Board overruled its decision in *Pepsi-Cola Bottling Co.*, and held that, when a union photographs employees engaged in Section 7 activity without explanation, such photographing is non-objectionable conduct unless accompanied by an express or implied threat or other coercion. On appeal, the District of Columbia Circuit, refused to enforce the Board's decision in *Randell I* and remanded the case "for further consideration and a reasoned opinion."[27]

Upon reconsideration, the Board reversed *Randell I* and held that union photographing of employees is objectionable conduct unless there is an accompanying explanation for the photographing (*Randell II*).[28] The *Randell II* Board looked to the three-part rationale underlying the rule articulated in *Waco, Inc.*[29] that unexplained employer photographing of employees engaged in Section 7 activities has a tendency to intimidate employees. In *Randell II*, the Board held that the same three *Waco, Inc.* factors are present when a union is taking the pictures of employees engaged in Section 7 activity: (1) during an election campaign, the union may be displeased with employees who exhibit support for the employer or fail to support the union's campaign; (2) the photographing and videotaping of employees engaged in such activity constitutes permanent record-keeping, which is more than "mere observation"; and therefore (3) employees could reasonably fear "that the record of their concerted activities might be used for some future reprisals." The *Randell II* Board, having found there to be the same concerns regardless of whether the union or the employer is taking the pictures, rejected the *Randell I* decision to treat union and employer conduct differently.[30] The Board also found that photography, unlike preelection

---

[25]289 NLRB 736, 737, 128 LRRM 1275 (1988).

[26]328 NLRB 1034, 1038, 161 LRRM 1265 (1999).

[27]252 F.3d 445, 449, 167 LRRM 2340 (D.C. Cir. 2001).

[28]*Randell Warehouse of Ariz.*, slip op. at 1.

[29]273 NLRB 746, 747, 118 LRRM 1163 (1984) (quoting NLRB v. Colonial Haven Nursing Home, 542 F.2d 691, 93 LRRM 2241 (7th Cir. 1976)).

[30] In *Randell I*, the Board relied on the fact that preelection polling by unions is treated differently than polling by employers in order to justify its holding that photographing of employees should vary depending on whether the union or employer was taking the pictures. 328 NLRB at 1035. The Board in *Randell II* specifically rejected the comparison of polling to photographing, stating, "[polls] show their obvious purpose to employees, is to solicit support for the union and/or to gauge the extent of such support. By contrast, the photographing of an employee (who, for example, is accepting or declining a union flyer) does not reveal an obvious purpose. Absent an explanation, employees are left to wonder why they are being photographed." 347 NLRB No. 56, slip. op. at 7, 180 LRRM 1017 (2006).

polling and card solicitation, is not a recognized traditional vehicle of organizing and serves no crucial union function.

In order to establish that a union is engaged in objectionable conduct by photographing or videotaping employees who come to the employer's premises to vote in an election, the employer must, as a general rule, present evidence that an agent of the union took photographs of the voters and that unit employees were aware that photos were being taken. For example, in *Chrill Care, Inc.*,[31] the Board overruled the employer's objection that the union had unlawfully photographed voters where the evidence was "vague and contradictory" and there was no credible evidence either that photographs were taken of the voters or that unit employees were aware of any photography.

III. REMEDIES

The Board ordered extraordinary remedies for a rerun election following extensive and serious unfair labor practices. In *Smithfield Packing Co., Inc.*,[32] the Board entered a broad cease-and-desist order and directed that notice of the rerun election be posted, mailed and read by a Board agent to all employees, in English and Spanish. The Board also directed the respondent employer, for a period of one year after its order, to provide upon request by the union a list of the names and addresses of current employees, and that such response be within 14 days of the request date.[33]

---

[31] 340 NLRB 1016, 174 LRRM 1237 (2003).
[32] 347 NLRB No. 109, 181 LRRM 1069 (2006).
[33] *See also* Food & Commercial Workers Local 204 v. NLRB, 447 F.3d 821, 179 LRRM 2708 (D.C. Cir. 2006), where extraordinary remedies were affirmed by the District of Columbia Circuit as appropriate in a previous case involving the same respondent in *Smithfield Packing*, 347 NLRB No. 109, 181 LRRM 1069.

CHAPTER 10

REPRESENTATION PROCEEDINGS AND ELECTIONS

I. Questions Concerning Representation

B. Petitions by Employers

2. History Under the Taft-Hartley Act

a. Unrecognized Unions

The Board continues to grant review of cases addressing whether different types of union conduct constitute a demand for recognition permitting the employer to file an election petition. In

Marriott Hartford Downtown Hotel,[1] the Board granted review (over vigorous dissent) to consider whether promotion of a "labor peace" agreement constituted a demand for recognition under Section 9(c) (1)(B). The Board noted that the case "presents many of the same issues" it is considering "in several pending cases currently under Board review" including *Dana Corp.*[2] and *Shaw's Supermarkets.*[3]

b. Incumbent Unions

(2) The Allentown Mack *and* Levitz Furniture *Decisions*

In further clarification of *Levitz Furniture,* the Board held in *Highland Regional Medical Center,* that an employer may unilaterally withdraw recognition from an incumbent union only where the union has actually lost the support of the majority of the unit.[4] The employee petition was a "showing of interest for decertification" and thus did not establish loss of majority status. Further, the Board held that an employer presented with evidence of loss of majority status, may poll its employees even while a decertification petition is pending.[5]

(3) Effect of Section 8(f) in the Construction Industry

A union can convert a Section 8(f) relationship to a 9(a) relationship by establishing majority status and obtaining the employer's agreement that it has done so. Thus, an employer's recognition of the union after the union offers evidence of majority status cannot be revoked simply because the employer does not take the union up on its offer to see the union's evidence of actual majority.[6]

---

[1] 347 NLRB No. 87, 180 LRRM 1057 (2006).
[2] 341 NLRB 1283, 174 LRRM 1521 (2004).
[3] 343 NLRB 963, 176 LRRM 1220 (2004).
[4] 347 NLRB No. 120, 180 LRRM 1414 (2006) (citing Levitz Furniture Co. of the Pac., 33 NLRB 717, 166 LRRM 1329 (2001)). *See also* Parkwood Dev. Ctr., Inc., 347 NLRB No. 95, 180 LRRM 1178 (2006) ("We shall no longer allow an employer to withdraw recognition from an incumbent union that retains the support of a majority of unit employees on a good faith belief that majority support has been lost.").
[5] Unifirst Corp., 346 NLRB No. 52, 179 LRRM 1116 (2006).
[6] M & M Backhoe Serv., Inc. v. NLRB, 469 F.3d 1047, 1050–51 (D.C. Cir. 2006).

II. Timeliness Of Petitions

A. The One-Election-per-Year Rule

2. The Certification Year

The Board continues to apply *Mar-Jac Poultry Co.*[7] by extending the presumption of majority status beyond 1 year when an employer's unlawful conduct interferes with union representation during the initial certification year.[8] It has clarified, however, that the duration of an extension depends "on the circumstances of the individual case" and that it will balance the nature of an employer's misconduct against an extension's interference with employees' Section 7 self-determination rights. For example, in *United Electrical Contractors Ass'n,*[9] the Board reduced a 1-year extension imposed by an Administrative Law Judge (ALJ), noting (1) that the Board is not always required to extend the certification year when faced with employer misconduct, and (2) that it would apply "remedial discretion" to determine whether and for how long an extension should apply. The Board has applied this standard in similar cases.[10]

Record evidence is essential to establish a case for extending the certification year. The Board requires that a record "support the need for an extension and the appropriate length of the extension," which is determined by "the nature of the violations; the number, extent, and dates of the collective-bargaining sessions; the impact of the unfair labor practices on the bargaining process; and the conduct of the union during negotiations."[11]

The Board's decision in *LTD Ceramics* was upheld by the Ninth Circuit.[12]

---

[7]136 NLRB 785, 49 LRRM 1854 (1962).
[8]*See, e.g.,* Goya Foods of Fla., 347 NLRB No. 103 (2006).
[9]347 NLRB No. 1 n.3 (2006).
[10]*See, e.g.,* Garden Ridge Mgmt., Inc., 347 NLRB No. 13, 180 LRRM 1030 (2006) (finding that an employer's refusal to meet at reasonable times was not sufficient to taint employee disaffection and overruling extension of the certification year).
[11]Mercy, Inc. dba American Med. Response, 346 NLRB No. 88, 179 LRRM 1205 (2006) (rejecting a 12-month period in favor of a more limited 3-month extension) (citing Northwest Graphics, Inc., 342 NLRB 1288, 176 LRRM 1188 (2004) and Metta Elec., 338 NLRB 1059, 172 LRRM 1298, *enforced in part,* 360 F.3d 904, 174 LRRM 2558 (8th Cir. 2004).
[12]341 NLRB 86, 174 LRRM 1105 (2004) (cited at footnote 109 in the Main Edition); 185 Fed. Appx. 581, 179 LRRM 2965 (9th Cir. 2006).

3. Voluntary Recognition Bar

The Board has not yet reached a decision in *Dana Corp.*,[13] in which it is to consider "the threshold issue" of whether voluntary recognition via a card-check agreement bars decertification petitions when the initial agreement preceded majority support.

B. Pendency of Unfair Labor Practice Charges

Under *Unifirst Corp.*,[14] an employer may not conduct its own "mock election" without following all other requirements applicable to employee polls under *Struksnes Construction Co.*[15]

C. Unlawful Employer Assistance

The Board does not require parties to establish with "mathematical certainty" that unlawful employer assistance reduced a union's showing of interest below the requisite level. In *Dairyland USA Corp.*,[16] it required only that the totality of the circumstances "demonstrate a pattern of unlawful assistance sufficient to taint a proposed card majority."

F. Clarification of Units

The Board generally dismisses unit-clarification petitions submitted during the term of a collective bargaining agreement, where the contract clearly defines the bargaining unit.[17] The Board recently reaffirmed an exception to this rule, however, where the parties cannot agree whether to include or exclude a disputed classification and do not wish to press the issue at the expense of reaching an agreement.[18]

The Board vigorously protects a party's right to seek a unit clarification through the Board's processes. In *United States Postal Service*,[19] for example, the Board allowed an employer to invoke the unit-clarification process following an adverse ruling by an arbitra-

---

[13] 341 NLRB 1283, 174 LRRM 1521 (2004).
[14] 346 NLRB No. 52, 179 LRRM 1116 (2006).
[15] 165 NLRB 1062, 65 LRRM 1385 (1967).
[16] 347 NLRB No. 30, 180 LRRM 1074 (2006).
[17] Wallace-Murray Corp., 192 NLRB 1090, 78 LRRM 1046 (1971).
[18] Sunoco, Inc. (R&M), 347 NLRB No. 38, 179 LRRM 1366 (2006).
[19] 348 NLRB No. 3, 180 LRRM 1227 (2006).

tor. The union filed a unit-clarification petition, seeking to include certain additional employee classifications in the bargaining unit. The employer and the union eventually signed a settlement agreement to "fully and completely resolve any and all issues, and all currently pending grievances" regarding the union's unit-clarification petition. Under the settlement agreement, the union agreed to withdraw its petition, and the parties agreed to arbitrate various classifications in dispute. The settlement agreement was silent regarding the parties' rights and obligations in the event that either of them disagreed with the results of the arbitration, and did not specify whether a party could file a unit-clarification petition with the Board under such circumstances.

When, pursuant to the settlement agreement, an arbitrator concluded that a particular classification should be included in the unit, the employer filed a unit-clarification petition seeking to exclude that classification. Relying on the Board's decision in *Verizon Information Systems*,[20] the regional director found that the settlement agreement estopped the employer from filing the petition. The Board disagreed, noting that any waiver of a statutory right must be "clear and unmistakable" and that the settlement agreement did not expressly provide that the arbitrator's decision would be final and binding. Thus, the employer's right to file a petition with the Board was not clearly and unmistakably waived. "Where, as here, the right involved is the statutory right of access to the Board, we would not lightly infer an agreement to forgo that right."[21]

G. Private Agreements

2. *Neutrality Agreements*

In *Heartland Industrial Partners, LLC*,[22] the Board held that an agreement to apply a neutrality and card-check agreement to business entities acquired by the employer in the future did not have a "cease doing business" object or effect, and thus did not violate Section 8(e) of the Act.

[**Editor's Note:** The Board currently is considering whether a union's efforts to obtain a neutrality agreement, including a card-

---

[20]335 NLRB 558, 168 LRRM 1136 (2001).
[21]*United States Postal Serv.* 348 NLRB No. 3, 180 LRRM 1227.
[22]348 NLRB No. 72 (2006).

check recognition procedure, constitutes a demand for recognition sufficient to support an employer's RM petition.[23]]

III. ELECTION PROCEDURES

A. Preelection Matters

3. Voter List and Eligibility

The Board continues to adhere to its standard that presumes that employee on sick leave or disability leave is eligible to vote absent an affirmative showing that the employee has resigned or been discharged.[24]

Receipt of the *Excelsor* list by a decertification petitioner 17 hours after receipt by the union was not found to be a significant delay.[25]

B. The Election Proper

1. Observers

The Board clarified that an employer need not treat its own observers the same as union observers with respect to pay and leave during the election. In *American Red Cross Missouri-Illinois Blood Services Region*,[26] the Board found acceptable the employer's compensating its own observers for time spent observing the election, but requiring the union observers to use accumulated paid time off. Further, the Board did not find objectionable the employer's preelection meeting with its own observers to explain the observers' role in the election process even though the union observers were not invited to the meeting. The Board explained that the employer was not obligated to provide similar explanations to the union's observers.

---

[23]Marriott Hartford Downtown Hotel, 347 NLRB No. 87, 180 LRRM 1057 (2006).
[24]Home Care Network, Inc., 347 NLRB No. 80, 180 LRRM 1044 (2006).
[25]Teamsters Local 705 (K-Mart), 347 NLRB No. 42 (2006).
[26]347 NLRB No. 33, 181 LRRM 1013 (2006).

D. Resolution of Challenges and Objections to the Election

2. *Objections to the Election*

The Board continues to require that objections contain a statement of the reasons for the objection. In *Factor Sales, Inc.*,[27] the Board overruled a union's objection because the wording of the objection and the course of the litigation pursued by the union failed to provide clear notice of the allegation.

---

[27]347 NLRB No. 66, 180 LRRM 1206 (2006).

CHAPTER 11

APPROPRIATE BARGAINING UNITS

I. BACKGROUND

When there is a dispute as to the inclusion of certain classifications, the Board continues to examine stipulated election agreements by applying the three-part test from *Caesar's Tahoe*[1] to determine the intent of the parties.[2]

III. TYPES OF UNITS

B. Unit Classifications in General

3. Plant and Employerwide Units

In determining whether the single-facility presumption has been rebutted, the Board continues to analyze such factors as centralized control over daily operations and labor relations and the extent of local autonomy; similarity of employee skills, functions, and working conditions; degree of employee interchange; distance between the locations; and bargaining history, if any.[3]

Without finding that the crude oil pipeline is a public utility, in *Alyeska Pipeline Service Co.*,[4] the Board concluded that the union failed to rebut the presumption of a systemwide unit.[5]

C. Specialized Units

1. Units in Health Care Institutions

g. Related Issues

(5) Supervisory Determinations

In *Oakwood Healthcare, Inc.*,[6] the Board set forth guidelines for determining supervisory status in light of the Supreme Court's *NLRB v. Kentucky River Community Care*[7] decision.

---

[1]337 NLRB 1096, 170 LRRM 1344 (2002).
[2]Columbia Coll., 346 NLRB No. 69, 179 LRRM 1129 (2006).
[3]Hilander Foods, 348 NLRB No. 82, 180 LRRM 1545 (2006); *see also* Prince Telecom, 347 NLRB No. 73, 180 LRRM 1310 (2006).
[4]348 NLRB No. 44, 180 LRRM 1345 (2006).
[5]*Id.* at 4.
[6]348 NLRB No. 37, 180 LRRM 1257 (2006).
[7]532 U.S. 706, 167 LRRM 2164 (2001).

The Board defined the statutory function "assign" as designating an employee to a place (such as a location, department, or wing), appointing an employee to a time (such as a shift or overtime period), or giving significant overall duties, i.e., tasks, to an employee.[8] However, choosing the order in which the employee will perform discrete tasks within those assignments would not be indicative of exercising the authority to assign.[9]

The Board also defined the term "responsibly to direct" by requiring the employee to be accountable for the performance of the task by the other, such that some adverse consequence may befall the employee.[10] In the companion case, *Golden Crest Healthcare Center*,[11] the Board explained that accountability requires that the putative supervisor must have an effect on the employee's terms and conditions of employment.[12]

The Board adopted the interpretation of the term "independent judgment" by requiring the judgment to be free from control by another authority and the exercise of judgment must involve a degree of discretion rising above the "routine or clerical."[13] In the context of nursing, the assignment of patients to nurses requires independent judgment if the charge nurse making the assignments considers the qualification and experience of the available nurses and the needs of the patients.[14]

Finally, the Board made clear that employees may be supervisors even if they do not possess these forms of authority whenever they are at work so long as they possess them a "regular and substantial" amount of the time.[15]

---

[8] *Oakwood Healthcare*, 348 NLRB No. 37, slip op. at 4.
[9] *Id.*
[10] *Id.* at 7.
[11] 348 NLRB No. 39, 180 LRRM 1288 (2006).
[12] *Id.* at 5.
[13] Oakwood Healthcare, Inc., 348 NLRB No. 37, slip op. at 8, 180 LRRM 1257 (2006).
[14] *Id.*
[15] *Id.* at 9.

2. Units in Colleges and Universities

b. Development of the Law: Basic Structure of Professional Units and the Impact of *Yeshiva*

(4) Other Specific Inclusions and Exclusions

(h) Part-Time Faculty

Part-time, nonstudent tutors in the writing and learning centers, who also work as part-time faculty members, were eligible to vote because of their substantial community of interest with other employees in the unit under the Board's dual-function employee analysis.[16]

D. Multi-Employer Bargaining Units

2. Establishment of the Multi-Employer Unit: Its Consensual Nature

In the construction industry, the Board continues to adhere to the principle established in *Casale Industries*,[17] that upon Section 9(a) recognition to a union as representative of a multi-employer unit, petitions for single-employer units of that multi-employer unit will not be entertained.[18]

---

[16]Columbia Coll., 346 NLRB No. 69, 179 LRRM 1129 (2006).

[17]311 NLRB 951, 143 LRRM 1291 (1993).

[18]Donaldson Traditional Interiors, 345 NLRB No. 117, 178 LRRM 1500 (2005).

CHAPTER 12

RECOGNITION AND WITHDRAWAL OF RECOGNITION WITHOUT AN ELECTION

I. Introduction

While the secret ballot election is still considered to be the "crown jewel" of the Board, there appears to be increasing efforts to obtain voluntary recognition in the context of a neutrality and card check agreement.[1]

III. Elements of a Bargaining Obligation in the Absence of an Election

A. Majority Representation

3. Status of the Solicitor

The Board continues to adhere to its *Harborside*[2] ruling that the solicitation of authorization cards by a supervisor constitutes objectionable conduct.[3] In *Chinese Daily News*,[4] the Board ruled that a supervisor's solicitation and collection of cards from his subordinates, including personally watching them sign the cards, was inherently coercive. However, a supervisor's pro-union conduct may not be deemed coercive when it is directed at employees over whom the supervisor does not have direct supervisory authority.[5]

---

[1]Burdney, *Neutrality Agreements and Card Check Recognition: Prospects for Changing Paradigms*, 90 Iowa L.Rev. 819 (2005); Cohen, *Resisting Its Own Obsolescence—How the National Labor Relations Board Is Questioning the Existing Law of Neutrality Agreements*, 20 Notre Dame J.L. Ethics & Pub. Pol'y 521 (2006).
[2]Harborside Healthcare Inc., 343 NLRB No. 100, 178 LRRM 1434 (2005).
[3]SNE Enters., Inc., 348 NLRB No. 69, 180 LRRM 1449 (2006).
[4]344 NLRB No. 132, 177 LRRM 1225 (2005). *See also SNE Enters.*, 348 NLRB No. 69, 180 LRRM 1449.
[5]Family Fare, Inc., 344 NLRB No. 25, 176 LRRM 1393 (2005), *enforced*, 205 Fed. Appx. 403, 180 LRRM 3046 (6th Cir. 2006). *See also* Northeast Iowa Tel. Co., 346 NLRB No. 47, 179 LRRM 1057 (2006).

C. Employer Unfair Labor Practices

1. Conduct Warranting a Gissel Bargaining Order

b. "Hallmark" Violations: Invasive Employer Conduct

The Board continues to recognize that certain violations of the Act are "hallmark" violations, those violations that are particularly coercive because of their tendency to destroy the laboratory conditions necessary for an election and that persist for longer periods than other unfair labor practices.

In *Evergreen America Corp.*,[6] the Board issued a *Gissel* bargaining order where the union lost the election 61 to 52 and the employer committed hallmark violations. Among a plethora of unfair labor practices, the employer granted an unprecedented and excessive wage increase, manipulated its promotion process so as to promote more unit employees, and threatened plant closure and job loss. The Board found the violations to have a long lasting effect that would preclude traditional remedies. The Board followed its traditional practice of not requiring as a remedy the withdrawal of a wage increase to employees.[7]

In *Concrete Form Walls, Inc.*,[8] the Board issued a *Gissel* bargaining order where the employer threatened employees with termination and following the election discharged four employees. The employer asserted that it fired the employees because they were undocumented aliens. The employer at the hearing sought to rely on an Internet database search that showed that the Social Security numbers did not match the names of the employees. The proffered evidence was found to be deficient as it did not identify to whom the Social Security numbers were properly assigned. The Board further ruled that there was no basis for the employer's claim that the four Hispanic employees were not statutory employees within the meaning of the Act. In eschewing traditional remedies, the Board found a bargaining order was warranted because the bargaining unit in which the discharges occurred was small and consisted of employees with questionable documentation, and, when coupled with an unlawful promise of a wage increase, the atmosphere could not possibly be cleansed so as to permit the holding of another election.

---

[6]348 NLRB No. 12, 181 LRRM 1288 (2006).
[7]Gerig's Dump Trucking, 320 NLRB 1017, 152 LRRM 1045 (1996), *enforced*, 137 F.3d 936 (7th Cir. 1998).
[8]346 NLRB No. 80, 179 LRRM 1193 (2006).

Similarly, in *California Gas Transport, Inc.*,[9] the Board issued a *Gissel* bargaining order based on the employer's hallmark violations that included unfair labor practices that occurred in Mexico. The Board held that it was proper to consider the violations occurring in Mexico as the effects of the unfair labor practices were on employees who primarily worked in the United States.

2. *Conduct Not Warranting a* Gissel *Bargaining Order*

The Board continues to hold that delay in case processing can make a bargaining order unenforceable.[10] However, the passage of time alone is insufficient to avoid a bargaining order.[11]

V. Defenses to the Remedial Bargaining Order

B. Change of Circumstances

The Board continues to assess the appropriateness of a *Gissel* bargaining order "based on the situation at the time the unfair labor practices were committed."[12] When a case has suffered "long and unjustified delay in processing" by the Board, proceeding directly to a second election remains the favored alternative in situations where a bargaining order may otherwise have been appropriate.[13] However, when an employer attempts to utilize passage of time not created by Board delay or turnover in the workforce to indicate changed circumstances as a defense to a bargaining order, the Board continues to reject these factors as insufficient, standing alone, to avoid a bargaining order.[14]

---

[9]347 NLRB No. 118, 181 LRRM 1114 (2006).
[10]Smithfield Foods, Inc., 347 NLRB No. 109, 181 LRRM 1132 (2006).
[11]*Id.* at n.7.
[12]Evergreen Am. Corp., 348 NLRB No. 12, slip op. at 6, 181 LRRM 1288 (2006).
[13]*Smithfield*, 347 NLRB No. 109, slip op. at 8. *But see* Cogburn Health Ctr., Inc., 335 NLRB 1397, 171 LRRM 1021 (2001), *enforcement denied in part*, 437 F.3d 1266, 179 LRRM 2065 (2006).
[14]California Gas Transp., Inc., 347 NLRB No. 118, 181 LRRM 114 (2006).

VI. WITHDRAWAL OF RECOGNITION

The Board continues to apply the standard announced in *Levitz Furniture Co.*[15] that an employer may lawfully withdraw recognition from an incumbent union only where the employer can demonstrate that "the union has actually lost the support of the majority of the bargaining unit employees. . . ."[16]

Withdrawal of recognition will ordinarily be precluded by law if the union has recently been certified or recognized. Not only is an employer prohibited from withdrawing recognition during the year after certification, an employer may not withdraw recognition outside the certification year on the basis of evidence of loss of majority status acquired within the certification year.[17] Although this remains the rule, the Board ruled in *LTD Ceramics Inc.*[18] that an employer's reliance on a disaffection petition was not improper where some of the signatures were obtained on the final day before the certification year expired. In that case, the employer did not receive the disaffection petition until after the certification year expired. Although the Board ruled in *LTD Ceramics* that the employer could rely on signatures that were obtained within the outer limits of the certification year, it remains to be seen how the Board would address a case where the employer based its withdrawal on less timely evidence.

An employer cannot unilaterally withdraw recognition from an incumbent union during the life of an existing collective bargaining agreement.[19] Under the "anticipatory withdrawal" line of cases, an employer may announce that it will not recognize the union after the contract expires if the employer can demonstrate that the union has lost majority support during the term of the agreement, provided that the employer complies with the existing agreement while it remains in effect.[20]

In *Parkwood Development Center Inc.*,[21] the Board reaffirmed the principles of anticipatory withdrawal but ruled that an employer can-

---

[15]333 NLRB 717, 166 LRRM 1329 (2001).

[16]*Id.*, 333 NLRB at 717.

[17]Chelsea Indus., Inc., 331 NLRB 1648, 165 LRRM 1118 (2000) (antiunion petition was circulated and presented to employer during certification year).

[18]341 NLRB No. 14, 174 LRRM 1105 (2004), *enforced*, 185 Fed. Appx. 581, 179 LRRM 2965 (9th Cir. 2006).

[19]Auciello Iron Works, Inc. v. NLRB, 517 U.S. 781, 786, 152 LRRM 2385 (1996).

[20]Abbey Med., 264 NLRB 969, 111 LRRM 1683 (1982), *enforced*, 709 F.2d 1514, 113 LRRM 3240 (9th Cir. 1983).

[21]347 NLRB No. 95, 180 LRRM 1178 (2006).

not follow through on its anticipatory withdrawal if the employer is confronted with conflicting evidence undermining its initial evidence that the union actually lost majority support. In that case, the employer received a disaffection petition from a majority of the bargaining-unit employees while the collective bargaining agreement was in effect. The employer announced that it would withdraw recognition effective on the expiration of the agreement. Prior to the expiration of the agreement, the union submitted a petition to the employer that contained a majority of the unit employees attesting that they desired continued representation and that they revoked any prior statements to the contrary. Despite this petition, the employer followed through on its announcement and withdrew recognition from the union on the date that the agreement expired. The Board ruled that the employer's withdrawal was improper because it relied solely on the disaffection petition and disregarded the subsequent petition submitted by the employees. In so ruling, however, the Board noted that the announcement of anticipatory withdrawal was not per se unlawful if it was based on objective evidence at the time of the announcement and that the employer could have followed through on its anticipatory withdrawal if it could have proved actual loss of majority support on the date that it subsequently withdrew recognition from the union. In *Parkwood*, the Board adhered to its ruling in *Caterair International*[22] that an affirmative bargaining order is the appropriate remedy for an employer's unlawful withdrawal of recognition. Recognizing that the District of Columbia Circuit has required the Board to justify the imposition of an affirmative bargaining order on a case-by-case basis, the Board determined that an affirmative bargaining order was required in that case under *Caterair* by balancing three considerations: "(1) the employees' Section 7 rights; (2) whether other purposes of the Act override the rights of employees to choose their bargaining representatives; and (3) whether alternative remedies are adequate to remedy the violations of the Act."[23]

In *HQM of Bayside LLC*,[24] the employer faced similar circumstances to those that the employer confronted in *Parkwood*. In that case, during the term of the collective bargaining agreement the employer received a disaffection petition signed by a majority of

---

[22] 322 NLRB 64, 153 LRRM 1153 (1996).

[23] *Parkwood*, 347 NLRB No. 95, slip op. at 3 (citing Vincent Indus. Plastics v. NLRB, 209 F.3d 727, 164 LRRM 2039 (D.C. Cir. 2000)).

[24] 348 NLRB No. 42, 181 LRRM 1003 (2006).

the bargaining-unit employees. The union subsequently submitted a petition indicating that it had majority support, thereby nullifying some of the employee signatures previously submitted on the disaffection petition. Despite receiving the subsequent petition from the union, the employer withdrew recognition from the union on the date the contract expired. Following its earlier decision in *Parkwood*, the Board ruled that the employer's withdrawal of recognition was unlawful. In doing so, the Board rejected the employer's argument that it was faced with a Hobson's choice of withdrawing recognition or bargaining with the union in violation of Section 8(a) (2). According to the Board, the employer could have avoided this dilemma by filing an RM petition after the expiration of the contract because the disaffection petition provided the employer with a "good-faith reasonable-uncertainty" about the union's majority support.[25]

A. Employee Activity or Inactivity as a Justifying Consideration

In *Highlands Regional Medical Center*,[26] the employer unlawfully withdrew recognition from the union based on a petition circulated by an employee-sponsored decertification committee. The employee decertification committee circulated a petition intended for a showing of interest to obtain a decertification election. After the petition was signed by a majority of the employees, the committee sent a letter to the employer stating that the majority of the unit employees did not wish to be represented by the union. Based on the letters from the committee and the petition, the employer withdrew recognition from the union. The Board held that the withdrawal of recognition was unlawful because the petition was circulated for the purposes of obtaining a decertification election and not for determining whether the employees desired union representation. The Board, however, noted that in some circumstances, which were not present in *Highlands Regional Medical Center*, there could be dual-purpose decertification petitions that reflect not only the desire for a decertification election but also nonsupport for the union.

---

[25] *Id.*, slip op. at 4 (quoting Levitz Furniture Co., 333 NLRB 717, 727–29, 166 LRRM 1329 (2001)).
[26] 347 NLRB No. 120, 180 LRRM 1414 (2006).

C. Filing of Decertification Petition

A pending decertification petition will not prohibit an employer from polling employees when it is presented with evidence that the union has actually lost majority support. In *Unifirst Corp.*,[27] the Board ruled that when an employer may lawfully withdraw recognition of a union under *Levitz*, then "it could, a fortiori, take the lesser step of polling employees."[28] The Board distinguished the facts involved in this case from those presented in *Struksnes Construction*,[29] in which the Board suggested that polling during the pendency of a Board election petition would be unlawful. The Board in *Unifirst* explained that polling was permissible in that case because the employer was presented with evidence that the union had lost majority support that would justify withdrawal of recognition; whereas, *Struksnes* was limited to a situation where the union was seeking recognition through an election petition. Accordingly, the Board held that the employer could lawfully withdraw recognition based on the polling results because the polling, itself, was lawful.

---

[27]346 NLRB No. 52, 179 LRRM 1116 (2006).
[28]*Id.*, slip op. at 6.
[29]165 NLRB 1062, 65 LRRM 1385 (1967).

Part IV

THE COLLECTIVE BARGAINING PROCESS

THE DUTY TO BARGAIN

I. Introduction

B. Elements of the Bargaining Obligation

1. The Duty to Meet, Confer, and Negotiate

There is still no per se standard to determine whether the bargaining parties have satisfied their Section 8(d) obligation to meet at reasonable times and confer in good faith with respect to wages, hours, and other terms and conditions of employment, or the negotiation of an agreement.[1]

---

[1] *See, e.g.,* Garden Ridge Mgmt., 347 NLRB No. 13, 180 LRRM 1030 (2006) (employer that met on 20 occasions with the union over 11 months nevertheless found to have unlawfully refused to meet with the union at reasonable times because of its repeated, unexplained refusals to meet more frequently as the union had requested, but not to have engaged in surface bargaining because the general counsel failed to prove that the employer did not intend to reach an agreement with the union).

2. The Obligation to Deal in Good Faith

The Board continues to take a case-by-case approach in determining whether a party's conduct at the bargaining table constitutes bad faith bargaining.[2]

II. PER SE VIOLATIONS

A. Unilateral Changes

The Board continues to regard an employer's material unilateral change to a mandatory subject of bargaining during the course of a collective bargaining agreement before an impasse is reached on that subject as a prima facie refusal to bargain.[3]

The Board also continues to find that an employer's unilateral implementation of final contract proposals involving the surrender of statutory rights or otherwise requiring agreement with the union is unlawful. Thus, in *Roosevelt Memorial Medical Center*,[4] the Board found the employer violated Section 8(a)(5) by unilaterally implementing its final proposal for dues checkoff, a no-strike clause, a grievance procedure with nonbinding arbitration that required the union to engage in the process of striking arbitrators' names from a list and paying half the cost of arbitration, and a 2-year term.[5]

While the Board continues to find unlawful unilateral implementation of a bargaining proposal where the parties have not bargained to overall impasse for an agreement, the Board will recog-

---

[2] *Id.* (employer's proposal seeking the union's agreement to refrain from organizing certain nonbargaining-unit employees, its initial proposal of a broad management-rights clause, its subsequent withdrawal of the broader proposal, and its resubmissions of more specific ones did not evince an intent to avoid reaching an agreement).

[3] *E.g.*, Park Maint., 348 NLRB No. 98 (2006) (employer's transfer of employees from a negotiated health plan to employer's own plan without offering to bargain with union or without union's consent unlawful); Vanguard Fire & Supply Co., Inc. v. NLRB, 468 F.3d 952, 180 LRRM 3137 (6th Cir. 2006), *enforcing* 345 NLRB No. 77 (2005) (strict enforcement of policy of charging employees for cell phone overages was unlawful unilateral change). *But see* Success Vill., 348 NLRB No. 28 (2006) (unilateral change to employer's parking policy requiring employees to walk an additional 200 yards not unlawful because it was immaterial).

[4] 348 NLRB No. 64 (2006).

[5] *See also* ACF Indus., LLC, 347 NLRB No. 99 (2006) (employer violated §8(a)(5) and (d) when it implemented its proposed early termination of the parties' separate insurance and pension agreements, which were nonmandatory subjects of bargaining).

nize an exception to this general requirement of an overall impasse. Under this exception, if a term or condition of employment concerns a discrete recurring event, such as an annually scheduled wage review, and that event is scheduled to occur during negotiations for an initial contract, the employer may lawfully implement a change in that term or condition if it provides the union with reasonable advance notice and an opportunity to bargain about the intended change in past practice.[6]

Thus, in *Neighborhood House Ass'n*,[7] the Board found that the employer lawfully withheld a regularly scheduled cost-of-living increase (COLA) from unit employees, and instead proposed a 2.2 percent COLA increase and then conditioned implementation on the union waiving its right to bargain over an increase in the COLA amount. The Board reasoned that the employer was free to implement its proposal even though no overall impasse existed because the COLA was a discrete event that was scheduled to recur during the negotiations for the initial collective bargaining agreement and the employer provided the union with reasonable advance notice and an opportunity to bargain about its proposal. The Board found that it was immaterial that the union protested the employer's proposal and that the employer's position was not prompted by economic considerations.

Similarly, in *St. Mary's Hospital of Blue Springs*,[8] the Board found that the employer's implementation of changes in health coverage for unit employees was permissible even though the parties had not reached an overall impasse. The Board reasoned that the employer was free to implement its proposal because the employer gave the union timely notice of the prospective changes and an opportunity to bargain over them, and also remained willing to bargain over the changes after implementation. Furthermore, the timing of the changes were consistent with a past practice established when the employees were unrepresented. Moreover, the employees would have suffered a disruption in coverage if the employer had not taken any action prior to the implementation date.

---

[6]Neighborhood House Ass'n, 347 NLRB No. 52 (2006).
[7]*Id.*
[8]346 NLRB No. 76 (2006).

C. Refusal to Execute Written Contract

The Board continues to follow the rule that a party's refusal to reduce to writing or sign a written memorandum of the agreement made is a per se refusal to bargain.[9]

D. Refusal to Meet at Reasonable Times

The Board continues to consider the totality of the circumstances and not just an examination of the number of bargaining sessions held in determining whether a party has satisfied its duty to meet at reasonable times. Thus, in *Garden Ridge Management*,[10] the Board found that the employer unlawfully refused to bargain in good faith, even though it met and negotiated on 20 occasions over 11 months, and reached agreement on 28 contract articles. The union had requested on approximately eight occasions for the employer to meet more frequently, and the employer refused each such request without an explanation. The Board relied heavily on the employer's repeated, unexplained refusals in finding that the employer violated its duty to meet at reasonable times.

The Board continues to find that face-to-face meetings are the bargaining norm. Thus, in *Success Village Apartments, Inc.*,[11] the Board held that the employer, by insisting on negotiating in separate rooms through a mediator, unlawfully refused to engage in face-to-face bargaining with the union. The Board found that the union bargaining representative's confrontational and derisive conduct towards management officials did not rise to the level of bad faith bargaining that would excuse the employer from bargaining or permit it to impose conditions on negotiations.

---

[9]Windward Teachers Ass'n, 346 NLRB No. 99, 179 LRRM 1217 (2006) (union unlawfully failed and refused to sign a successor collective bargaining agreement submitted to it by the employer because the parties reached a "meeting of the minds" on the terms of a contract, including the bonus clause at issue, and the document submitted to the union for signature by the employer accurately reflected that agreement. The parties' dispute over the interpretation of the scope of the bonus clause contained in the agreement was found not to justify the union's refusal to execute the agreement).

[10]347 NLRB No. 13, 180 LRRM 1030 (2006).

[11]347 NLRB No. 100 (2006).

III. THE GOOD FAITH REQUIREMENT

B. Indicia of Good or Bad Faith

1. Surface Bargaining

The Board continues to review all of the evidence regarding the parties' negotiations, including the employer's total conduct both away from and at the bargaining table, to decide whether the employee is engaging in hard but lawful bargaining to achieve a contract that it considers desirable or is unlawfully endeavoring to frustrate the possibility of reaching agreement. Thus, in *Garden Ridge Management*,[12] the Board found that the general counsel failed to satisfy its burden of proving that the employer harbored an intent to avoid reaching an agreement. The employer's management-rights proposal and its proposal seeking the union's agreement to refrain from organizing certain nonbargaining-unit employees were found not to evidence an unlawful intent, and there was no slight-of-hand gamesmanship found in the employer's submission of a more narrowly tailored management-rights proposal after withdrawing its broad management-rights proposal. The employer's failure to meet more frequently, while a violation of its duty to meet at reasonable times in the circumstances where the refusals were unexplained, also did not warrant finding an unlawful surface bargaining motive, because, as the Board reasoned, "the fact that a party does not meet with sufficient frequency does not necessarily mean that it does not want to agree to contract."[13] Finally, statements made by the employer's managers prior to the representative election, that "we would basically tie the union up at the bargaining table and we would not come to an agreement" and that if the union were voted in "there's all kinds of things that we could do and...bargaining would go on and the union is not going to get anything that we don't want to give them" were insufficient to establish surface bargaining because these statements were made before the union was certified, the manager who made the first statement did not "call the shots" during the negotiation, and agreement was reached during negotiations on many substantive contract provisions.[14]

---

[12]347 NLRB No. 13, 180 LRRM 1030.
[13]*Id.*, slip op. at 3.
[14]*Id.*

2. Concessions, Proposals, and Demands

a. Concessions

The Board continues to find that a refusal to compromise may support an inference of bad faith.[15]

b. Proposals and Demands

The Board continues to examine the context of the entire negotiation in evaluating whether the process of making concessions and proposals is evidence of a lack of good faith. In *Garden Ridge Management*,[16] the Board found that the employer's proposal seeking the union's agreement to refrain from organizing certain nonbargaining-unit employees was not unlawful and did not evidence an unlawful motive. The Board also addressed the argument that the employer's handling of its management-rights proposal was evidence of surface bargaining. The employer had proposed a broad management-rights clause, to which the union made specific objections. The employer and union reached agreement on the proposal after the objectionable portions were withdrawn, though the employer reintroduced some of the "objectionable" portions in connection with other provisions, as it had advised the union it might do. The Board rejected the argument that this amounted to the tactic of pretending to concede to a matter particularly objectionable to the union, while reintroducing its substance in another portion of its bargaining proposal. The Board found that there was no "gamesmanship" because the employer had clearly advised the union it would agree to the modified management-rights clause but reserved the right to reintroduce the points where agreement had not been reached. The employer's "effort to secure agreement, where possible, while voicing its intent not to retreat from the substance of its bargaining position, is not inconsistent with an intent to reach agreement."[17]

---

[15]TNT Logistics N. Am., Inc., 346 NLRB No. 109, 179 LRRM 1257 (2006) (finding bad faith where employer held one brief negotiating session and failed to make a counterproposal to union).

[16]347 NLRB No. 13, 180 LRRM 1030 (2006).

[17]*Id.*, slip op. at 3.

3. Dilatory Tactics: Refusing to Confer at Reasonable Times and Intervals

The Board continues to find that a party may not engage in dilatory bargaining tactics to frustrate negotiations.[18]

4. Bargaining Representatives

The District of Columbia Circuit, agreeing with the Board, held that an employer unlawfully interfered with its employees' choice of bargaining representation by refusing to grant employee-members of the bargaining committee unpaid leave to attend negotiations.[19] In *Ceridian*, the court found that the employer's unreasonable insistence on meeting during the work day and charging employees leave against their entitlement of paid leave for participating in bargaining was unlawful. The court observed that an employer may bargain during work hours and grant unpaid leave, or bargain after work hours where no leave is required, but that the employer's attempt to have it both ways was unlawful.

As to who the representative is, the Board in *Alan Ritchey, Inc.*,[20] found that an employer's poll of its drivers concerning whether they wanted an employee to represent them was not unlawful.

7. Unilateral Changes[21]

The Board continues to find that during negotiations an employer may not implement proposed changes or those tenta-

---

[18] *See, e.g.,* Pavilion at Forrestal Nursing & Rehab., 346 NLRB No. 46, 179 LRRM 1007 (2006) (employer refused to bargain in good faith when it, inter alia, canceled eight consecutively scheduled bargaining sessions between the first and second meetings); *Garden Ridge,* 347 NLRB No. 13 (employer that met with the union on 20 occasions over 11 months nevertheless was found to have unlawfully refused to meet with the union at reasonable times where the union repeatedly requested more frequent bargaining sessions and the employee repeatedly refused these requests without explanation); Teamsters Local 287 (Granite Rock), 347 NLRB No. 32, 180 LRRM 1007 (2006) (union violated §8(b)(3) by delaying a ratification vote for 8 weeks). *But see* Washoe Med. Ctr. Inc., 348 NLRB No. 22, 180 LRRM 1502 (2006) (no bad faith bargaining when the employer attended 30 negotiating sessions in 15 months).

[19] Ceridian Corp. v. NLRB, 435 F.3d 352, 356 (D.C. Cir. 2006), *enforcing* 343 NLRB 571 (2004).

[20] 346 NLRB No. 26, 178 LRRM 1421 (2006).

[21] *See also* related discussion on unilateral changes in Section II.A., *supra.*

tively agreed to by the parties absent impasse or waiver.[22] However, the Board continues to allow employers to make unilateral changes where a union expressly waives the right to bargain about the issue under a collective bargaining agreement.[23]

IV. The Duty to Furnish Information

A. The Role of Information in the Collective Bargaining Relationship—An Overview

3. Refusal to Furnish Information as an Unfair Labor Practice

In addition to being an unfair labor practice in its own right, the Board continues to find that an unlawful refusal to provide requested information necessary for the other party to create counterproposals and, as a result, engage in meaningful bargaining, will preclude a lawful impasse.[24] Thus, in *DuPont*, the Board found no lawful impasse regarding subcontracting where the employer asserted that subcontracting milling and finishing work would save $1 million over a 12-month period and challenged the union to formulate a proposal that would provide for similar savings without subcontracting, but the employer refused to provide the information upon which it relied in making the decision to subcontract. By unlawfully refusing to provide the information upon which it relied in making the decision to subcontract, the Board found the employer prevented the union from effectively creating a counterproposal, which in turn precluded a lawful impasse on this issue.

---

[22]Beverly Health & Rehab. Servs., Inc., 346 NLRB No. 111, 179 LRRM 1284 (2006) (employer unlawfully based changes on an expired management-rights clause, which did not survive the expiration of the contract, and unproven past practice); Children's Ctr. for Behavioral Dev., 347 NLRB No. 3, 179 LRRM 1321 (2006) (employer could not unilaterally eliminate pay and hours of employees after expiration of contract, but before good faith impasse); Ivy Steel & Wire, Inc., 346 NLRB No. 41, 179 LRRM 1060 (2006) (employer unlawfully lowered employee's wages, because it did not bargain with union over change); New Seasons, Inc., 346 NLRB No. 57, 179 LRRM 1214 (2006) (employer unlawfully changed provision that was not subject to contract's reopener clause).

[23]Budd Co., 348 NLRB No. 85, 181 LRRM 1001 (2006) (an employer could unilaterally ban radios relying on an unmistakable waiver in parties' collective bargaining agreement).

[24]*E.g.*, E.I. DuPont & Co., 346 NLRB No. 55, 179 LRRM 1227 (2006).

However, the Board will not find a violation where the union's information request is designed as a bad faith, tactical ploy to forestall an otherwise lawful implementation of terms.[25]

B. Nature of the Duty to Furnish Information

1. Request or Demand

The Board has held that an employer did not act unlawfully by providing a delayed response to an information request made 3 days before its deadline for implementing its final offer where the information request was found "purely tactical" and "submitted solely for purposes of delay." [26]

2. Relevance or Necessity

The Board continues to hold that relevance is determined by a broad, liberal, "discovery type" standard.[27] It also continues to hold that information regarding wages, including overtime wages, as well as other working conditions, such as employee training, is presumptively relevant.[28]

3. Availability

a. Good Faith Effort to Respond to Request

The Board continues to hold that the recipient of an appropriate information request must make "a reasonable good-faith effort to respond to the request as promptly as circumstances allow."[29]

---

[25]ACF Indus., LLC, 347 NLRB No. 99, 180 LRRM 1303 (2006) (employer lawfully delayed information requested by union when the union requested information after months of extensive bargaining, after contract expiration, after its rejection of the employer's final offer, and after the employer declared that it had nothing left to offer).

[26]Id., slip op. at 4.

[27]North Star Steel Co., 347 NLRB No. 119 (2006) (employer unlawfully refused to provide union with requested information regarding transferred production work).

[28]Pavilion at Forrestal Nursing & Rehab., 346 NLRB No. 46, 179 LRRM 1007 (2006) (overtime wages); Southern Calif. Gas Co., 346 NLRB No. 45, 179 LRRM 1135 (2006) (employee training).

[29]United Elec. Contractors Ass'n, 347 NLRB No. 1, slip op. at 3, 180 LRRM 1336 (2006). But see ACF Indus., 347 NLRB No. 99, 180 LRRM 1303.

5. Employer Defenses

a. Claims of Confidentiality or Privilege Based on Employer Interests

The Board continues to hold that a party may refuse to furnish confidential information to the other party under certain circumstances. Thus, in *Northern Indiana Public Service Co.*,[30] the Board concluded that the employer did not act unlawfully by refusing, on confidentiality grounds, to provide the union with copies of interview notes because the information requested was confidential and the employer's interest in confidentiality outweighed the union's need for information. An employee had complained that his supervisor made threats to his personal safety. The employer subsequently interviewed the supervisor, the employee, and another supervisor about the allegation. The union filed a grievance alleging that the employer had violated its contractual guarantee of a safe workplace and simultaneously requested the employer's notes of the interviews. The employer objected on the ground that the interviewees had been promised confidentiality. The Board found this to be a legitimate confidentiality concern and held that it outweighed any need for the interview notes, given that the union had been provided the names of the interviewees and that the notes would "provide, at best, corroboration, denials, or assertions of mitigation regarding what was said."[31]

C. When the Duty Exists

The duty to furnish information attaches immediately when a construction industry employer voluntarily recognizes the union as the Section 9(a) representative of its employees after expiration of the Section 8(f) contract.[32]

Once an employer lawfully withdraws recognition from a union, the duty to furnish information immediately ceases.[33]

---

[30]347 NLRB No. 17, 179 LRRM 1305 (2006).
[31]*Id.*, slip op. at 4.
[32]M & M Backhoe Serv., Inc. v. NLRB, 469 F.3d 1047, 180 LRRM 3201 (D.C. Cir. 2006).
[33]Renal Care of Buffalo, Inc., 347 NLRB No. 112, 181 LRRM 1095 (2006).

D. Information That Must Be Furnished

1. Financial Information

The Board continues to draw a distinction between claims of "inability to pay" and "claims of competitive disadvantage," the former entitling the union to request and review the employer's financial records to assess the employer's representations about its financial condition.[34] In *North Star Steel*, the Board found statements such as " 'extremely low' future orders were 'a cause of great concern' "; "several competitors were 'effectively bankrupt' "; and that "business was really going south in a hurry" constituted claims of competitive disadvantage and did not entitle the union to company financial information.[35] The Board reasoned that the employer's statements stayed completely clear of the subject of company assets and its ability to pay employees and merely relayed the message that it was losing money and would not pay, as opposed to could not pay, in order to stay competitive.

Nevertheless, where an employer premises its bargaining proposals on specific assertions of relative competitiveness, the union is entitled to targeted financial information (not general access to financial records) where that information would assist the union in evaluating the employer's assertions and developing its own proposals.[36] Thus, where the employer claimed that the plant at issue was less competitive than its others, the union was entitled to cost data it had requested for each of the plants.[37]

In another case, the Ninth Circuit held that the union was entitled to financial information because the employer was asked, "So are you saying you cannot afford the Union's proposals?" and responded, "No, I can't. I'd go broke."[38] In this regard, the court overruled the Board, which had excused the employer because the comment was made "in the heat of bargaining."[39] The court concluded that there was insufficient evidence to support the Board's conclusion that the employer did not assert an inability to pay. The Board had also found that the employer withdrew its claim of inabil-

---

[34]North Star Steel Co., 347 NLRB No. 119 (2006).
[35]*Id.*, slip op. at 6–7.
[36]Caldwell Mfg. Co., 346 NLRB No. 100, 180 LRRM 1053 (2006).
[37]*Id.*, slip op. at 2 n.6.
[38]Chemical Workers v. NLRB, 467 F.3d 742, 750–55 (9th Cir. 2006).
[39]American Polystyrene, 341 NLRB 508, 174 LRRM 1305 (2004).

ity to pay, but the court disagreed and found this attempted withdrawal was bad faith bargaining.[40]

2. Other Information

b. Hours and Terms and Conditions of Employment

The duty to provide information continues to encompass the duty to allow the union to conduct a time-and-motion study to validate a claim of work overload.[41] Thus, the Board found that the employer unlawfully denied the union access to its warehouse to conduct a time and motion study on the work performed by forklift drivers who complained of work overload. The Board found that time study was plainly relevant to the union's representation of forklift drivers on the work-overload issue and the employer failed to carry its burden of showing that there were alternative means by which the union could represent employees on this issue.

V. ECONOMIC PRESSURE DURING BARGAINING

A. Lockout[42]

Contrary to the Board, the District of Columbia Circuit, in *Steelworkers v. NLRB*, recently held that an employer's lockout of unit employees, while allowing probationary employees with fewer contractual rights to work who were not union members, was unlawful.[43] The court granted the union's petition for review and remanded the case for the Board to "determine whether the union decertification process was tainted by the unlawful lockout and, if so, whether Bunting violated [Section] 8(a)(5)...by relying on this petition to withdraw recognition from the union."

The Board had determined that the employer's partial lockout—refusing to allow unit employees to work, while continuing to employ probationary employees with dramatically reduced rights under the contract who were not union members—was lawful because it distinguished between two classes of employees on a non-

---

[40]467 F.3d at 753–55.
[41]Nestle Purina Petcare Co., 347 NLRB No. 91 (2006).
[42]For a more detailed discussion, see Chapter 20, "The Lockout."
[43]Steelworkers v. NLRB, 179 Fed. Appx. 61, 179 LRRM 2896 (D.C. Cir. 2006), *reversing and remanding* Bunting Bearings Corp., 343 NLRB 479 (2004).

discriminatory basis. Thus, the Board had found the decertification petition was not tainted.

However, on review, the District of Columbia Circuit rejected the Board's conclusion that the union had failed to establish that the employer's conduct was discriminatory. Instead, the court approvingly quoted dissenting Member Walsh's conclusion that "no authority holds that [the union] must initially do more than what [it] has done here: show a perfect correlation between union membership and which employees were locked out." Accordingly, the court held, "the burden was on [the employer] to present evidence showing that the lockout was motivated by legitimate objections [and the employer] did not even attempt to do this."[44]

[**Editor's Note**: The updated citation for *Midwest Generation*, 343 NLRB No. 12, 175 LRRM 1461 (2004) is: *Midwest Generation*, 343 NLRB No. 69, 175 LRRM 1461 (2004), *rev'd sub nom. Electrical Workers(IBEW) Local 15 v. NLRB*, 429 F.3d 651, 178 LRRM 2385 (7th Cir. 2005), *writ of cert. denied, Midwest Generation, EME, LLC v. Electrical Workers (IBEW) Local 15*, 127 S. Ct. 42, 180 LRRM 2832 (2006).]

B. Responses to Strikes

The Second Circuit has recently indicated that an employer may violate the Act by replacing strikers if motivated by an independent unlawful motive. In *New England Healthcare Employees District 1199 v. NLRB*,[45] the Second Circuit granted the union's petition for review and vacated the Board's decision to the extent that it dismissed the general counsel's Section 8(a)(3) complaint that the employer had an "independent [and hence] unlawful motive for hiring permanent replacements for the striking workers—to break the union—and that its refusal to reinstate therefore violated the Act."[46] The court "accept[ed] the Board's premise that an employer has no legal obligation to inform striking workers before hiring permanent replacements."[47] However, the court found that the Board erred in concluding, "based on that observation alone—that an employer's decision to keep the hiring of permanent replacements secret is not probative of whether the employer had an independent unlawful

---

[44]*Id.*, 179 Fed. Appx. at 62.

[45]448 F.3d 189, 179 LRRM 2577 (2d Cir. 2006) *remanding sub nom.* Church Homes Inc., 343 NLRB 1301 (2004).

[46]*Id.* at 190.

[47]*Id.* at 194.

purpose for the hiring."[48] The court observed that "logic suggests that an employer seeking to enhance its bargaining leverage by hiring permanent replacements would have every incentive to publicize the effort" and that "it would appear that employers with an illicit motive to break a union have a strong incentive to keep the ongoing hiring of permanent replacements secret."[49] In remanding, however, the court made clear that its "opinion does not preclude the Board on remand from reaching th[e] same conclusion through adequate reasoning."[50]

As to employers not being required to finance strikes, the Board continues to find that an employer is generally not required to continue paying health insurance premiums for employees who are on strike.[51]

VI. Bargaining Impasses

A. Elements of Impasse

The Board continues to hold that an impasse occurs when both parties would be warranted in believing that further bargaining would be futile.[52] Thus, in *Richmond Electrical Services*,[53] the Board concluded that an impasse existed where the union conceded that the most-favored-nations clause in its other collective bargaining agreements effectively precluded it from agreeing with the employer on a wage rate that was lower than the one in its multi-employer agreement, the union never proposed a wage rate lower than the one in its multi-employer agreement, and the employer consistently made clear that it would not agree to the wage rates contained in the multi-employer agreement. In these circumstances, the Board

---

[48]*Id.* at 195.

[49]*Id.*

[50]*Id.* at 196; in Church Homes, Inc. dba Avery Heights and New England Health Care Employees Dist. 1199, 350 NLRB No. 21 (2007), the Board accepted the court's holding as law of the case and a violation.

[51]*But see* Beverly Health & Rehab. Servs., Inc., 346 NLRB No. 111, 179 LRRM 1284 (2006) (employer acted unlawfully because it did more than simply cease paying its share of the insurance premiums; instead it paid the premiums and then deducted from the strikers' payments the sum that it paid for their insurance premiums).

[52]Richmond Elec. Servs., Inc., 348 NLRB No. 62, 181 LRRM 1029 (2006); ACF Indus., LLC, 347 NLRB No. 99 (2006); Washoe Med. Ctr., Inc., 348 NLRB No. 22, 180 LRRM 1502 (2006).

[53]348 NLRB No. 62, 181 LRRM 1029 (2006).

found that the parties' course of bargaining demonstrated that an agreement on wages was critically important to an overall agreement, and thus the impasse over wages led to a complete breakdown in negotiations.

Similarly, in *ACF Industries, LLC*,[54] the Board concluded the parties had reached an impasse where the employer had informed the union that its economic conditions necessitated major concessions in wages and benefits and the parties engaged in hard but good faith bargaining in 12 sessions over a 2-month period. By the time the employer declared impasse, the Board found that the parties had engaged in extensive bargaining but still remained far apart on a number of major issues. The employer had nothing left to offer beyond that which had already been rejected, and the union similarly had offered no new proposals to demonstrate that further progress was possible. Although the union had stated, shortly after the employer had declared impasse, that it had additional proposals, the union failed to divulge any specifics regarding those proposals and gave the employer no reason to conclude that further bargaining would have been fruitful.

In determining whether an impasse has occurred the Board continues to rely on numerous factors.[55]

These factors include:

1. Fluidity of position.[56]
2. Statements or understandings of the parties concerning impasse.[57]
3. The nature and importance of issues and the extent of difference or opposition.[58]

---

[54]347 NLRB No. 99 (2006).

[55]Ead Motors E. Air Devices, Inc., 346 NLRB No. 93, 180 LRRM 1192 (2006) (relevant factors in determining the validity of an impasse such as bargaining history, whether the parties acted in good faith during negotiations, the length of the negotiations, the significance of the issue or issues where disagreement exists, and the parties' beliefs regarding the state of negotiations evinced that the impasse declared by the employer was invalid).

[56]*ACF Indus.*, 347 NLRB No. 99, 180 LRRM 1303 (impasse finding where no movement was attempted by the parties after employer submitted its best and final economic proposal and employer stated it had no more room to move and it was not going to make any further offers, membership rejected the offer, and where parties were far apart on a number of significant issues).

[57]Day Auto. Res., Inc., 348 NLRB No. 90, 181 LRRM 1047 (2006) (employer statement that parties at impasse insufficient).

[58]*Id.* (no impasse because importance of issues warranted more extensive discussion than took place during the parties' few meetings); *Richmond Elec.*, 348

4. Demonstrated willingness to consider the issue further.[59]
5. Number and duration of bargaining sessions.[60]
6. The presence of a federal mediator during bargaining.[61]
7. Other actions inconsistent with impasse.[62]

B. Effect on the Bargaining Obligation

The Board continues to hold that when an impasse is reached, the duty to bargain is not terminated but only suspended.[63] An impasse may be "broken" if one of the parties makes new substantive proposals.[64]

The Board continues to recognize that in certain circumstances, impasse on a single issue can result in an overall impasse if the particular issue is of such overriding importance that impasse on that issue alone causes a breakdown in the overall negotiations.[65]

NLRB No. 62, 181 LRRM 1029 (impasse over a single issue (wages) resulted in overall impasse because the wage issue was so important that impasse on that issue frustrated overall bargaining).

[59]*ACF Indus.*, (union's statements that it had additional proposals without providing any specifics insufficient to preclude finding of impasse); *Ead Motors*, 346 NLRB No. 93, 180 LRRM 1192 (2006) (union's stated intention to return to negotiations rather than strike following members' rejection of employer's offer a factor in finding that parties not at impasse); Coastal Cargo Co., Inc., 348 NLRB No. 32, 180 LRRM 1520 (2006) (no impasse where employer demonstrated movement possible by presenting union with multiple final offers after indicating it had reached a point where it could not bargain further).

[60]Washoe Med. Ctr., Inc., 348 NLRB No. 22, 180 LRRM 1502 (2006) (impasse; 30 meetings, some with mediator, over 16-month period); ACF Indus., LLC, 347 NLRB No. 99, 180 LRRM 1303 (2006) (parties reached a valid impasse where they negotiated in hard, but good faith, bargaining in 12 sessions over a 2-month period); Ead Motors E. Air Devices, Inc., 346 NLRB No. 93, 180 LRRM 1192 (no impasse; seven meetings insufficient to allow for meaningful negotiations given complexity of issues and because the parties had only generally discussed economic issues).

[61]*Washoe Med.*. 348 NLRB No. 22, 180 LRRM 1502 (mediator present at "some" of 30 bargaining sessions supports impasse finding).

[62]*Ead Motors*, 346 NLRB No. 93, 180 LRRM 119 (employer's final offer included provision that called for additional negotiations over proposed new job classification system; also, employer presented its final offer before union had sufficient time to respond to employer's previous economic proposal); *see also Coastal Cargo*, 348 NLRB No. 32, 180 LRRM 1520 (no impasse where employer presented final offer on an issue prior to any bargaining on that issue).

[63]Richmond Elec. Servs., Inc., 348 NLRB No. 62, 181 LRRM 1029 (2006).

[64]ACF Indus., LLC, 347 NLRB No. 99, 180 LRRM 1303 (2006).

[65]*Richmond Elec.*, 348 NLRB No. 62, 181 LRRM 1029 (deadlock on wages resulted in overall impasse).

The Board also has continued to develop the exception allowing implementation of a change with absence of overall impasse.
Under this exception, "if a term or condition of employment concerns a discrete recurring event, such as an annually scheduled wage
review, and that event is scheduled to occur during negotiations for
an initial contract,"[66] the employer may implement a change in that
term or condition "if it provides the union with reasonable advance
notice and an opportunity to bargain about the intended change in
past practice."[67] In *Neighborhood House Ass'n*,[68] the Board concluded
that an employer did not violate Section 8(a)(5), when, absent an
overall impasse, it implemented its proposal to withhold a cost-of-
living adjustment. The Board reasoned that the cost-of-living adjustment was a discrete annually occurring event, and that the employer
made clear during bargaining that if no decision was reached by
the time the cost-of-living adjustment had to be in place, then the
employer would withhold the increase and continue to bargain over
the amount of the increase. The Board found these actions by the
employer evinced that the union had received reasonable advance
notice and an opportunity to bargain on this issue. The dissent, in
contrast, found that the employer acted unlawfully because it found
that the employer's actions were not motivated by economic concerns, but rather by the impermissible negotiating tactic of requiring
the union to waive its right to negotiate the cost-of-living adjustment.
The Board has not yet ruled on whether an employer must first bargain to impasse over the particular matter before implementation
under this exception.[69]

In addition, in *E.I. DuPont de Nemours & Co.*,[70] the Board made
clear that the holding of *Sierra Bullets LLC*[71] only applies when information requests are unrelated to the key issues dividing the parties
during negotiations. Specifically, in *DuPont*, the Board found that
an employer violated the Act by not responding to an information
request prior to declaring impasse on the issue of subcontracting

---

[66]Neighborhood House Ass'n, 347 NLRB No. 52, slip op. at 2, 180 LRRM 1101
(2006).
[67]*Id.*
[68]347 NLRB No. 52, 180 LRRM 1101 (2006). *See also* St. Mary's Hosp. of Blue
Springs, 346 NLRB No. 76, 179 LRRM 1221 (2006) (employer did not violate the
Act by implementing a proposal pre-impasse, because the employer gave the union
proper notice of the prospective changes and the chance to bargain over them).
[69]*St. Mary's Hosp.*, slip op. at 1 n.4; Saint-Gobain Abrasives, Inc., 343 NLRB No.
68, 176 LRRM 1466 (2004).
[70]346 NLRB No. 55, 179 LRRM 1227 (2006).
[71]340 NLRB 242, 173 LRRM 1283 (2003).

milling and finishing work, as the request related to the subcontract issue negotiations and thus the failure to provide this information possibly hindered potential negotiation progress on this issue.[72]

The Board continues to recognize that an employer may make unilateral changes upon impasse.[73] However, the Board also continues to recognize the exception to this rule set forth in *McClatchy Newspapers*,[74] under which an employer may not implement a proposal upon impasse that would be inherently destructive to the principles of collective bargaining.[75] In addition, the Board continues to hold that parties retain a duty to bargain following impasse.[76]

The Board continues to hold that if a party's unlawful bargaining or unfair labor practice precludes agreement, the impasse is not a valid one, and any unilateral changes by that party will be illegal.[77] Similarly, unremedied unfair labor practices may preclude impasse. In determining whether there is a lawful impasse, the Board continues to look at the effects of the conduct at issue in the particular circumstances.[78]

---

[72] *See also* Caldwell Mfg. Co., 346 NLRB No. 100, 180 LRRM 1053 (2006) (employer violated §8(a)(5) by unilaterally declaring impasse prior to providing the requested information that was key to the development of the union's bargaining position).

[73] *See, e.g., DuPont*, 346 NLRB No. 55, 179 LRRM 1227.

[74] 321 NLRB 1386 (1996), *enforced*, 131 F.3d 1026 (D.C. Cir. 1997), *cert. denied*, 524 U.S. 937 (1998).

[75] Roosevelt Mem'l Med. Ctr., 348 NLRB No. 64, 181 LRRM 1084 (2006) (employer unlawfully implemented dues checkoff, no-strike provision, and grievance arbitration provisions). *But see E.I. DuPont de Nemours & Co.*, 346 NLRB No. 55, 179 LRRM 1227, where the Board found the exception set forth in *McClatchy* inapplicable where an employer did not seek to implement a broad discretionary policy over which it had total discretion, but instead sought to implement a narrow provision regarding healthcare benefits that did not give it total discretion because it set limits on the employer's discretion to act with respect to healthcare. The Board reasoned that implementation of this narrow provision was permissible as it would not destroy the principles of collective bargaining.

[76] *Id.* (despite a lawful impasse, employer violated §8(a)(5) by unilaterally implementing its contract proposal for a 2-year term as this was tantamount to a 2-year refusal to bargain).

[77] Day Auto. Res., Inc., 348 NLRB No. 90, 181 LRRM 1047 (2006) (employer's adamant insistence that union accept its proposed health plan without any changes before it would bargain about any other economic issues precluded lawful impasse); Success Vill. Apartments, Inc., 347 NLRB No. 100 (no lawful impasse where employer refused to meet with union face-to-face in mediation sessions and insisted on meeting in separate rooms with mediator as go-between; use and format of mediation sessions is a permissive subject of bargaining).

[78] ACF Indus., LLC, 347 NLRB No. 99, 180 LRRM 1303 (2006) (no showing that inclusion of nonmandatory subject in employer's final offer contributed to deadlock).

VII. DEFENSES AND EXCEPTIONS: WAIVER, SUSPENSION, AND
TERMINATION OF BARGAINING RIGHTS

A. Waiver of Bargaining Rights

1. Waiver by Express Agreement

The District of Columbia Circuit continues to apply the less rigid "contract coverage" analysis.[79] Under that approach, the proper inquiry is whether the subject matter in dispute is "covered" by the collective bargaining agreement; if so, "questions of waiver normally do not come into play."[80] The District of Columbia Circuit has continued to deny enforcement of Board orders premised on the "clear and unmistakable" waiver standard, noting that "the Board's doctrine imposes an artificially high burden on an employer that claims its authority to engage in an activity is granted by such an agreement."[81] In *Enloe Medical Center v. NLRB*,[82] the court applied its "contract coverage" analysis in the context of effects bargaining and reiterated its view that questions of "waiver" normally do not come into play with respect to subjects already covered by a collective bargaining agreement. The court stated that it would be "rather unusual" to interpret an agreement as granting an employer the unilateral right to make a decision while reserving the union's right to bargain over the effects." The court therefore found no effects bargaining obligation.

Relatedly, courts continue to recognize that the "clear and unmistakable" waiver standard does not apply in cases where the union alleges an unlawful modification under Section 8(d).[83] In

---

[79]Enloe Med. Ctr. v. NLRB, 433 F.3d 834, 178 LRRM 2718 (D.C. Cir. 2005).
[80]*Id.* at 838.
[81]*Id.*
[82]433 F.3d 834, 178 LRRM 2718 (D.C. Cir. 2005).
[83]In *Bath Marine Draftsmen Ass'n v. NLRB*, 475 F.3d 14, 24, 181 LRRM 2267 (1st Cir. Jan. 29, 2007), *enforcing* 345 NLRB No. 33, slip op. at 3, 178 LRRM 1183 (2005), the court cited the Board's decision in describing the fundamental differences between §8(a)(5) and 8(d) allegations, noting "the 'unilateral change' case and the 'contract modification' case are fundamentally different in terms of principle, possible defenses, and remedy. In terms of principle, the 'unilateral change' case does not require the General Counsel to show the existence of a contract provision; he need only show that there is an employment practice concerning a mandatory bargaining subject, and that the employer has made a significant change thereto without bargaining. The allegation is a failure to bargain. In the 'contract modification' case, the General Counsel must show a contractual provision, and that the employer has modified the provision."

such cases, the issue is not whether the union waived its right to bargain over the unilateral change, but instead whether the change modified the agreement, and whether the employer has a "sound arguable basis" for its actions.[84]

b. "Management-Rights" Clauses

An employer may not rely on an expired contract's management-rights clause as support for a "clear and unmistakable waiver" unless there is some indication the parties' intended such clause to continue in effect beyond contract expiration.[85]

3. Waiver by Inaction

Although a union's inaction may constitute a waiver of its right to bargain,[86] a union will not waive its right to bargain by failing to request negotiations, where such an act would be futile.[87] The Board also continues to hold that a party must have "clear notice" of an intended change in order to have been found to waive its right to bargain by inaction.[88] To be timely, notice must be given sufficiently in advance to allow the union the reasonable opportunity to request bargaining.[89]

C. Union Loss of Majority

The Board and courts continue to follow the standard set forth in *Levitz Furniture*[90] to assess whether an employer is privileged to withdraw recognition and/or refuse to bargain with an incumbent union. Under this standard, the employer must demonstrate objective evidence of an "actual loss of support" by the incumbent

---

[84]*Id.*

[85]Clear Channel Outdoor, Inc., 346 NLRB No. 66, 179 LRRM 1189 (2006).

[86]Budd Co., 384 NLRB No. 85 (2006) (union failed to follow contractual procedures to challenge employer's right to implement work rule, which supported finding it waived its right to bargain over the issue).

[87]National Steel & Shipbuilding Co., 348 NLRB No. 23, 180 LRRM 1423 (2006) (no waiver where union was presented with "fait accompli"); Berkshire Nursing Home, LLC, 345 NLRB No. 14, 178 LRRM 1015 (2005).

[88]Waste Mgmt. de Puerto Rico, 348 NLRB No. 26, 181 LRRM 1159 (2006) (no waiver of right to bargain over bonuses, where union had no notice of employer's intent to change past practice regarding payment).

[89]Peerless Pump Co., 345 NLRB No. 20, 178 LRRM 1307 (2005); *National Steel & Shipbuilding*, 348 NLRB No. 23, slip op. at 5 (2006) ("when the union receives notice of the action contemporary with the action itself, there can be no waiver").

[90]333 NLRB 717 (2001).

union—and the employer acts at its own peril if it is mistaken.[91] Three Board members have noted, however, that they did not participate in *Levitz Furniture* and expressed no view as to whether it was correctly decided.[92]

The Board has suggested that when confronted with inconclusive evidence of the loss of the union's majority status, the better approach is for an employer to file an RM petition rather than unilaterally withdraw recognition.[93] In this regard, the Board has repeat-

---

[91]Port Printing Ad & Specialties, 344 NLRB No. 34, 176 LRRM 1495 (2005), *enforced*, 192 Fed. Appx. 290, 180 LRRM 2512 (5th Cir. 2006) (employer unlawfully withdrew recognition from union where it did not have evidence of union's "actual loss of support," but erroneously believed the union had lost such support); Vanguard Fire & Sec. Sys., 345 NLRB No. 77, 178 LRRM 1447 (2005), *enforced*, 468 F.3d 952, 180 LRRM 3137 (6th Cir. 2006) (employer unlawfully withdrew recognition based on disaffection petition it believed was signed by majority of bargaining-unit members, where several signatures were of individuals not performing bargaining-unit work and, thus, not counting those signatures, the union continued to enjoy majority support); Flying Foods Group, Inc., 345 NLRB No. 10, 178 LRRM 1244 (2005), *enforced*, 471 F.3d 178, 181 LRRM 2001 (D.C. Cir. 2006) (where employer withdrew recognition based on petition signed by 96 out of 164 unit employees, and 16 of those signatures turned out to be invalid, the employer failed to satisfy the *Levitz* standard, and unlawfully withdrew recognition from the union); HQM of Bayside, LLC, 348 NLRB No. 42, 181 LRRM 1003 (2006) (employer unlawfully withdrew recognition based on disaffection petition signed by majority of employees, when group of employees later "rescinded" disaffection and signed a petition supporting union; Board held that employer could not rely on signatures of "crossover" employees who later reversed themselves and declared support for the union, as evidence of loss of majority status); Parkwood Dev. Ctr., 347 NLRB No. 95, 180 LRRM 1178 (2006) (employer's anticipatory withdrawal of recognition from the union unlawful, where it relied on earlier petition of disaffection signed by majority of employees, but union later presented a petition supported by majority of employees' signatures); LTD Ceramics, Inc., 341 NLRB 86 (2004), *aff'd*, 185 Fed. Appx. 581 (9th Cir. 2006).

[92]*See HQM*, 348 NLRB No. 42, 181 LRRM 1003 (Member Schaumber) and *Parkwood*, 347 NLRB No. 95, 180 LRRM 117 (Chairman Battista and Member Kirsanow). For a fuller discussion, see Chapters 10, "Representation Proceedings and Elections" and 12, "Recognition and Withdrawal of Recognition Without an Election."

[93]Several Board cases since *Levitz* have emphasized that an employer faced with a petition indicating loss of support for an incumbent union can avoid the apparent "Hobson's choice" of continuing to recognize an incumbent minority union, thus violating §8(a)(2), and unilaterally withdrawing recognition, in violation of §8(a)(5), by filing an RM petition to determine the union's majority status. *HQM*, 348 NLRB No. 42, 181 LRRM 1003 (employer unlawfully withdrew recognition, and should have instead filed an RM petition and continued to recognize incumbent union); Dura Art Stone, 346 NLRB No. 14, 179 LRRM 1217 (2005) (employer violated §8(a)(2) by continuing to negotiate with incumbent union where employer had demonstrable, objective evidence of an "actual loss of support," and no petition was filed to clarify the union's status).

edly found that the employer is not entitled to rely on the signatures of employees who sign both antiunion and union petitions.[94]

The Board continues to apply *Lee Lumber II*[95] in determining whether a causal connection exists between the employer's unfair labor practice(s) and the ensuing events indicating a loss of majority support, thereby tainting or precluding a lawful withdrawal of recognition.[96] In this regard, the temporal nexus between the employer unfair labor practice(s) and employee petition continues to be an important factor. Thus in *Goya Foods of Florida*,[97] the Board found that the employer unlawfully withdrew recognition from the union where the employer's substantial and continuing unfair labor practices had a strong temporal nexus with the employee petitions.

On the other hand, in *Garden Ridge Management*,[98] the Board found that the employer did not act unlawfully when it withdrew recognition from the union, even though it violated Section 8(a)(5) by refusing to meet at reasonable times with the union. The Board found that the 5-month period, between the employer's last refusal to hold additional bargaining sessions and the time the disaffection petition was presented to it, weighed against finding that the unfair labor practice caused employee sentiment against the union. It also found that the nature of the violation did not support a finding of taint. Member Liebman dissented in relevant part because she would find that the employer's unlawful refusal to meet with the union was enough, by itself, to taint the employer's withdrawal of recognition and she would also find that the employer engaged in surface bargaining.[99]

---

[94]*HQM*, 348 NLRB No. 42, 181 LRRM 1003; *Parkwood*, 347 NLRB No. 95, 180 LRRM 11; Highlands Reg'l Med. Ctr., 347 NLRB No. 120, 180 LRRM 1414 (2006).

[95]322 NLRB 175, 153 LRRM 1158 (1996), *enforced in relevant part and remanded in part*, 117 F.3d 1454, 155 LRRM 2748 (D.C. Cir. 1997). *See also* Master Slack Corp., 271 NLRB 78, 116 LRRM 1324 (1984) (setting forth a four-part test to determine whether a causal relationship exists).

[96]Goya Foods of Fla., 347 NLRB No. 103 (2006).

[97]*Id.*

[98]347 NLRB No. 13, 180 LRRM 1030 (2006).

[99]*Id.*

VIII. THE CONSTRUCTION INDUSTRY: SECTION 8(f)

B.   The *Deklewa* Decision: Binding Section 8(f) Agreements and the Duty to Bargain

In *M & M Backhoe Service, Inc. v. NLRB*,[100] the District of Columbia Circuit reaffirmed its holding in *Nova Plumbing v. NLRB*[101] that contract language and intent, standing alone, does not dispositively modify a union's Section 8(f) status to that of Section 9(a) status where record evidence contains strong indications that the union lacked majority status, continuing the disagreement between the District of Columbia Circuit and the Board on this issue. However, in *M & M Backhoe Service*, this disagreement was immaterial because the record evidence showed that a majority of the employees had voluntarily signed union authorization cards.[102]

IX. NOTICE TO TERMINATE OR MODIFY THE LABOR AGREEMENT

A.   Notice Requirements Generally

Whether the conduct of negotiations alone—and absent any manifestation of an intent to terminate a collective bargaining agreement—stops the operation of an automatic-renewal evergreen clause remains a developing area of the law. In *Long Island Head Start v. NLRB*,[103] the Second Circuit vacated the Board's decision and remanded the case to the Board for further proceedings consistent with the court's opinion. The court rejected the Board's holding that, the extant collective bargaining agreement did not automatically renew although timely notice to terminate had not been given, because face-to-face negotiations had already commenced. The Board had concluded that by commencing these negotiations, the "parties waive[d] contractual requirements of timely or written notice of ter-

---

[100]469 F.3d 1047, 180 LRRM 3201 (D.C. Cir. 2006), *denying petition for review and granting cross petition for enforcement*, 345 NLRB No. 29, 178 LRRM 1510 (2005).

[101]330 F.3d 531, 538 172 LRRM 2700 (D.C. Cir. 2003), *granting petition for review and denying cross petition for enforcement*, 336 NLRB 633, 169 LRRM 1276 (2001).

[102]*M & M Backhoe*, 469 F.3d at 1050–51, 180 LRRM at 3204.

[103]460 F.3d 254, 180 LRRM 2161 (2nd Cir. 2006), *vacating and remanding*, 345 NLRB No. 74 (2005).

mination or modification," thereby disabling the evergreen clause.[104] In the court's view, however, neither the cases upon which the Board relied nor the analysis the Board supplied "explain[ed] why the rule granting relief from the formalities of notice should be extended to grant relief from notice altogether."[105]

XI. Bargaining During the Term of an Existing Agreement

The Board continues to hold that an employer violates Section 8(a)(5) if it makes a midterm unilateral change in wages, hours, or other terms and conditions of employment without first giving the union notice and an opportunity to bargain.[106] In *Allied Aviation Fueling of Dallas, LP*,[107] the Board held that the employer violated Section 8(a)(5) when it unilaterally implemented a modified drug and alcohol testing policy—a mandatory subject of bargaining—without consulting the union. That the employer's amendment was motivated by economic pressures rather than union animus did not excuse the employer's obligation to bargain prior to implementing a unilateral change in the terms and conditions of employment.[108]

Where the collective bargaining agreement waives a union's right to bargain over a particular subject, however, the Board continues to hold that the employer has no obligation to bargain over midterm modifications of that subject.[109] In *Budd Co.*, the Board held that the union clearly and unmistakably waived its right to request bargaining over the implemented change in safety rules,[110] where the collective bargaining agreement gave management the right "to make and enforce rules and regulations . . . to provide for the safety of associates and equipment" and provided a specific method for the union to contest such rule alterations. Because the union failed to seek recourse under the bargained-upon procedures, it therefore had no additional Board remedy.[111]

---

[104]345 NLRB No. 74, slip op. at 1.
[105]460 F.3d at 259.
[106]Allied Aviation Fueling of Dallas, LP, 347 NLRB No. 22, 180 LRRM 1255 (2006).
[107]*Id.*
[108]*Id.*
[109]Budd Co., 348 NLRB No. 85, 181 LRRM 1001 (2006).
[110]*Id.*, slip op. at 7–8.
[111]*Id.*, slip op. at 8.

When bargaining under a reopener provision, the parties are required to bargain only over those mandatory subjects covered by the contract's reopener provision.[112] A subject outside the scope of the reopener provision is considered a permissive subject of bargaining during reopened negotiations, even if that subject would be mandatory if the parties were bargaining for a new agreement.[113] While the parties may bargain about subjects outside the reopener, they are not required to do so. Thus, an impasse in reopener negotiations is not a defense to an employer's unilateral changes to employment terms outside the reopener.[114]

In *New Seasons, Inc.*,[115] the Board held the employer unlawfully implemented a change to the notice of leave provision that was not covered by the reopener. The contract contained a reopener provision covering wages, health insurance benefits, and an attendance bonus. During reopened negotiations, the employer sought changes to a contractual term that addressed the number of days' notice an employee needed to provide management to obtain requested leave. This notice for leave provision, while not specifically covered by the reopener provision, was contained in the same contractual article as the attendance bonus program. Although it was lawful for the employer to make proposals regarding the notice for leave provision, the Board held that the attendance bonus program and the notice for leave provision were separate contractual terms.[116]

XII. DUAL EMPLOYER OPERATIONS: THE "DOUBLE-BREASTED" ISSUE

The Board and courts continue to hold that in determining whether two nominally separate business entities are a single employer, the following four factors must be analyzed: (1) interrelation of operations, (2) common management, (3) centralized control of labor relations, and (4) common ownership.[117] In addition,

---

[112]New Seasons, Inc., 346 NLRB No. 57, 179 LRRM 1214 (2006); Campo Slacks, Inc., 266 NLRB 492, 112 LRRM 1432 (1983).

[113]*New Seasons*, 346 NLRB No. 57, 179 LRRM 1214.

[114]*Id.*

[115]*Id.*

[116]*Id.*

[117]*See* Asher Candy, Inc., 348 NLRB No. 60, at n.1, 181 LRRM 1214 (2006); Flat Dog Prods., 347 NLRB No. 104, 180 LRRM 1383 (2006); Central Ill. Carpenters Health & Welfare Trust Fund v. Olsen, No. 03-3250, 2006 WL 1520273, at *5 (C.D. Ill. June 1, 2006).

the Board and courts continue to find that no single factor in the single-employer inquiry is controlling, and that all four elements need not be present for the Board to find that two entities are a single employer.[118] "Rather, single-employer status depends on all the circumstances, and is characterized by the absence of the arm's-length relationship found between unintegrated entities."[119] In *Leb-anite Corp.*,[120] the Board clarified that the presence or absence of an "arm's-length relationship" between the two companies alleged to be a single employer is not an additional factor to those noted above, but instead bears on the factor of the interrelation of operations.[121]

Courts continue to hold that when two entities are found to be a single employer, for one company to be bound by a collective bargaining agreement made by another company it must be shown that the relevant employees of the two nominal employers together represent an appropriate bargaining unit.[122] Some courts have also found that they have jurisdiction to decide the appropriate bargaining unit because they may decide labor law questions that emerge as collateral issues in suits brought under independent federal remedies.[123] Courts also continue to find that ownership of two entities by close family members can establish the element of common ownership.[124]

In determining whether one entity is the alter ego of another, courts continue to examine whether there is substantially identical management, business purpose, operation, equipment, customers, and supervision, as well as ownership and a purpose to evade responsibilities under the Act.[125] Courts also continue to hold that

---

[118]*Id.*

[119]*See Flat Dog*, 347 NLRB No. 104, 180 LRRM 1383; Engelhardt v. S.P. Richards Co., 472 F.3d 1 (1st Cir. 2006).

[120]346 NLRB No. 72, 179 LRRM 1166 (2006).

[121]*Id.*, slip op. at n.5.

[122]*See* Fuchs v. Cristal Concrete Corp., No. CV 04-1555, (ETB), 2006 WL 2548169, 180 LRRM 2426 (E.D.N.Y. July 18, 2006).

[123]Laborers Dist. Council Health & Welfare Trust Fund No. 2 v. Comet Contracting LLC, Civil No. RWT-03-2196, 2006 WL 2085847, at *8 (D. Md. July 25, 2006).

[124]*See* Sheet Metal Workers Local 67 v. Todd-Ford Mgmt. Co., No. SA-03-CA-290-XR, 2006 WL 1044240, at *2 (W.D. Tex. Mar. 9, 2006) ("familial control constitutes common ownership and control").

[125]*See* Electrical Workers (IBEW) Local 159 v. Circuit Elec., L.L.C., No. 05-CV-613-S, 2006 WL 623792, at *5, 179 LRRM 2421 (W.D. Wis. Mar. 10, 2006).

in an alter ego analysis, no factor is controlling and all need not be present.[126]

Some courts continue to follow the rule that it is not essential that there be an intention to evade responsibilities under the Act in order to find alter ego status.[127] Finally, certain courts continue to refuse to find alter ego status in situations where the union was not receiving less than that for which it bargained after the creation of the second company.[128]

---

[126] *See* Yolton v. El Paso Tenn. Pipeline Co., 435 F.3d 571, 587, 178 LRRM 2918 (6th Cir.), *cert. denied,* 127 S. Ct. 555, 180 LRRM 3040 (2006).

[127] *See* NLRB v. Crossroads Elec., Inc., 178 Fed. Appx. 528, 534, 179 LRRM 2835 (6th Cir. 2006) ("Although this circuit does not require the Board to show that an employer intended to circumvent its labor obligations in order to establish that one company is the alter ego of another, such a showing lends considerable support to an alter ego finding."); Burke v. Hamilton Equip. Installers, Inc., 2006 U.S. Dist. LEXIS 74850, at *16 (W.D.N.Y. Oct. 16, 2006) (not cited in Westlaw) ("Evidence of an anti-union animus is also relevant, although not essential."); *Sheet Metal Workers Local 67,* 2006 WL 1044240, at *2 ("The Fifth Circuit has not expressly stated that unlawful motive is a necessary requirement for finding alter ego status, and this Court concludes it is not."); *see also* Flynn v. Interior Finishes, Inc., 425 F. Supp. 2d 38, 53 (D.D.C. 2006).

[128] *See Flynn,* 425 F. Supp. 2d at 53 ("the alter ego doctrine—an equitable doctrine—should not be invoked in the absence of inequity"); Cement Masons Pension Trust Fund v. McCarthy, 2006 WL 770444, at *5 (E.D. Mich. Mar. 24, 2006).

EFFECT OF CHANGE IN BARGAINING REPRESENTATIVE DURING THE TERM OF A COLLECTIVE BARGAINING AGREEMENT

I. CONTEXT IN WHICH THE ISSUE ARISES

The Board has reiterated that the disaffiliation of a parent labor organization from the AFL-CIO, standing alone, does not create a schism.[1]

---

[1]New York Rehab. Care Mgmt., 346 NLRB No. 44 (2006).

III. MERGERS AND TRANSFERS OF AFFILIATION

A. Due Process

The Board's approach to due process issues continues, although its post-*Seattle-First* existence and exact scope remains open. The Board continues to hold that nonunion bargaining-unit employees have no right to notice of, or to vote in, an affiliation matter.[2]

B. Continuity of Representation

The fact that eight of 11 local unions merged to form a new larger local union does not demonstrate discontinuity of representation.[3] The Board found continuity when the locals retained a voice in collective bargaining and each local remained a unit of the larger local. Similarly, the merger of two or more locals of the same international union did not present any continuity issues where the international itself was the certified bargaining representative and had not given up its right to represent the bargaining-unit employees.[4]

---

[2] *See* Deposit Tel. Co., 349 NLRB No. 21 (2007).
[3] *Id.*
[4] Kindred Healthcare, Inc., 346 NLRB No. 28 (2006).

CHAPTER 15

EFFECT OF CHANGE IN THE EMPLOYING UNIT: SUCCESSORSHIP

III. SUCCESSORSHIP AND THE BARGAINING OBLIGATION

A. Continuity of the Work Force: "The Concept of Majority"

1. The Applicable Yardstick

The Board, with court approval, continues to apply its customary standards for defining bargaining units in determining whether the successor employer has a bargaining obligation.[1]

2. The Appropriate Time for Measuring Majority Status

An employer who expresses a clear intention to staff a facility with the predecessor's employees and bargains with the employees' designated representative will be considered to be a "perfectly clear" successor under Burns.[2]

4. Discriminatory Refusals to Hire Predecessor's Employees

In Planned Building Services,[3] the Board clarified that it will apply Wright Line when analyzing refusal-to-hire allegations in a successorship context, rather than the FES analytical framework utilized in other refusal-to-hire situations. The Board also reaffirmed its Love's Barbeque[4] rule that an employer that discriminatorily refuses to hire the employees of the predecessor may not unilaterally set the initial terms and conditions of employment. However, the Board modified its historical remedial order in such cases where the respondent

---

[1]Marine Spill Response Corp., 348 NLRB No. 92, 181 LRRM 1047 (2006); Shares, Inc. v. NLRB, 433 F.3d 939, 178 LRRM 2836 (7th Cir. 2006).

[2]Road & Rail Servs., Inc., 348 NLRB No. 77, 181 LRRM 1057 (2006).

[3]347 NLRB No. 64, 180 LRRM 1081 (2006).

[4]245 NLRB 78, 102 LRRM 1546 (1979), enforced in relevant part sub nom. Kallman v. NLRB, 640 F.2d 1094, 107 LRRM 2011 (9th Cir. 1981).

employer, in a compliance proceeding presents evidence to establish that it would not have agreed to the monetary provisions of the predecessor employer's collective bargaining agreement, and further to establish either the date on which it would have bargained to agreement and the terms of the agreement that would have been negotiated, or the date on which it would have bargained to good faith impasse and implemented its own monetary proposals. If the respondent employer carries its burden of proof on these points, its make-whole obligations are to be adjusted accordingly.[5]

B. Continuity of Identity in the Business Enterprise or Employing Industry

The Board continues to hold that a change in the scope of operations is not material.[6] The Board also continues to focus on whether changes to the business would affect employee attitudes about representation.[7]

D. The Effect of Hiatus

In line with the Supreme Court's decision in *Fall River Dyeing Corp. v. NLRB*,[8] the Board and the courts have continued to view hiatus in a successorship scenario as having a limited effect on the bargaining obligation of the new employer. Thus, a hiatus in operations is "relevant only when there are other indicia of discontinuity."[9]

---

[5] *Planned Bldg. Servs.*, slip op. at n.5.

[6] Marine Spill Response Corp., 348 NLRB No. 92, 181 LRRM 1047 (2006) (fact that successor is a larger organization with larger customer base than predecessor not determinative when there are no significant changes at the facilities where the affected employees work); M. Mogul Enter., Inc., 348 NLRB No. 73 (2006) (affirming ALJ's determination that successorship is not defeated by operation of only one of prior employer's two facilities).

[7] *Id.* (modification of working conditions, including introduction of new equipment that was similar to equipment employees had used before, use of computer terminals for record-keeping, requirement that employees be on call at all times, and infrequent temporary assignments away from permanent duty station, were "minor alterations" that would not alter employees' attitudes about representation).

[8] 482 U.S. 27, 125 LRRM 2441 (1987).

[9] *Id.* at 45.

E. Determining When the Bargaining Obligation Attaches

The basic principle that a successor employer's bargaining obligation attaches when it employs a substantial and representative complement of employees, a majority of whom were employed by the predecessor, remains unchanged.[10]

In general, a successor employer may unilaterally set the initial terms of employment, subject to two recognized exceptions: where it is "perfectly clear" that the successor plans to hire all of the employees in the predecessor's unit and where the successor forfeits that right by refusing to hire union employees or informing them that union representation will not be accepted.[11]

In *Road & Rail Services, Inc.*,[12] the Board expressly adopted the administrative law judge's (ALJ's) finding that the employer was a "perfectly clear" successor where, although the company did not hire "all" of the predecessor's employees, it hired 20 of 23, and repeatedly made clear that it intended to negotiate desired changes to terms and conditions of employment with the union. In fact, the new collective bargaining agreement was reached before the employer hired the predecessor's employees and commenced operations, which the Board found determinative.[13]

In *Planned Building Services, Inc.*,[14] the Board considered and clarified the analytical framework for determining the appropriate remedy in circumstances where an employer unlawfully refused to hire its predecessor's employees so as to avoid a bargaining obligation. In that case, the successor, a commercial cleaning company, chose not to employ most of its predecessor's workforce at three locations and instead staffed each building with employees transferred from its other worksites. The ALJ found that the refusal to hire the predecessor's employees was motivated by a desire to avoid an obligation to recognize and bargain with the union representing those employees. In fashioning the remedy, the ALJ applied the analysis set forth in *FES*[15] that generally applies in cases involving a discrimi-

---

[10] *See generally* Shares, Inc. v. NLRB, 433 F.3d 939, 178 LRRM 2836 (7th Cir. 2006).

[11] *See* NLRB v. Burns Int'l Sec. Servs., 406 U.S. 272, 80 LRRM 2225 (1975); Waterbury Hotel Mgmt., LLC v. NLRB, 314 F.3d 645, 171 LRRM 2781 (D.C. Cir. 2003).

[12] 348 NLRB No. 77, 181 LRRM 1057 (2006).

[13] *Id.*, slip op. at 2.

[14] 347 NLRB No. 64, 180 LRRM 1081 (2006).

[15] 331 NLRB 9, 164 LRRM 1063 (2000).

natory failure to hire or refusal to consider for hire, and requires evidence, in addition to unlawful motive, relating to the employer's hiring plans and applicant's experience and training.

The Board rejected application of the *FES* approach to refusals to hire in the successorship context, instead holding that the well-established *Wright Line*[16] analysis was more appropriate. In so doing, the Board noted that in the successorship situation, the predecessor's employees presumptively meet the successor's qualifications for hire because the business is generally the same as the predecessor's, and because a successor employer must fill vacant positions in starting up its business, it is of little use to demonstrate that the employer had plans to hire.[17]

The Board also addressed the make-whole remedy to be issued in successorship refusal-to-hire cases. Under the prior standard, the make-whole remedy, including back pay and benefits, was measured in reference to the predecessor's terms and conditions of employment, and extends from the date of the unlawful refusal to bargain until the successor reaches a new agreement or bargains to impasse with the union. The Board recognized that a significant degree of uncertainty exists as to both what the new terms would be, and when they would go into effect. In order to strike a better balance between placing the burden of uncertainty on the wrongdoer and avoiding a punitive penalty, and in consideration of conflicting circuit court pronouncements on the issue, the Board held that

> [A]lthough genuine uncertainty in successorship-avoidance cases will continue to be resolved against the successor as the wrongdoer, where the successor can provide the Board with an adequate factual basis for resolving the uncertainty created by its misconduct, it should be permitted to do so. Placing the burden of proof on the successor is both equitable (the successor is the wrongdoer) and practical (the successor has superior access to the relevant evidence).[18]

The Board further determined that the compliance proceeding is an appropriate forum for introduction of such evidence.[19]

---

[16]Wright Line, Wright Line Div., 251 NLRB 1083, 105 LRRM 1169 (1980), *enforced*, 602 F.2d 899, 108 LRRM 2513 (1st Cir. 1981), *cert. denied*, 455 U.S. 989, 109 LRRM 2779 (1982).

[17]*Planned Bldg. Servs.*, slip op. at n.17.

[18]*Id.*, slip op. at 9.

[19]*Id.*

IV. SUCCESSORSHIP AND THE CONTRACTUAL OBLIGATION

A. The "Alter Ego" Employer

2. The Defining Factors of the Alter Ego Employer

The Board continues to apply the following standards to determine whether two entities are "alter egos": the two enterprises have "substantially identical" management, business purpose, operation, equipment, customers, and supervision.[20]

a. The Factor of Common Ownership

The Board also continues to hold that "where members of the same family are the owners of two nominally distinct entities, which are otherwise substantially the same, ownership and control of both of the entities is considered substantially identical...."[21]

b. The Factor of Employer Motive to Evade Labor Obligations

Additionally, the Board and courts continue to hold that although an employer's motive to evade labor law obligations is an important factor to consider in determining alter ego status, it is not a required element.[22] Individual Board members continue to express the view that such a motive is required.[23]

4. Individual Liability: "Piercing the Veil" of the Alter Ego Employer Entity

Following *White Oak Coal Co.*,[24] the Board continues to pierce the corporate veil to hold individual shareholders individually liable for corporate remedial obligations in the exceptional situation where: "(1) there is such unity of interest, and lack of respect given to the separate identity of the corporation by its shareholders, that the personalities and assets of the corporation and the individu-

---

[20]Park Maint., 348 NLRB No. 98 (2006).

[21]*Id.*

[22]*Id.*, slip op. at 11; NLRB v. Crossroads Elec., Inc., 179 LRRM 2835, 2839–40 (6th Cir. 2006).

[23]*Park Maint.*, slip op. at 1 n.3 (2006) (Chairman Battista repeated his view that to prove alter ego status, "the General Counsel must show, among other things, an intent to avoid legal obligations under the Act * * *."); SRC Painting, LLC, 346 NLRB No. 67, slip op. at 1 n.6, 179 LRRM 1224 (2006).

[24]318 NLRB 732 (1995), *enforced*, 81 F.3d 150 (4th Cir. 1996).

als are indistinct, and (2) adherence to the corporate form would sanction a fraud, promote injustice, or lead to an evasion of legal obligations."[25]

The Board has reaffirmed that "the mere receipt of corporate payments for noncorporate purposes does not establish" that a given respondent participated in an abuse of the corporation and should be exposed to personal liability.[26]

In *Carpenters Local 2471 v. NLRB*,[27] the District of Columbia Circuit remanded that portion of the case involving the Board's failure to pierce the corporate veil of the employer as had been recommended by the ALJ. The court chastised the Board for failing to cite evidence sufficient to support its findings as well as failing to explain why it disregarded conflicting record evidence.

5. Application of Alter Ego Test in Section 301 Actions and in Arbitration

Alter ego issues continue to arise in the context of Section 301 actions to enforce collective bargaining obligations. For example, in *Yolton v. El Paso Tennessee Pipeline Co.*,[28] the court affirmed the use of alter ego factors in a labor contract dispute regarding retiree health benefits liability.

VI. LIABILITY OF SUCCESSOR FOR PREDECESSOR'S UNFAIR LABOR PRACTICES

Consistent with the Supreme Court's decision in *Golden State Bottling Co. v. NLRB*,[29] the courts and the Board continue to hold that where a successor continues business without interruption or

---

[25]Flat Dog Prods., Inc., 347 NLRB No. 104, slip op. at 4, 180 LRRM 1383 (2006) (finding no misuse of corporate assets, the Board reversed an ALJ's decision and held it was not appropriate to pierce the corporate veil).

[26]*SRC Painting*, 346 NLRB No. 67, slip op. at 2–3 (finding it was improper to impose personal liability on the wife and daughter-in-law of the corporate owner where, even though they received corporate assets, they did not play an active role in the corporation).

[27]No. 05-1416, 06-1098, 2007 WL 776859, 181 LRRM 2609 (D.C. Cir. Mar. 16, 2007), *enforcing in part and remanding in relevant part*, A.J. Mechanical, Inc., 345 NLRB No. 22, 178 LRRM 1093 (2005).

[28]435 F.3d 571, 586, 178 LRRM 2918 (6th Cir. 2006).

[29]414 U.S. 168, 84 LRRM 2839 (1973).

without substantial change in form, the successor is liable for the predecessor's unfair labor practices if circumstances charge the successor with notice of the practices at the time of acquisition.[30]

---

[30]JLL Rest., Inc. dba Smokehouse Rest., 347 NLRB No. 16, 180 LRRM 1537 (2006) (successor employer jointly and severally liable for predecessor's unfair labor practices where successor continued business without significant interruption or substantial change in operations and where successor previously was made aware that unfair labor practice charges had been filed against predecessor); Dearborn Gage Co., 346 NLRB No. 71, 179 LRRM 1250 (2006) (*Golden State* successor held jointly and severally liable for unfair labor practices of predecessor where successor president was aware of such practices); *but see* Lebanite Corp., 346 NLRB No. 72, 179 LRRM 1166 (2006) (no joint and several liability where successor was unable to protect itself from potential unfair labor practices liability by reflecting potential liability in the transaction price or addressing such liability in an indemnity clause).

CHAPTER 16

SUBJECTS OF BARGAINING

III. DEVELOPMENT OF THE DISTINCTION BETWEEN "MANDATORY" AND "PERMISSIVE"

B. *Pittsburgh Plate Glass*—The "Vitally Affects" Test

As noted in the Main Edition, benefits for current retirees are not mandatory subjects of bargaining. Nonetheless, the union may challenge unilateral changes through a Section 301 action (as noted in footnote 41 of the Main Edition), or represent consenting retirees in arbitration where a grievance procedure is applicable.[1]

D. *First National Maintenance Corp.*—The Balancing Test

In *Washington Metropolitan Area Transit Authority v. Office & Professional Employees Local 2*,[2] the court enforced an arbitration award in which the arbitrator found that the unilateral closure of an employee cafeteria amounted to the termination of a longstanding and significant benefit. The arbitrator determined that if the parties were unable to resolve their dispute through collective bargaining, which the arbitrator also ordered, the closure would be subject to future interest arbitration.[3] The court rejected the employer's argument that the dispute involved a permissive subject of bargaining and found *First National Maintenance Corp. v NLRB*[4] inapplicable to the dispute. The court instead applied *Ford Motor Co. v. NLRB*,[5]

---

[1] *See* Cleveland Elec. Illuminating Co. v. Utility Workers Local 270, 440 F.3d 809, 815, 179 LRRM 2211 (6th Cir. 2006).

[2] 465 F.3d 151, 180 LRRM 2785 (4th Cir. 2006).

[3] *Id.* at 155–56, 180 LRRM at 2789.

[4] 452 U.S. 666, 107 LRRM 2705 (1981).

[5] 441 U.S. 488, 101 LRRM 2222 (1979).

noting that decisions interpreting *First National* "appear to be confined to major operational changes...."[6]

IV. MANDATORY SUBJECTS OF BARGAINING

A. Wages

2. *Specific Forms of Compensation*

a. Bonuses

Most Board cases assessing whether a bonus is a gift (and therefore a nonmandatory subject of bargaining) do so in the context of the situation where an employer ceases granting a bonus it gave in the past without first bargaining with the union. In 2006, the relatively rare situation came up where a union challenged an employer that *initiated* a grant of a benefit to employees without first bargaining with the union. A divided Board panel held in *North American Pipe Corp.*[7] that the employer did not violate Section 8(a)(5) when it made a unilateral grant of a companywide stock award worth over $1,400 to its bargaining-unit employees. The panel majority focused on the fact that this was a one-time grant made to all employees at each of the employer's facilities in connection with an initial public stock offering of its parent corporation, and each employee received the same amount of stock regardless of position with the company. Because the stock grant was "without regard to any employment-related factors, including work performance, wages, hours worked, seniority, or productivity," the panel majority concluded that the award was free of any tie to employee remuneration, and therefore was a gift, and not subject to bargaining.[8]

---

[6] *Washington Metro.*, 465 F.3d at 156, 180 LRRM at 2789 (citing Arrow Auto. Indus., Inc. v. NLRB, 853 F.2d 223, 225–32, 128 LRRM 3137, 3139–45 (1988) and Dorsey Trailers, Inc. v. NLRB, 233 F.3d 831, 841–44, 165 LRRM 3003, 3009–10 (4th Cir. 2000)).

[7] 347 NLRB No. 78, 180 LRRM 1125 (2006).

[8] *Id.*, slip op. at 3.

h.   Other Miscellaneous Benefits

In *Vanguard Fire & Supply Co., Inc.*,[9] the Board ruled that the employer violated Section 8(a)(5) by enforcing its written policy to bill employees for cell phone charges in excess of their allotted monthly minutes. The policy had been in place for one year before the employer began stringently enforcing the policy. The Board held that the employer's change from lax enforcement of the cell phone policy to stringent enforcement was a mandatory subject of bargaining.

C.   Other Terms and Conditions of Employment

2.   *Specific Terms and Requirements*

e.   Plant Rules and Discipline

The Board continues to hold that, generally, plant rules are considered subjects of mandatory bargaining, which means that an employer cannot unilaterally implement or change such rules.[10] The Board also continues to carve out exceptions to this general proposi-

---

[9]345 NLRB No. 77, 178 LRRM 1446 (2005), *enforced*, 468 F.3d 952, 180 LRRM 3137 (6th Cir. 2006).

[10]*See* Goya Foods of Fla., 347 NLRB No. 103, 180 LRRM 1553 (2006) (Board adopted the ALJ's decision and recommended order finding that respondent violated §8(a)(5) by the unilateral discontinuance of the personal cellular phone privilege); WGE Fed. Credit Union, 346 NLRB No. 87, 179 LRRM 1314 (2006) (unilaterally implementing a rule prohibiting employees from participating, in their capacity as employees, in the election of individuals to the respondent's board of directors); Mail Contractors of Am., 347 NLRB No. 88, 180 LRRM 1467 (2006) (unilaterally setting the routes and relay points for drivers are working conditions that may not be changed without first giving the collective bargaining representative of those drivers notice of the change and an opportunity to bargain); United Cerebral Palsy of N.Y. City, 347 NLRB No. 60, 180 LRRM 1140 (2006) (unilateral changes to the following terms and conditions of employment: (i) vacation scheduling policy; (ii) floating holidays policy; (iii) schedules; (iv) vacancy posting policy; (v) transfer policy; (vi) discipline or discharge for cause; (vii) grievance and arbitration procedures; (viii) employees' access to their personnel files; (ix) separation from employment; and (x) documentation of absences); Success Vill. Apartments, Inc., 348 NLRB No. 28, 180 LRRM 2758 (2006) (unilaterally changing existing terms and conditions of employment for bargaining-unit employees by implementing a "Conflict of Interest" policy concerning off-duty employee participation in residential co-op resales and including the sanction of termination for violation, by prohibiting employees from making personal local calls during work time, and by removing the telephone from an employee work area); Asher Candy, Inc., 348 NLRB No. 60, 181 LRRM 1214 (2006) (failure to pay severance and vacation pay is a unilateral change in violation of §8(a)(5)).

tion in cases where a change in a plant rule had little or no impact on the employees as a group or on their working conditions.[11]

The Board continues to narrow and limit the "the core purposes of the enterprise" exception[12] to the general rule that an employer may not unilaterally change plant rules that are mandatory subjects of bargaining by strictly construing the notion of what constitutes a "core purpose of the enterprise."[13]

Finally, although the Board continues to hold that the unilateral institution of new rules can be rendered lawful by a sufficiently broad contractual management-rights clause giving the employer the right to promulgate and to enforce rules of conduct, the management-rights clause must clearly and unequivocally waive the right to bargain.[14]

f.   Drug and Alcohol Testing

The Board continues to hold that testing of current employees is a mandatory subject of bargaining.[15]

---

[11] See Success Vill, 348 NLRB No. 28, 180 LRRM 2758 (unilateral change to parking policy did not constitute a substantial change in conditions of employment where the only change resulting from the new policy was that employees had to walk approximately 200 additional yards from their vehicles to the main building).

[12] See Capital Times Co., 223 NLRB 651, 91 LRRM 1481 (1976); Peerless Publ'ns (Pottstown Mercury), 231 NLRB 244, 95 LRRM 1611 (1977), remanded, 636 F.2d 550, 105 LRRM 2001 (D.C. Cir. 1980), modified by 283 NLRB 334, 124 LRRM 1331 (1987).

[13] See WGE Fed. Credit Union, 346 NLRB No. 87, 179 LRRM 1314 (2006). The Board affirmed the decision of the ALJ that respondent could not establish a viable "core purpose" defense. Respondent had unilaterally implemented a new rule prohibiting employees from campaigning, in their capacity as employees, for the board of directors. The ALJ found that the rule at issue did not protect a "core purpose" but rather purported to prohibit electioneering activity in order to "keep [the employer's] reputation" as a "respected financial institution."

[14] See Success Vill., 348 NLRB No. 28, 180 LRRM 2758 (the Board adopted the ALJ's decision holding that a general management-rights clause did not constitute a clear, unequivocal, and unmistakable waiver by the union of its statutory right to bargain about the employer's implementation of a work rule not specifically mentioned in the clause. The employer had not presented bargaining history evidence indicating that the particular matter at issue was fully discussed and consciously explored during negotiations, or that the union consciously yielded or clearly and unmistakably waived its interest in the matter).

[15] See Allied Aviation Fueling of Dallas, LP, 347 NLRB No. 22, 180 LRRM 1255 (2006) (respondent's admitted unilateral change in the company drug-testing policy violated §8(a)(5)).

g. Grievance Procedures and Arbitration

The Board continues to hold that arbitration and grievance procedures are mandatory subjects for collective bargaining.[16]

j. Work Assignments

The duty to bargain over changes in operations continues to challenge employers. In *EAD Motors*,[17] the elimination of a part-time position in the toolroom and the transfer of the incumbent part-time employee to a full-time position in the stockroom without notice or bargaining was not unlawful. The Board concluded the change was not a "material, substantial or significant change" in the employee's terms and conditions of employment as the incumbent employee had been working part-time in the stockroom prior to the change. Conversely, in *Goya Foods*,[18] the continued unilateral reassignment of drivers' routes following the union's certification was unlawful. The Board rejected the argument that a historical right predating the union's certification survived that certification and became a past practice without negotiations.

Finally, in *Southern Mail*,[19] the Board held that a subcontractor lawfully dropped two stops from a driver's route when the customer demanded these stops be dropped. However, the subcontractor violated the Act by extending the driver's route by 100 miles because this decision was discretionary.

m. Major Business Changes

(1) Subcontracting and Removal of Work From the Bargaining Unit

The Board continues to apply the Supreme Court's long standing *Fibreboard*[20] decision and analysis to issues involving employers' subcontracting of bargaining-unit work, absent evidence of a clear change in the scope, nature, and direction of the employer's overall business enterprise. In *Dallas & Mavis Specialized Carrier Co.*,[21] the Board held that the employer violated Section 8(a)(5) terminat-

---

[16]*See* United Cerebral Palsy of N.Y. City, 347 NLRB No. 60, 180 LRRM 1140 (2006) (unilateral changes to grievance and arbitration procedures violated §8(a)(5)).

[17]346 NLRB No. 93, 180 LRRM 1192 (2006).

[18]347 NLRB No. 103, 180 LRRM 1553 (2006).

[19]345 NLRB No. 43 n.8, 178 LRRM 1480 (2005).

[20]Fibreboard Paper Prods. Corp. v. NLRB, 379 U.S. 203, 57 LRRM 2609 (1964).

[21]346 NLRB No. 27, 178 LRRM 1489 (2006).

ing all bargaining-unit drivers and transferring the specific route runs to independently contracted nonunion owner-operators who owned their own trucks, without providing notice to the union or an opportunity to bargain over the subcontracting decision. It found no change in the scope or nature of the employer's business, noting instead that the transfer of runs to the owner-operators involved "nothing more than the substitution of one group of workers for another to perform the same work."

The Board continues to limit the situations in which it will permit subcontracting without bargaining during a hiatus between contracts to situations where such subcontracting is in line with established past practice. For example, in *Clear Channel Outdoor Inc.*,[22] the Board found that the employer violated Section 8(a)(5) by unilaterally subcontracting and assigning unit work to nonunit employees following expiration of the existing contract, since the employer did not have an established past practice of taking this action, the management-rights clause in the parties' collective bargaining contract had expired with the contract, and the union had not waived its right to bargain over this issue.

(c) Otis Elevator (II).[23] In another case, *Yeshiva Ohr Torah Community School, Inc. dba Manhattan Day School*,[24] the Board found that the employer violated Section 8(a)(1) by informing unit employees that it intended to subcontract work because of their support for the union. The employer later claimed its motivation for the subcontracting, which was allowed under the collective bargaining agreement if justified by economic circumstances, was the financial difficulty it was experiencing and the anticipated cost savings of subcontracting maintenance work. The employer also subcontracted kitchen work because it was unable to find adequate replacements after two employees quit. However, the Board held the employer did not violate 8(a)(3) or (5) by subcontracting unit work and terminating unit employees, because the employer gave the union advance notice and would have subcontracted the work for legitimate business reasons even in the absence of union activity. The evidence showed an anticipated cost savings of $22,000 by subcontracting maintenance work, and the employer subcontracted kitchen work because it was unable to find adequate replacements.

---

[22]346 NLRB No. 66, 179 LRRM 1189 (2006).
[23]270 NLRB 232, 116 LRRM 1075, *correcting* 269 NLRB 891, 115 LRRM 1281 (1984).
[24]346 NLRB No. 89, 179 LRRM 1241 (2006).

(*f*) *Transfer of Unit Work.* In a follow up case, *St George Warehouse, Inc.*,[25] the employer argued that the Board's order to restore the bargaining unit should not be enforced, due to an alleged loss of majority support among the remaining unit employees. The Board rejected this argument, finding that the alleged loss of majority support was tainted by the employer's unlawful unilateral transfer of unit work to nonunit (temporary) employees.

However, in *North Star Steel Co.*,[26] the Board did not require the company to bargain over the transfer of unit work. The company transferred production of 175 tons of steel, less than 1 percent of a single month's production, from one facility to another without notice to the union or an opportunity to bargain over the transfer. The company argued there was no duty to bargain because the transfer was an isolated incident that caused a minimal loss of business to the losing plant. The administrative law judge (ALJ) concluded, however, that the company violated Sections 8(a)(5) and (1) by failing to bargain over the transfer. The Board reversed the ALJ, finding no duty to bargain because the transfer was not material or substantial and did not significantly affect the terms and conditions of employment, noting that the general counsel offered no evidence that the transfer adversely affected any employee.

V. PERMISSIVE SUBJECTS OF BARGAINING

A. In General

The Supreme Court has held that when a permissive subject is included in a collective bargaining agreement, that subject is not transformed into a mandatory one even for the term of that agreement.[27] However, until the collective bargaining agreement expires, the courts will enforce the parties' promise, even if it is a promise to perform a permissive subject.[28]

---

[25] 348 NLRB No. 67, 180 LRRM 1465 (2006).

[26] 347 NLRB No. 119 (2006).

[27] Allied Chem. & Alkali Workers Local 1 v. Pittsburgh Plate Glass Co., 404 U.S. 157, 78 LRRM 2974 (1971). As a consequence, the Court held that unilateral midterm modification of a permissive subject that had been included in the agreement did not constitute an unfair labor practice under the Act. *Accord* Midwest Television, Inc. dba KFMB Stations, 343 NLRB No. 83, 176 LRRM 1483 (2004). *See also* Section III.B., *supra.*

[28] Kalmar Indus. USA v. Teamsters Local 838, 452 F. Supp. 2d 1154, 181 LRRM 2535 (D.C. Kan. 2006).

In determining the appropriate remedy in a case where the union unlawfully refused to ratify a collective bargaining agreement because there was no meeting of the minds regarding a belatedly raised permissive subject of bargaining, the Board held that the contract was to be given effect as of the date the ratification vote would have taken place but for the union's unfair labor practice.[29]

B. Specific Subjects

3. Selection of Bargaining Representative

In *Alan Richey, Inc.*,[30] the Board held that although an employer generally may not inject itself into the selection of the bargaining unit's representative for contract negotiations, an employer's polling of bargaining-unit members in order to determine which one of them would be their representative for contract negotiations did not violate Sections 8(a)(1), (2), or (5) because "unique circumstances" were present. The union in that case was a "loose-knit, informal group with no officers, no constitution or bylaws, no dues structure, and no regular meetings." The employer had a bona fide doubt about with whom it was to negotiate, as well as a need to get the agreement negotiated quickly because of a strict deadline imposed by the employer's customer for the completing of negotiations.

7. Interest Arbitration and Bi-Level Bargaining

Courts continue to hold that where a contract at least arguably binds parties to interest arbitration, a union may lawfully submit unresolved issues to arbitration and seek court enforcement of the award.[31]

---

[29]Teamsters Local 287 (Granite Rock Co.), 347 NLRB No. 32, 180 LRRM 1007 (2006).

[30]346 NLRB No. 26, 178 LRRM 1421 (2006).

[31]Robert S. Bortner, Inc. v. Sheet Metal Workers Local 19, 2006 WL 1000025 (M.D. Pa. Apr. 13, 2006) ("[A]n interest arbitration clause cannot be invoked solely because of an impasse over a nonmandatory subject of bargaining;" however, where the disputed issues go beyond nonmandatory subjects, a party may invoke interest arbitration even if [the] negotiations [leave] some nonmandatory issues unresolved") (internal quotation marks omitted); *see also* M.R.S. Enter., Inc. v. Sheet Metal Workers Local 40, 429 F. Supp. 2d 72, 79 (D.D.C. 2006) ("These Articles have been interpreted to represent the parties' agreement to negotiate a renewal agreement, and, if no agreement is forthcoming, to submit their dispute to the NJAB for interest arbitration.") (internal quotation marks omitted); *Kalmar Indus.*, 452 F. Supp. 2d 1154, 1164 ("Moreover, contrary to the Company's claim

Although such provisions are judicially enforceable, it is well established that a party may not use an existing interest-arbitration clause to perpetuate that clause; otherwise, "a party having once agreed to the provision, may find itself locked into that procedure for as long as the bargaining relationship endures."[32]

Courts continue to hold that an employer did not violate Section 8(a)(5), by refusing to implement the contract unless the union complied with its agreement to seek ratification. In such circumstances, bargaining has concluded and the employer may lawfully seek compliance with the ratification agreement.[33]

13. Tape Recordings, Stenographers, and Other Technical Preconditions on the Bargaining Process

The Board and the courts continue to hold that a party may not insist upon the other party's providing a written agenda as a precondition to bargaining.[34]

Finding that face-to-face meetings are the "bargaining norm," the Board held that mediation is a permissive subject, and the particular mediation format is also a permissive subject. The parties had agreed on mediation, but the employer refused to meet directly with the union once mediation began, preferring instead to send the mediator between rooms. The Board found that the union had the right to decline this method, and the employer's insistence to impasse was a refusal to bargain.[35]

---

that permissive subjects are not arbitrable, federal courts have routinely enforced permissive subject awards where a union and company bargain for the permissive benefits and include the benefits in their contract.").

[32] M.R.S. Enter., 429 F. Supp. 2d 72, 79 n.4 ("The Agreement only requires the parties to negotiate for one successor term. If the ... negotiations reach a deadlock, no agreement imposed by an arbitrator can contain an interest arbitration clause.") (internal quotation marks omitted).

[33] Granite Rock, 347 NLRB No. 32, 180 LRRM 1007 ("The parties, however, may agree that employee ratification is a condition precedent to a final and binding contract... [w]here there is such an express bilateral agreement, the Board finds that a contract cannot become effective until ratification occurs.")

[34] Vanguard Fire & Supply Co., Inc. v. NLRB, 468 F.3d 952, 962, 180 LRRM 3137 (6th Cir. 2006) (court enforced Board order where there was substantial evidence that employer insisted upon a nonmandatory agenda as a precondition to bargaining on mandatory subjects, thereby violating the union's collective bargaining rights).

[35] Success Vill. Apartments, Inc., 347 NLRB No. 100, 180 LRRM 2758 (2006).

14. Miscellaneous

The Board found that if a reopener clause of a collective bargaining agreement is narrow, a bona fide impasse cannot be reached if one of the parties insists on terms outside the scope of the reopener. Thus, subjects outside the opener become permissive subjects, even if they would be mandatory subjects in another context.[36]

The Board found that the inclusion of a permissive subject of bargaining in a final offer does not necessarily invalidate an impasse. It depends on whether the union has objected to the permissive subject or the employer's insistence on that subject has contributed to the impasse.[37]

The Board declined to rule whether a training program for individuals who might become employees was a permissive or mandatory subject of bargaining. It did, however, find that an information request concerning the program was presumptively relevant to the union's representational duties.[38]

The Sixth Circuit confirmed the Supreme Court's holding in *Allied Chemical & Alkali Workers Local 1 v. Pittsburgh Plate Glass Co.,*[39] that retired workers' benefits were a permissive subject of bargaining. The court went on to state, however, that where the employer and union have bargained over such benefits and included provisions in the collective bargaining agreement, the union has standing to represent the retirees in connection with any dispute over those benefits.[40]

The Board enforced an ALJ's decision that changes to retiree benefits effective after the collective bargaining agreement's expiration were mandatory subjects of bargaining. The judge rejected the argument that under *NLRB v. Columbus Printing Pressmen Local 252,*[41] the change had no impact on the unit employees. The clause in *Columbus Printing* involved a contract arbitration provision.[42]

---

[36]New Seasons, Inc., 346 NLRB No. 57, 179 LRRM 1214 (2006).
[37]ACF Indus. LLC, 347 NLRB No. 99, 180 LRRM 1303 (2006).
[38]Southern Cal. Gas Co., 346 NLRB No. 45, 179 LRRM 1135 (2006).
[39]404 U.S. 157, 78 LRRM 2974 (1971).
[40]Cleveland Elec. Illuminating Co. v. Utility Workers Local 270, 440 F.3d 809, 179 LRRM 2211 (6th Cir. 2006).
[41]543 F.2d 1161 (5th Cir. 1976), *affirming* 219 NLRB 268 (1975).
[42]Southern Nuclear Operating Co., 348 NLRB No. 95 (2006).

VI. ILLEGAL SUBJECTS OF BARGAINING

A. Relationship to Duty to Bargain

In *BellSouth Telecommunications, Inc.*,[43] the Board held on remand from the Fourth Circuit that an employer violated Sections 8(a)(1), (2), and (3) and a union violated Sections 8(b)(1)(A) and (2) by agreeing to a contract provision requiring employees to wear a uniform bearing the union's logo. Initially, the Board held that the requirement did not violate the Act because although compelling employees to wear the union logo implicated Section 7 rights, it did so to a lesser extent than a unilateral employer rule prohibiting the display of union insignia.[44] On appeal, the Fourth Circuit reversed, reasoning that the provision interfered with an employee's right to refrain from concerted activity.[45] The court rejected the argument that the requirement did not violate the Act because it was mutually agreed to as part of the collective bargaining process. Recognizing that a union may waive certain statutorily protected rights of the employees it represents, the court nevertheless concluded that the exclusive representative "may not surrender rights that impair the employees' choice of their bargaining representative." On remand, the Board ordered that the contract provision containing the logo requirement be rescinded.

---

[43]346 NLRB No. 59, 179 LRRM 1134 (2006).
[44]BellSouth Telecomms., Inc., 335 NLRB 1066, 168 LRRM 1049 (2001).
[45]Lee v. NLRB, 393 F.3d 491 (4th Cir. 2005).

PART V

ARBITRATION AND THE ACT

Chapter 17

RELATION OF BOARD ACTION TO ENFORCEMENT OF AGREEMENTS UNDER SECTION 301

I. INTRODUCTION

Scholars continue to write on the subject of the role of the National Labor Relations Board (NLRB, or the Board) to the enforcement of the contracts.[1]

II. SECTION 10(a) POWER OF THE BOARD

In light of *Litton Financial Printing Division v. NLRB*, the First Circuit analyzed the standard of review in a contract modification claim holding that the Board does not have broad powers to interpret collective bargaining agreements. The court adopted a "sound arguable" standard for Section 8(d) contract modification claim cases.[2]

III. SCOPE AND PURPOSE OF SECTION 301

C. The *Steelworkers Trilogy*

The courts continue to recognize the strong presumption in favor of arbitration of labor disputes established by the Supreme Court in the *Steelworkers Trilogy* and its progeny.[3] This presumption is tempered by the court's acknowledgement that an award granted by an arbitrator acting outside the scope of his authority does not mandate such deference.[4] The public policy exception to the presumption in favor of arbitration, as reiterated by the Supreme Court in *Paperworkers v. Misco Inc.*,[5] continues to receive varying interpretations by the circuit courts.[6]

---

[1]For bibliographic materials, see: Gould, *Kissing Cousins?: The Federal Arbitration Act and Modern Labor Arbitration*, 55 EMORY L.J. 609 (2006).

[2]*See* Bath Marine Draftsmen's Ass'n v. NLRB, 475 F.3d 14, 181 LRRM 2267 (1st Cir. 2007).

[3]*See e.g.*, Star Tribune Co. v. Minnesota Newspaper Guild, 450 F.3d 345, 348, 179 LRRM 2945 (8th Cir. 2006) (court review of arbitration reward is narrow and decision will not be disturbed even if court is convinced a serious error was committed).

[4]The Seventh Circuit held that the district court properly found the employer lawfully terminated the CBA before negotiations began for a new agreement, and accordingly, was not bound by the new agreement. Stevens Constr. Corp. v. Chicago Reg'l Council of Carpenters, 464 F.3d 682, 180 LRRM 2589 (7th Cir. 2006).

[5]484 U.S. 29, 126 LRRM 3113 (1987).

[6]*See* Main Edition at footnote 93; *see also* Midamerican Energy Co. v. Electrical Workers (IBEW) Local 499, 345 F.3d 616, 619–23, 173 LRRM 2353 (8th Cir. 2003).

F.   Overlapping Jurisdiction: Conflict or Accommodation?

1.   Federal and State Courts

b.   Statutes of Limitations

In *Lee v. Cytec Industries, Inc.*,[7] the Fifth Circuit considered the application of equitable tolling of the 6-month statute of limitations in a hybrid Section 301 claim where employees were suing their union for breach of its duty of fair representation. The employees' claim against the union did not arise within the usual context of the union's mishandling a grievance, but rather, a challenge to the union's adoption of a bumping procedure which was immiscible to their seniority rights. Failing to file a grievance with the union within 6 months of the union's posting of the bumping procedures, the employees contended that the statute of limitations should have been equitably tolled until they knew, or reasonably should have known, that the union would no longer process their grievance. The Fifth Circuit found that in this "non-grievance" context, the statute of limitations commences when the employees knew or should have known of the union's breach, rather than when they knew, or should have known, that the union would no longer process their grievance. Otherwise, the court reasoned, the employees could wait until the statute of limitations had passed and then file a grievance against the union to circumvent the applicable 6-month statute of limitations.

2.   The Board and the Courts

In challenges to federal district courts' concurrent Section 301 jurisdiction based on the Board's exclusive jurisdiction over representation issues, the courts continue to closely examine whether the Section 301 claims are primarily a matter of contract interpretation or are primarily representational in nature. In *Electrical Workers (IBEW) Local 71 v. Trafftech, Inc.*,[8] the union sought to arbitrate the employer's assignment of covered work to a different union with whom the employer also had a collective bargaining agreement. Refusing to arbitrate, the employer filed a representation petition with the Board prior to the union bringing its Section 301 action to compel arbitration. Pending resolution by the Board, the union filed a Section 301 claim, and subsequently, the Board "administratively

---

[7]460 F.3d 673, 180 LRRM 2185 (5th Cir. 2006).
[8]461 F.3d 690, 180 LRRM 2370 (6th Cir. 2006).

deferred" the matter in light of the court's concurrent jurisdiction. Finding that the employer's filing of a representational matter with the Board to be of no consequence to its decision and the union's action to compel arbitration to be primarily a matter of contract interpretation rather than representational in nature, the Sixth Circuit upheld the lower court's ruling to compel arbitration.

IV. INJUNCTIONS IN AID OF ARBITRATION: SECTION 301 VERSUS NORRIS-LAGUARDIA

B. The *Boys Markets* Injunction: Halting Strikes Over Arbitrable Grievances

2. *Sympathy Strikes Not Enjoinable:* Buffalo Forge

In addition to routinely denying injunctions enjoining strikes in support of strikes or pickets of other unions, courts have also denied injunctions barring unions from engaging in strikes in support of the union's pension funds.[9]

Courts have also denied injunctions barring a union's secondary area-standards picket in support of employees of an employer's subcontractor, which later developed into a refusal of overtime with the primary employer.[10] In *Central Illinois Public Service Co. v. Electrical Workers (IBEW) Local 702*, the contract contained a promise by the union "to provide the Company with proper and adequate services to enable the Company to continue operation of its property without interruption or other injurious effect."[11] While this case did not relate to a traditional sympathy strike, but rather a refusal of overtime due to a secondary area-standards picket in support of employees of the employer's subcontractor, the court did not interpret the contractual union promise as a vehicle allowing a court injunction. Instead, the court determined that there was no "strike" because the underlying dispute was expressly excluded from the contract and, therefore, not arbitrable.

---

[9]Chicago Dist. Council of Carpenters Pension Fund v. K & I Constr., Inc., 270 F.3d 1060 (7th Cir. 2001).

[10]Central Ill. Pub. Serv. Co. v. Electrical Workers (IBEW) Local 702, No. 05-cv-4140, 2005 WL 2094747 (S.D. Ill. Aug. 24, 2005).

[11]*Id.; cf.* Kroger v. Teamsters Local 89, No. 3:06-CV165-5, 2006 WL 1382290 (W.D. Ky. May 15, 2006) (enjoining picket union characterized as an "area standards" picket).

4. Injunctions Against Employers to Preserve the Status Quo

Circuit courts continue to deny injunctions against employers to preserve the status quo where the court determines that an arbitrator could grant appropriate relief and effectively restore the status quo ante, therefore, demonstrating that the harm to the union is not irreparable. For example, courts have denied injunctions based on lack of irreparable harm for the termination of employment;[12] management decisions to sell the company;[13] layoffs;[14] and layoffs due to successor company restructuring.[15]

5. Injunctions Against Employers in Aid of Employee Choice During Safety Investigations [New Topic]

Pursuant to the Mine Safety and Health Act, the Secretary of the U.S. Department of Labor is authorized to perform safety investigations in mines where explosions or accidents have occurred.[16] By law, representatives of both the mining company and the miners are authorized to participate in any investigation conducted by the Secretary.[17] In the wake of the January 2006 explosion at Wolf Run Sago Mine in West Virginia, which killed 12 miners, several miners made anonymous requests to the Mine Safety Administration that,

---

[12]State, County & Mun. Employees Dist. Council 1707 v. New York Ass'n for New Ams., Inc., No. 03 Civ. 9536 RCC, 2003 WL 22871926, 174 LRRM 2537 (S.D.N.Y. Dec. 4, 2003) (denying union's TRO to enjoin employer from terminating five employees pending arbitration because no irreparable harm would be suffered to the union's collective bargaining sessions even if one of the terminated employees was a senior union representative on its bargaining team).

[13]North Carolina Mail Haulers (Postal Workers Local 8001) v. East Coast Leasing, Inc., No. 1:06CV00840, 2006 WL 3068497, 181 LRRM 2523 (M.D.N.C. Oct. 27, 2006) (holding that the union's grievance over the employer's contractual and inherent managerial right to decide to go out of business was not arbitrable and would be futile under the grievance provision and, therefore, could not be enjoined).

[14]Auto Workers Local 1069 v. Boeing Rotorcraft, No. 04-3603, 2004 WL 1969680 (E.D. Pa. Sept. 1, 2004) (refusing to enjoin employer from laying off employees during arbitration process where it would not frustrate the arbitral process and where the employer was not attempting to evade the arbitral process).

[15]Steelworkers Local 13702 v. Mikocem Corp., No. 05-73184, 2005 WL 2090884 (E.D. Mich. Aug. 30, 2005) (after granting TRO, denying union's request for preliminary injunction to enjoin a successor employer from laying off bargaining-unit members in a companywide restructuring where there was a concurrent arbitration in process and successful arbitration award for the union could reinstate the members and provide back pay).

[16]30 U.S.C. §813.

[17]Id.

although the workers at Wolf Run were not unionized, their interests be represented by the United Mine Workers of America during the investigation.[18] The Fourth Circuit upheld a preliminary injunction brought by the Mine Safety Administration against the mining company and enjoined it from refusing to allow union representatives on its property for the purpose of representing these anonymous, nonunion miners during the safety investigation.[19] The court also held that it would not be a violation of Section 8(a)(2) of the NLRA for the employer to deal with UMWA representatives pursuant to the Mine Safety Act investigation even though the union did not represent a majority of employees. Furthermore, the court determined that the employer was not entitled to know the identity of the anonymous mine workers requesting union representation.

C. Injunction Suits in State Courts

Federal courts continue to honor state court orders issued prior to removal to federal courts as binding until they are set aside. However, once the case is removed to a federal court, a party may modify or seek to dissolve a TRO issued in a state court pursuant to Rule 65(b) of the Federal Rules of Civil Procedure.[20]

---

[18]U.S. Dep't of Labor v. Wolf Run Mining Co., Inc., 452 F.3d 275 (4th Cir. 2006).

[19]*Id.; see also* Thunder Basin Coal Co. v. Federal Mine Safety and Health Review Comm'n, 56 F.3d 1275 (10th Cir. 1994) *and* Kerr-McGee Coal Corp. v. Federal Mine Safety and Health Review Comm'n, 40 F.3d 1257 (D.C. Cir. 1994).

[20]Napleton Auto Werks, Inc. v. Auto Mechanics Local 701, No. 2:06-cv-160, 2006 WL 1128653 (N.D. Ill. Apr. 26, 2006).

CHAPTER 18

ACCOMMODATION OF BOARD ACTION TO THE ARBITRATION PROCESS

175

II. PREARBITRAL DEFERRAL: APPLYING THE *COLLYER* DOCTRINE

A. The Parties' Relationship

The Board continues to refuse to defer under *Collyer* when an employer's conduct amounts to a rejection of the collective bargaining process.[1]

B. The Parties' Willingness to Arbitrate and Arbitrability

The Board has refused to defer representation issues under *Collyer* where the underlying dispute turns on statutory policy.[2]

C. Whether the Dispute Centers on the Collective Bargaining Agreement

4. Demands for Information

The Board continues to exclude from *Collyer* deferral alleged refusals to furnish information. The Board will refuse to defer where

---

[1]United Cerebral Palsy of New York City, 347 NLRB No. 60, 180 LRRM 1140 (2006).

[2]Advanced Architectural Metals, Inc., 347 NLRB No. 111, 180 LRRM 1490 (2006) ("Where... resolution of the issue does not implicate statutory policy, the Board's procedures need not and should not supplant the parties' contractual dispute resolution procedure.").

the agreement contains no provision with respect to information disputes.[3]

III. POST-ARBITRAL DEFERRAL: APPLYING THE *SPIELBERG* STANDARDS

B. Fair and Regular Proceedings

1. *The Arbitral Procedure*

The Board continues to hold that fair and regular proceedings are a prerequisite to deferral.[4]

D. The Award Is Not Repugnant to the Policies of the Act

In *Kvaerner Philadelphia Shipyard, Inc*,[5] the Board upheld an administrative law judge's (ALJ's) deferral to arbitration in a wrongful discharge action, even though the ALJ indicated that he would have found the discharge to violate the Act. There, an employee distributed letters to co-workers, stating that the employer was taking additional deductions out of employee paychecks, and was earning interest on that money. The employee signed the letters with his name and the title, "The Silent Steward." Later that day, the employee was terminated.

The matter went to arbitration, where the arbitrator found that the employer had not violated the Act, and that the termination was lawful. Specifically, the arbitrator concluded that the employee's conduct was unprotected because he had demonstrated a reckless disregard for the truth, and had made statements that were tantamount to defamation.

In considering the arbitrator's decision, the ALJ and the Board both acknowledged that the holding was not wholly without basis in the Act, and that there was precedent in which an employee's misconduct had the effect of removing otherwise protected activity from the Act. As such, they both concluded that the arbitrator's deci-

---

[3]Team Clean, Inc., 348 NLRB No. 86, 181 LRRM 1024 (2006); Daimler Chrysler Corp., 344 NLRB No. 154, 178 LRRM 1083 (2005), but see Main Edition, p. 1528 for discussion of positions taken by the general counsel in particular cases.
[4]Kvaerner Phila. Shipyard, Inc., 347 NLRB No. 36, 180 LRRM 1147 (2006).
[5]*Id.*

sion was not "palpably wrong," and therefore, deferral was appropriate. Member Liebman dissented, arguing that the arbitrator's decision had no basis in the Act, and contradicted the Board's own precedent.

PART VI

ECONOMIC ACTION

THE PRIMARY STRIKE

I. INTRODUCTION: THE RIGHT TO STRIKE

A. Constitutional Protection

Courts continued to parse out a delicate balance between con-stitutional rights and private property rights. For example, in *Utah Gospel Mission v. Salt Lake City Corp.*,[1] the Tenth Circuit held that a church plaza that was formerly a public street was not a "public forum" and upheld a church's prohibition of soliciting, begging, demonstrations, protests, leafleting, and other such activities in the plaza because the asserted purpose of the plaza was to act as an ecclesiastical park, there was no deed requiring the church to allow public access, and the plaza was not seamlessly connected to public sidewalks.

II. STRIKES PROTECTED UNDER THE ACT

B. Economic and Unfair Labor Practice Strikes

1. Unfair Labor Practice Strikes

The Board reaffirmed that employees who engage in an unfair labor practice strike must be reinstated to their former positions upon their unconditional offers to return to work.[2] The Board con-tinues to place the burden on the general counsel to demonstrate the existence of unfair labor practices to support a finding of an unfair labor practice strike.[3]

---

[1]425 F.3d 1249 (10th Cir. 2005).

[2]Pennant Foods Co., 347 NLRB No. 41, 180 LRRM 1040 (2006) (holding that reinstatement of first-shift strikers to second-shift positions violated the Act).

[3]Basic Indus., Inc., 348 NLRB No. 89 (2006) (noting that the general counsel failed to establish any reason the discriminatee had joined a strike).

2. Economic Strikes

One recognized legitimate and substantial business justification for refusing to reinstate economic strikers is that their jobs are occupied by workers hired as permanent replacements.[4] The burden is on the employer to prove that the replacement workers are permanent.[5]

In *Sutter Roseville Medical Center*,[6] the employer was found to have unlawfully delayed the reinstatement of strikers. The strike lasted one day and the employer closed its cafeteria for five days thereby delaying reinstatement. The employer contended that it should have been given five days to reinstate the strikers arguing that there is "no principled reason" for not allowing a 5-day grace period for reinstating economic strikers. The Board rejected the employer's contention finding the case to be a particularly good example of a situation where five extra days was not needed.

In *Roosevelt Memorial Medical Center*,[7] a Board majority dismissed an allegation that the employer's action in reducing the hours of employees who had previously announced an intention to strike was "inherently destructive" of employee rights. The employer was a health care institution that had arranged for strike replacements. When the union postponed the strike four days before it was to commence, the employer offered, and the union did not respond to, a request to bargain about the return of the intended strikers to the employment schedule.

III. UNPROTECTED AND PROHIBITED STRIKES

A. Unlawful or Wrongful Means

4. Picket Line Misconduct; Strike Violence

In *Universal Truss, Inc.*,[8] the Board found that the employer did not violate the Act when it discharged strikers who had assaulted and threatened other employees and vandalized nonstrikers' vehicles.

---

[4]Supervalu, Inc., 347 NLRB No. 37, slip op. at 2, 180 LRRM 1421 (2006).
[5]Capehorn Indus., 336 NLRB 364, 168 LRRM 1400 (2001).
[6]348 NLRB No. 29 (2006).
[7]348 NLRB No. 64 (2006).
[8]348 NLRB No. 41 (2006).

CHAPTER 20

THE LOCKOUT

II. CONTEMPORARY LAW OF LOCKOUTS

A. The Offensive Economic Lockout—In General

2. *The Use of Replacements*

In *Bud Antle Inc.*,[1] the Board considered the rights of locked out workers after a 14-year lockout. This case is discussed in Chapter 7, "Discrimination in Employment," Section II.B.2.

5. *The Partial Lockout*

After publication of the Main Edition, the Board requested the positions of the parties in *Midwest Generation EME, LLC*[2] on the issue remanded from the Seventh Circuit. In *Midwest Generation*, the Board found lawful a lockout of strikers during which crossovers and nonstrikers were allowed to work. On review, the Seventh Circuit reversed the Board on the lockout and remanded to determine whether the illegal lockout coerced union members into ratifying a contract.[3]

Briefs and reply briefs were filed with the Board in March and April 2007.

---

[1] 347 NLRB No. 9, 180 LRRM 1507 (2006).

[2] 343 NLRB No. 12, 175 LRRM 1461 (2004), *reversed and remanded sub nom.* Electrical Workers (IBEW) Local 15 v. NLRB, 429 F.3d 651, 178 LRRM 2385 (7th Cir. 2005).

[3] *See* discussion at Main Edition, p. 1669.

CHAPTER 21

PICKETING FOR ORGANIZATION AND RECOGNITION

II. PICKETING DEFINED

B. Patrolling or Carrying Placards

In two cases arising under Section 8(b)(4)(B), the Board found, despite the absence of picket signs, unlawful picketing to exist as a result of patrolling behavior. In *Laborers Eastern Region Organizing Fund (Ranches at Mt. Sinai)*,[1] the Board found that two or three people who were at times distributing handbills, engaged in patrolling

---

[1]346 NLRB No. 105, 180 LRRM 1109 (2006).

by walking back and forth across entrances to the worksite, effectively formed a barrier. In addition, at least one person momentarily blocked an employee (of a neutral contractor) from entering the worksite. In *Sheet Metal Workers Local 15 (Brandon Regional Medical Center)*,[2] the Board found that within the context of Section 8(b)(4)(ii) (B), a "mock funeral procession" on the public sidewalk in front of the medical center, complete with faux casket, an individual dressed as the Grim Reaper, and accompanied by leafleting, created a barrier that constituted patrolling and therefore unlawful picketing. Of note, the Board left open the issue of whether "[i]t may be that other conduct, short of a barrier, can be 'conduct' that is picketing or at least 'restraint or coercion' within the meaning of Section 8(b)(4)(ii)(B)."[3]

In a series of cases still pending before the Board, the general counsel has alleged that the display of large banners at neutral sites is picketing and thus within the proscriptions of Section 8(b)(4). On February 15, 2006, the general counsel directed the regions, in an effort to assure nationwide consistency, to submit to the Division of Advice all cases involving bannering or the display of an inflated rat until the Board resolves bannering issues in pending cases.[4] In their submissions, the regional offices are instructed to include evidence such as the location of the banner (or inflatable rat), the language on or near the banner, and whether it follows lawful or unlawful

---

[2]346 NLRB No. 22, 178 LRRM 1393 (2006).

[3]*Id.* at 1394.

[4]Regional Office Procedures for Handling Pending Section 8(b)(4)(ii)(B) Charges Involving Union "Bannering" of Neutral Persons and the Display of Inflatable Rats, Operations Management Memo. 06-42 (Feb. 15, 2006), *available at* www.nlrb.gov.

Several recent Advice Memoranda also address the issue of bannering, handbilling, and inflatable rats and other objects. *See* SEIU Local 32 BJ (Planned Bldg. Servs.), NLRB Gen. Counsel Advice Memo., Case Nos. 2-CC-2663 and 2-CP-1062 (2006) (union did not violate §8(b)(7) or 8(b)(4) using inflated turkey and Santa Clause costume where these objects have no significance in labor movement and protesting members only handbilled and milled about in an uncoordinated fashion, but did not patrol across the building entrance); Carpenters Local 971 (Gore Acoustics), NLRB Gen. Counsel Advice Memo., Case No. 32-CC-1531 (2006) (union did not violate §8(b)(4)(ii) by displaying banners and handbilling some distance from job site of neutral employer where conduct was not equivalent of picketing or other confrontational conduct); Electrical Workers (IBEW) Local 269 (Kay Constr., Inc.), NLRB Gen. Counsel Advice Memo., Case No. 4-CC-2447 (2006) (union did not violate §8(b)(4) by stationing individuals with placards and an inflatable rat on a main road, 250 feet past an access road to job site because mere presence of placards and/or patrolling does not constitute inducement or coercion without an element of confrontation).

picketing and the duration of any hiatus between them. The resolution of these issues in pending cases may also have implications for Section 8(b)(7) cases where bannering is alleged to be picketing.

III. PROSCRIBED ORGANIZATIONAL OR RECOGNITIONAL OBJECTIVE

A. Evidence of Proscribed Object

The Board continues to hold that recognitional picketing for fewer than 30 consecutive days may be unlawful where the picketing, albeit intermittent, spans a period longer than 30 days.[5]

C. Area-Standards Picketing

1. Area-Standards Object Not Proscribed

The Board continues to examine the truthfulness of a union's assertion that the picketed employer is maintaining subnormal wages and benefits, and the burden remains on the union to investigate and determine what the area standards are and whether the employer is meeting them.[6] The ostensible purposes of area-standards picketing may be deemed pretextual and evidence of improper motive found.[7]

VI. PICKETING OF UNREASONABLE DURATION ABSENT A PETITION

A. Reasonable Period of Time

The Board continues to carefully examine recognitional picketing that is intermittent to ascertain whether its duration is reasonable. In *Laborers Eastern Region Organizing Fund (Ranches at Mt. Sinai)*,[8]

---

[5] *Laborers E. Region Org. Fund*, 346 NLRB No. 105, 180 LRRM 1109.

[6] *See* Machinists Lodge 1173 (Future Ford), NLRB Gen. Counsel Advice Memo, Case No. 32-CP-487-1 (Although union obtained information from employees, its failure "to attempt to obtain such information directly from the Employer before picketing suggests that it was interested in obtaining something other than comparable labor costs").

[7] *See* Sheet Metal Workers Local 7 (Andy J. Egan Co.), 345 NLRB No. 119, 178 LRRM 1321 (2005).

[8] *Laborers E. Region Org. Fund*, 346 NLRB No. 105, 180 LRRM 1109.

the Board held that recognitional picketing for 28 days was unreasonable under Section 8(b)(7)(C) when the picketing was spread out over a 4-month period.

While the Board continues to recognize an exception to Section 8(b)(7), when picketing is for recognition in a one-person bargaining unit, the District of Columbia Circuit declined to recognize this exception. In *International Transportation Service, Inc. v. NLRB*,[9] the District of Columbia Circuit denied enforcement of a Board order finding that an employer committed an unfair labor practice when it fired an employee who engaged in recognitional picketing for a single-employee bargaining unit. The court disagreed with the Board's adherence to its ruling in *Vila-Barr*[10] and reiterated that recognitional picketing of any duration violates Section 8(b)(7)(C) of the Act where the bargaining unit sought would be improper. Because a single-employee bargaining unit will not be certified by the Board, the employee's recognitional picketing was not protected activity. Thus, the court concurred with the Seventh Circuit's holding that called *Vila-Barr Co.* into question.[11]

---

[9]449 F.3d 160, 179 LRRM 2897 (D.C. Cir. 2006).
[10]Teamsters Local 115 (Vila-Barr Co.), 157 NLRB 588, 61 LRRM 1386 (1966).
[11]Teamsters v. NLRB (Purolator Sec.), 568 F.2d 12 (7th Cir. 1977).

CHAPTER 22

SECONDARY ACTIVITY: HANDBILLS, PICKETS, AND STRIKES

II. SECTION 8(b)(4)(B): PROHIBITED SECONDARY ACTIVITY DEFINED

A. Definitions of Terms

1. *"Doing Business" [New Topic]*

In *T.H. Eifert Inc. v. Plumbers & Pipe Fitters,*[1] a Section 303 proceeding, the district court held that a union did not violate Section 8(b)(4) when it allegedly coerced an employer's workers to quit their jobs prior to the sale of the business to another company with whom the union had a labor dispute. The court noted that generally the sale of one company to another does not constitute "doing business"

---

[1]422 F. Supp. 2d 818, 179 LRRM 2354 (W.D. Mich. 2006).

under Section 8(b)(4). The court distinguished the Third Circuit's holding in *Taylor Milk Co. v. Teamsters*[2] that the union's interference with the lengthy acquisition negotiations, by direct interference in the related labor negotiations, provided the basis for a finding that the "doing business" factor had been satisfied.[3]

2. *"Picketing" [New Topic]*

In *Sheet Metal Workers Local 15 (Brandon Regional Medical Center),*[4] the Board found that a "mock funeral procession" constituted picketing. Accompanied by leafleting, the procession involved four union members patrolling on the public sidewalk in front of a medical center while carrying a faux casket and accompanied by a member dressed as the Grim Reaper. Although the Board found that the procession created a barrier, two members noted that "[i]t may be that other conduct, short of a barrier, can be 'conduct' that is picketing or at least 'restraint or coercion' within the meaning of Section 8(b)(4)(ii)(B)."[5]

B. The Elusive Distinction Between Primary and Secondary Conduct

In *Gotham Logistics v. Teamsters Local 917,*[6] the district court noted that the "distinction between primary activity which is lawfully aimed at the union's employer, and unlawful secondary activity can, at times, be difficult to draw." A trucking company had entered into an agreement with a liquor distributor to provide trucking services. At the time of the agreement, the liquor distributor was a party to a collective bargaining agreement that provided for the use of outside general trucking contractors. Following a purchase of the distributor and the negotiation of a new collective bargaining agreement, the distributor began to hire more employees to perform the trucking services that the outside company had previously performed. The outside trucking company alleged that the union's negotiation of an

---

[2]248 F.3d 239, 167 LRRM 2087 (3d Cir.), *cert. denied,* 534 U.S. 1055, 168 LRRM 2960 (2001).

[3]*T.H. Eifert,* 422 F. Supp. 2d at 833.

[4]346 NLRB No. 22, 178 LRRM 1393 (2006).

[5]*Id.;* Laborers E. Region Org. Fund (Ranches at Mt. Sinai), 346 NLRB No. 105, 180 LRRM 1109 n.5 (2006) (neither patrolling alone nor patrolling combined with the carrying of placards are essential to the existence of picketing; the essential feature of picketing is the posting of individuals at entrances to a place of work).

[6]446 F. Supp. 2d 130 (E.D.N.Y. 2006).

agreement allowing the distributor to hire more in-house, unionized employees amounted to secondary coercive activity in violation of Section 8(b)(4). The district court disagreed, noting that the distinction between preserving work and obtaining additional work is not determinative of whether activity is prohibited. Rather, "the issue is whether the activity is sanctioned primary activity aimed at putting pressure on an employer with respect to his own employees, or activity with respect to the employees of another, unrelated third party."[7] In dismissing the claim, the court stated that "[w]hile it is true that the Union's negotiation of a new CBA affects the business of the Plaintiffs, that negotiation was aimed at [the distributor], the union member's employer, and not at Plaintiffs or with respect to Plaintiffs' treatment of its employees."[8]

In *Chicago District Council of Carpenters Pension Fund v. Reinke Insulation Co.*,[9] a Section 303 proceeding, the Seventh Circuit affirmed the district court's decision that a union had engaged in lawful primary picketing when it picketed a construction company at its various construction sites with signs accusing the company of failing to make fringe-benefit contributions. The employer had withdrawn from a multi-employer bargaining association. A preliminary audit of the employer's pension and welfare contributions found some delinquencies. The union filed suit against the employer and began to picket its various job sites with signs accusing the employer of failing to make fringe benefit contributions. After a court had enjoined the picketing, the union began distributing handbills stating that the employer had "cheated" its employees. The activity resulted in various homeowners terminating their construction contracts with the employer. The employer argued that the union picketed with the prohibited object of forcing the employer to return to the multi-employer bargaining association. The Seventh Circuit found that the record indicated that the picketing, and later handbilling, was directed solely at the employer's failure to make the required payments and there was no evidence that the picketing would have stopped if the employer had rejoined the multi-employer bargaining association. Accordingly, the union had not engaged in unlawful secondary activity.[10]

---

[7] *Id.* at 133.
[8] *Id.* at 134.
[9] 464 F.3d 651, 180 LRRM 2584 (7th Cir. 2006).
[10] *Id.* at 659.

In *T.H. Eifert*, the court found that, even if the contemplated sale of the business had amounted to "doing business," the alleged coercion was not a violation of Section 8(b)(4) because the union's conduct was primary in that it was directed at affecting the decision of prospective employees to accept employment with the purchaser.[11]

F. Applying the Primary-Secondary Tests

1. Conduct Other Than Picketing

Picketing may occur even if there is not patrolling or patrolling with placards. Picketing includes the union's agents walking back and forth, without picket signs, in front of an entrance to a construction site and momentarily blocking one worker's access to the site.[12] A letter to a neutral employer that stated that, if a nonunion contractor worked on the project, leafleting and protesting would occur, also constituted primary activity.[13]

G. Bannering

Replacing an earlier directive, the general counsel instructed the regions to submit all cases involving union bannering or the display of an inflated rat to the Division of Advice.[14]

III. HANDBILLING

B. Standards for Lawful Handbilling

2. Location of Handbilling

See discussion at Chapter 6, "Interference With Protected Rights," Section II.B.1.g. and h.

---

[11]T.H. Eifert Inc. v. Plumbers & Pipe Fitters, 442 F. Supp. 2d 818, 833–34, 179 LRRM 2354 (W.D. Mich. 2006).

[12]Laborers E. Region Org. Fund (Ranches at Mt. Sinai), 346 NLRB No. 105, 180 LRRM 1109 (2006).

[13]Sheet Metal Workers Local 15 (Brandon Reg'l Med. Ctr.), 346 NLRB No. 22, 178 LRRM 1393 (2006), cited in Main Edition, Section II.F.1. at 1815 n.347.

[14]Regional Office Procedures for Handling Pending Section 8(b)(4)(ii)(B) Charges Involving Union "Bannering" of Neutral Persons and the Display of Inflatable Rats, Operations Management Memo. 06-42 (Feb. 15, 2006), *available at* www.nlrb.gov.

V. ACTIONS FOR DAMAGES UNDER SECTION 303

A. Nature of the Action

1. Relationship to Section 8(b)(4)

Section 303 of the Labor Management Relations Act confers a private right of action for damages resulting from any unfair labor practice under Section 8(b)(4) of the National Labor Relations Act and that there is no liability under Section 303 in the absence of a violation of Section 8(b)(4).[15]

Section 303 cases continue to follow the Section 8(b)(4) principle that literal compliance or noncompliance with the *Moore Dry Dock*[16] standards neither precludes nor establishes a violation. However, where *Moore Dry Dock* common situs rules are observed, there is a presumption that picketing has a lawful purpose.[17] Cases continue to look to the totality of the circumstances, placing the burden on the employer to establish that secondary effects were the intended consequence of union activity.[18]

3. Effect of Arbitration Clause

Courts continue to hold that an employer may be required to arbitrate its Section 303 damage claim if an applicable collective bargaining agreement provides for an arbitration procedure with an extremely broad scope. However, in a case where a multi-employer association, rather than the plaintiff employers, negotiated the col-

---

[15]Chicago Dist. Council of Carpenters Pension Fund v. Reinke Insulation Co., 464 F.3d 651, 657–59, 180 LRRM 2584 (7th Cir. 2006) (affirming summary judgment dismissing §303 claim because the record presented no genuine issue of fact that picketing had secondary object of forcing employer to rejoin multi-employer bargaining association). *Cf.* Frito-Lay, Inc. v. Teamsters Local 137, 623 F.2d 1354, 104 LRRM 2931 (9th Cir. 1980), *cert. denied*, 449 U.S. 1013, 105 LRRM 3327 (1980) *and* 449 U.S. 1112, 106 LRRM 2200 (1981) (§303 damages were recovered for a strike that forced three employers to negotiate in a multi-employer bargaining unit.).

[16]Sailors Union of the Pac. (Moore Dry Dock Co.), 92 NLRB 547, 27 LRRM 1108 (1950).

[17]Tri-Gen Inc. v. Operating Eng'rs Local 150, 433 F.3d 1024, 1038, 1042, 178 LRRM 2897 (7th Cir. 2006) (affirming grant of summary judgment dismissing §303 claims because there was no material issue that union's intent in picketing site was to force drilling company's customer to terminate contract and hire another driller).

[18]*Id. See also* T.H. Eifert Inc. v. Plumbers & Pipe Fitters, 422 F. Supp. 2d 818, 833–84, 179 LRRM 2354 (W.D. Mich. 2006).

lective bargaining agreement, the court found that contract language did not require the employers to arbitrate because the contract did not include a clear and unmistakable waiver of the employer's statutory right to litigate a Section 303 claim.[19]

C. The Measure of Damages

In a contempt proceeding for continuing violations of Section 8(b)(4), a court refused to allow, as part of the remedy for the contempt, damages suffered by the neutral employers.[20]

---

[19] *T.H. Eifert*, 422 F. Supp. 2d at 829–31.
[20] NLRB v. Electrical Workers (IBEW) Local 3, 471 F.3d 399, 181 LRRM 2069 (2d Cir. 2006).

Chapter 23

SECTION 8(e): THE "HOT-CARGO" AGREEMENT

III. INTERPRETATION AND APPLICATION

A. Definitions and Coverage

In *Heartland Industrial Partners, LLC*,[1] the Board addressed whether a union recognition agreement between an investment firm and a union violated Section 8(e). The agreement required the investment firm to "cause" any manufacturing company that it acquired to sign a "framework" governing unionization within six months of the acquisition, assuming that the union notified the investment firm of its intent to unionize the acquired company. Under the framework, the acquired company was required to remain neutral during any union-organizing drive, grant the union access to its premises, and recognize and bargain with the union based upon a card showing of majority support. Issues that remained open after 90 days of bargaining were subject to interest arbitration. The agreement between the investment firm and the union contained an arbitration clause, but failed to specify the arbitrator's remedial authority.

The general counsel alleged that the agreement had a prohibited "cease doing business object" because it "operate[d] as a restriction" on the firm's "investments."[2] Rejecting the general counsel's position, a divided three-member panel of the Board (with Chairman Battista dissenting) concluded that the agreement was lawful because it did not have a cessation-of-business object within the meaning of Section 8(e).[3]

---

[1] 348 NLRB No. 72, 180 LRRM 1473 (2006).

[2] *See id.*, slip op. at 3–4.

[3] Having reach that conclusion, the Board declined to consider whether the agreement had a secondary object—that is, whether it met §8(e)'s "with another person" criterion. *See id.*, slip op. at 3 n.5.

Critical to the Board's conclusion was that, *on its face*, the agreement did not require the investment firm to cease doing business with any company it might acquire. The Board also noted the absence of any evidence that the clause had that effect. The Board emphasized that, unlike other agreements it had found unlawful in prior cases, the agreement before it did not require the investment firm "to choose between inducing" a company it acquired to sign the framework or to sever its relationship with the company.[4] That was true, the Board explained, despite the possibility that an arbitrator *might* remedy a breach of the agreement by ordering the investment firm to cease doing business with the acquired company by divestiture or otherwise. The Board rejected the "chain of contingencies" that might result in an arbitrator's divestiture order, noting that a challenged agreement must be interpreted " 'to require no more than what is allowed by law,' when it is not 'clearly unlawful on its face,' "[5] and the agreement at issue "*on [its] face* contain[ed] no provision that would allow an arbitrator to order" the investment firm "to cease doing business" with an acquired company.[6]

---

[4] *Id.*, slip op. at 2.

[5] *Id.*, slip op. at 4 (citing Teamsters Local 982 (J.K. Barker Trucking Co.), 181 NLRB 515, 517 (1970), *aff'd*, 450 F.2d 1322 (D.C. Cir. 1971)).

[6] *See id.* (emphasis added). The Board did, however, leave open the possibility that an arbitral remedy that required the investment firm to cease doing business with an acquired company *might* render the agreement unlawful in application. *Id.* at 4 n.6.

CHAPTER 24

JURISDICTIONAL DISPUTES AND "FEATHERBEDDING"

II. JURISDICTIONAL DISPUTES

C. Procedure in Jurisdictional Dispute Cases

3. Disclaimer

In *Miron Construction Co.*,[1] the Seventh Circuit held that the pursuit of contractual remedies without a demand for reassignment of the work is not inconsistent with a Section 10(k) award.

D. Factors Determining Jurisdictional Disputes

The Board continues to rely on the five basic factors announced in *Jones Construction*[2] in deciding jurisdictional disputes.[3] The Board's analysis includes, as part of its consideration of relative economies and efficiencies, weighing whether its decision will cause the employer to hire additional employees unnecessarily.[4]

E. Post-Hearing Procedure

The Board continues to refuse to issue broad prospective awards unless there is evidence both that (a) the disputed work has been a continuous source of controversy in the relevant geographic area and that similar disputes may recur and (b) the offending union has a proclivity to engage in unlawful conduct to obtain work similar to that in dispute.[5]

---

[1] 44 F.3d 558, 148 LRRM 2199 (7th Cir. 1995) (finding union can bring subcontracting grievance against general contractor even after work is awarded to another union).

[2] Machinists Lodge 1743 (J.A. Jones Constr. Co.), 135 NLRB 1402, 49 LRRM 1684 (1962). For the list of *Jones Construction* factors, see Main Edition at pp. 1961–62.

[3] Operating Eng'rs Local 150 (Royal Components, Inc.), 348 NLRB No. 97, 181 LRRM 1081 (2006).

[4] *Id.*

[5] *Id.* (refusing to award broad injunctive relief because "[t]he Employer has presented no evidence that the disputed work in this case is likely to be a continuous source of controversy or that Local 150 has a proclivity to engage in unlawful conduct to acquire the disputed work").

F. Relationship of Section 8(b)(4)(D) Proceedings to Other Actions and Unfair Labor Practice Proceedings

Courts continue to hold that the Board's decision following a Section 10(k) hearing overrides a conflicting arbitration award.[6] Relying on this same reasoning, one court preliminarily enjoined a union from even pursuing its claims in arbitration where it was required to utilize the building and construction trades department arbitration procedures.[7]

---

[6]Eshbach Bros., L.P. v. Operating Eng'rs Local 542, Nos. Civ.A.04-0089 & Civ. A.04-0102, 2006 WL 557683 (E.D. Pa. Mar. 2, 2006) ("the NLRB's finding in its determination precludes enforcement of the arbitrator's award").

[7]Competitive Interiors, Inc. v. Laborers Local 1015, No. 5:06-cv-370, 2006 WL 1967378 (N.D. Ohio July 12, 2006).

Part VII

RELATIONS BETWEEN EMPLOYEE
AND UNION

CHAPTER 25

THE DUTY OF FAIR REPRESENTATION

II. JURISDICTION AND PROCEDURES TO ENFORCE THE DUTY

A. The Courts

1. Exhaustion of Contractual Remedies

Courts continue to hold that, in a hybrid Section 301 breach of contract/duty of fair representation case, the plaintiff must establish both that the employer breached the collective bargaining agreement and that the union breached its duty of fair representation in representing the plaintiff with respect to the alleged collective bargaining agreement violation. Thus, courts granted summary judgment for employers, even when there were genuine issues of material fact with respect to the violation of the collective bargaining agreement, when there were no genuine issues of material fact with respect to the union's breach of the duty of fair representation;[1] and granted summary judgment in favor of unions when there were no genuine issues of material fact as to whether the employer violated the collective bargaining agreement, without deciding whether

---

[1]White v. Detroit Edison Co., 472 F.3d 420, 181 LRRM 2065 (6th Cir. 2006); Taafe v. BellSouth Telecomms., Inc., 204 Fed. Appx. 823, 181 LRRM 2370 (11th Cir. 2006); Benson v. Potter, 210 Fed. Appx. 530 (7th Cir. 2006) (strategic decisions by union not made on a discriminatory basis or in bad faith do not breach the duty of fair representation); Nicholls v. Brookdale Univ. Hosp. & Med. Ctr., 204 Fed. Appx. 40, 180 LRRM 3075 (2d Cir. 2006) (mere negligence by union not enough to establish breach of duty of fair representation).

there were genuine issues of material fact as to whether the union breached its duty of fair representation.[2]

In *Bianchi v. Roadway Express, Inc.*,[3] the Eleventh Circuit followed the First Circuit's decision in *Early v. Eastern Transfer*,[4] and held that the plaintiff had waived any argument that his union representative at the grievance hearing, or any of the union members on the grievance panel, were biased against him by stating at the grievance hearing that he had presented everything in his favor and that the union representative "represented me properly and fully."[5] While not finding a waiver, the Eighth Circuit in *Jones v. United Parcel Service, Inc.*[6] noted that the plaintiffs had stated that their union representatives had afforded them adequate representation at their grievance hearings. The court held that the alleged bias and failure to present evidence did not rise to the level of a breach of the duty of fair representation.[7]

B. The Labor Board

1. Unfair Labor Practice Cases

In *Letter Carriers Branch 1227 (United States Postal Service)*,[8] the Board did not reach the issue of whether the union owed a duty of fair representation to retirees in allocating a grievance settlement between retirees and active employees. The Board found that the union did not breach any duty it may have had to the retirees in deciding to allocate a half share of the settlement to retirees. The union had relied in good faith on advice of counsel.[9]

---

[2]Bliesner v. Communications Workers, 464 F.3d 910, 180 LRRM 2593 (9th Cir. 2006); Suter v. Louisiana Philharmonic Orchestra, No. 05-30824, 2006 WL 1877220, 179 LRRM 3294 (5th Cir. July 5, 2006); Hollowell v. Bakery, Confectionery, Tobacco Workers & Grain Millers Local 280, 191 Fed. Appx. 499 (7th Cir. 2006); Kellhoffer v. Columbus S. Power Co., 192 Fed. Appx. 383, 180 LRRM 2133 (6th Cir. 2006).
[3]441 F.3d 1278, 179 LRRM 2203 (11th Cir. 2006).
[4]699 F.2d 552, 112 LRRM 3381 (1st Cir. 1983), *cert. denied*, 464 U.S. 824, 114 LRRM 2568 (1983). See Main Edition at footnotes 220 and 321.
[5]*Bianchi v. Roadway Express*, 441 F.3d at 1281.
[6]461 F.3d 982, 180 LRRM 2298 (8th Cir. 2006).
[7]*Id.*
[8]347 NLRB No. 27 (2006).
[9]*Id.*, slip op. at 2.

The Sixth Circuit enforced a Board order because it found that substantial evidence supported the Board's determinations that a union had breached its duty of fair representation by not investigating a grievance and that the grievance would have been meritorious if brought by the union.[10]

3. Preemption and Accommodation

Courts continue to hold that state causes of action, such as claims for breach of contract or fraud, are preempted by Section 301 if they require interpretation of the collective bargaining agreement,[11] and that the breach of duty of fair representation counts of the complaint are the only claims that are appropriate.[12]

IV. STATUTES OF LIMITATIONS

In *Adorno v. Crowley Towing & Transportation Co.*,[13] the First Circuit joined those circuits that held that the cause of action for breach of duty of fair representation cases accrues when the "prospective plaintiffs knew, or reasonably should have known of the alleged wrongful acts."[14] That case involved a union negotiating with an employer over which employees would remain to fulfill residual contract obligations and complete closing of operations after most of the workforce was laid off. The court held that the cause of action accrued when the layoffs took place, because at that point the employees knew they had been terminated and knew that employees with less seniority were among those retained to complete closing of operations.[15]

The court also accepted arguendo the parties' agreement that the statute of limitations was tolled for employees not among the initial plaintiffs to the action, during the pendency of a class certifi-

---

[10]NLRB v. State, County & Mun. Employees Local 1640, Nos. 05-2122, 05-2163, 2006 WL 2519732, 180 LRRM 2519 (6th Cir. Aug. 30, 2006) *enforcing* State, County & Mun. Employees Local 1640 (Children's Home of Detroit), 344 NLRB No. 53, 177 LRRM 1019 (2005).

[11]Eddy v. Radar Pictures, Inc., No. 04-56993, 2006 WL 3821078, 181 LRRM 2284 (9th Cir. Dec. 22, 2006).

[12]*Id.* (court held that the union had not breached its duty of fair representation, and dismissed the other counts of the complaint as preempted).

[13]443 F.3d 122, 179 LRRM 2385 (1st Cir. 2006).

[14]*Id.* at 126.

[15]*Id.* at 127.

cation motion.[16] The court did not have to decide the tolling issue definitively as based on the accrual date found by the court; the additional plaintiffs claims were time-barred even if the statute was tolled for the class certification motion.[17] The Fifth Circuit held that equitable tolling could apply to a claim for the period that the plaintiffs are seeking to resolve the matter though the grievance procedure, but in order to invoke equitable tolling the grievance must be brought within six months of the event giving rise to the grievance, even if the contract allows for a longer period.[18]

---

[16]*Id.* at 126 (citing Basch v. Ground Round, Inc., 139 F.3d 6, 10 (1st Cir. 1998)).

[17]*Id.* at 126–27.

[18]Lee v. Cytec Indus., Inc., 460 F.3d 673, 180 LRRM 2185 (5th Cir. 2006).

UNION SECURITY

IV. SECTION 14(b) AND STATE "RIGHT-TO-WORK" LAWS

Labor contract provisions that assess nonunion employees "fair share" amounts for the costs of union representation have been found to violate right-to-work laws, regardless of the fact that the required amount is less than the full equivalent of union dues.[1]

---

[1]Plumbers & Pipe Fitters Local 141 (International Paper Co.) v. NLRB, 675 F.2d 1257, 110 LRRM 2027 (D.C. Cir. 1982) (finding that "fair share" clauses violated the right-to-work laws of Arkansas, Florida, Mississippi, and Louisiana); State, County & Mun. Employees Local 2384 v. City of Phoenix, 142 P.3d 234, 180 LRRM 2325 (Ariz. 2006) (clause precluded under Arizona law); *see* Florida Educ. Ass'n/ United v. Public Employees Relations Comm'n, 346 So. 2d 551, 94 LRRM 2607 (Fla. Dist. Ct. App. 1977) (clause prohibited under Florida law).

V. Hiring-Hall and Job-Referral Practices

A. General Rules

The courts continue to prohibit discrimination on the basis of protected activity in operating hiring-hall referral systems.[2] The courts also continue to prohibit referrals made to reward "good" members or to punish "bad" ones.[3] Finally, the courts continue to hold that the prohibition against discrimination operates not only as to the ultimate referral, but also at the intermediate steps in the referral process.[4]

VI. The Dues Checkoff

C. The NLRB

1. Jurisdiction of the Board

The Board continues to hold that an employer may engage in illegal domination under Section 8(a)(2), or illegal interference under Section 8(a)(1), or both, if it encourages its employees to execute checkoff authorizations.[5]

---

[2]Plumbers & Pipe Fitters Local 420 (Carrier Corp.), 347 NLRB No. 53, 180 LRRM 1015 (2006) (union violated §8(b)(1)(A) and (2) when it caused the employer not to hire union member because he worked for a nonunion company).

[3]Cf. Iron Workers Local 350 (Consumers Energy Co.), 347 NLRB No. 57, 180 LRRM 1166 (2006) (union did not violate LMRA when it failed to refer union dissident to a two-person team where dissident had long-standing hostility toward other potential team member).

[4]Plumbers & Pipe Fitters Local 32 (Anthony Constr. Co.), 346 NLRB No. 95, 179 LRRM 1213 (2006) (union violated §8(b)(1)(A) by denying employee's request for photocopying of referral records where employee had reasonable belief that he had been unfairly treated by hiring hall's classification of his position as pipefitter, rather than steamfitter).

[5]Planned Bldg. Servs., Inc., 347 NLRB No. 64, 180 LRRM 1081 (2006) (supervisor's statement that he "needed" authorization forms to be filled out, and that the "office" needed them violated §8(a)(1) and (2) of the Act).

VII. Constitutional Dimensions and Other Statutory Requirements

B. Effect of Political Expenditures

In calculating the remedy to dissenters for unlawful political expenditures over their objection, courts continue to hold that the union has the burden of proof regarding establishing the proportion of political expenditures as compared to the proportion of union expenditures.[6]

Courts continue to apply the *Hudson* standards to determine whether a union's system to collect fair-share fees is constitutional.[7]

In *Liegmann v. California Teachers Ass'n,*[8] the court held that a midyear fee increase that plaintiffs claimed the union assessed to address a state ballot initiative and for other political purposes did not represent "extraordinary circumstances," such that the court would require more exacting notice procedures that those required under *Hudson.*

Courts have held with respect to agency fees in public sector employment, unions are not prohibited by *Lehnert* from including extra-unit litigation costs as part of chargeable fees.[9]

A lack of judicial review of an independent arbiter's decision was held not to render union objection procedures constitutionally defective.[10]

Following *Beck,* the Board has continued to require unions to inform employees of their right to become nonmembers and, thus,

---

[6]Wessel v. City of Albuquerque, 463 F.3d 1138, 1145, 180 LRRM 2577, 2581 (10th Cir. 2006) (because the union "did not identify the various components" making up the fees, and the union has the "burden of proof" regarding these components, the trial court was correct in ordering the union to refund the entire fee); Wright v. Cincinnati, 450 F. Supp. 2d 831, 839, 180 LRRM 2546, 2551 (S.D. Ohio 2006) (impartial arbiter's "arbitrary and capricious" level of review of union's determination of what proportion of its fees went to political expenditures and what proportion went to union expenditures was insufficient, because this standard did not impose the burden of proof upon the union).

[7]Locke v. Karass, 425 F. Supp. 2d 137, 144–45, 179 LRRM 2457, 2462 (D. Me. 2006) (union notice that included a notice of service fee, a breakdown of chargeable and nonchargeable categories, and information on how to challenge the fee was constitutional under *Hudson* and dismissing plaintiffs' argument that the financial data used in the service fee calculation must be from the immediately prior fiscal year rather than the most recent fiscal year for which data is available).

[8]No. C 05-03828 JW, 2006 WL 1795123 (N.D. Cal. June 28, 2006).

[9]*Locke v. Karass,* 425 F. Supp. 2d at 147, 179 LRRM at 2463.

[10]*Wright v. Cincinnati,* 450 F. Supp. 2d at 838, 180 LRRM at 2551.

to pay reduced agency fees as part of the union's duty of fair representation under Section 8(b)(1)(A).[11] The Board has also cited *Beck* as requiring unions to apply liquidated damages to offset chargeable, as well as nonchargeable fees.[12]

Currently, there is a split among the circuit courts regarding whether *Hudson's* independent audit verification requirement applies to small unions. In *Harik v. California Teachers Ass'n*,[13] the Ninth Circuit determined that a local union with under $50,000 in estimated annual revenues was not required to obtain independent auditor verification of its expenditures. The court held that a small union could either disclose the full financial material necessary to verify its expenditures or an independently sanctioned verification of the local union's chargeable and nonchargeable expenditures.[14] To the contrary, in *Otto v. Pennsylvania State Education Ass'n*,[15] the Third Circuit held that local unions, regardless of their size, are required to obtain independent audits of their financial expenditures.

In *Washington v. Washington Education Ass'n*,[16] the Washington Supreme Court considered a state law that required unions to receive affirmative assent from nonmembers in order to use agency funds collected for political causes. The court held that this requirement was not narrowly tailored and unconstitutionally burdened the rights of supporting nonmembers, because of the administrative burden necessary to obtain assent.[17] The Washington Supreme Court distinguished *Miller*, noting that the statute at issue there applied not just to unions, but also to corporations, nonprofits, and other enti-

---

[11]Teamsters Local 492 (United Parcel Serv., Inc.), 346 NLRB No. 37, 179 LRRM 1062 (2006); Food & Commercial Workers Local 648 (Safeway, Inc.), 347 NLRB No. 83, 180 LRRM 1230 (2006).

[12]Teamsters Local 399 (Hilltop Servs., Inc.), 346 NLRB No. 32, 179 LRRM 1024 (2006).

[13]326 F.3d 1042, 172 LRRM 2193 (9th Cir.), *cert. denied sub nom.* Sheffield v. Aceves, 540 U.S. 965, 173 LRRM 2512 (2003).

[14]*Id.* at 1047, 172 LRRM at 2196–97.

[15]330 F.3d 125, 134, 172 LRRM 2452, 2459 (3d Cir.) (declining to find a "small local union" exception to *Hudson* safeguards), *cert. denied*, 540 U.S. 982, 173 LRRM 2576 (2003).

[16]130 P.3d 352, 179 LRRM 2518 (Wash. 2006).

[17]*Id.* at 360, 364, 179 LRRM at 2525, 2528. *See also* Sanger v. Dennis, 148 P.3d 404 (Colo. Ct. App. 2006) (cited to *Washington v. Washington Educ. Ass'n* in granting plaintiffs' motion for a preliminary injunction against a similar opt-in requirement, but applied intermediate scrutiny, holding that the requirement would unduly burden union members' First Amendment rights in the imminent November 2006 elections).

ties, whereas the Washington law only targeted unions.[18] In *Davenport v. Washington Education Ass'n*,[19] the U.S. Supreme Court vacated that decision and held that it does not violate the First Amendment for a state to require that its public-sector unions receive affirmative authorization from a nonmember before spending that nonmember's agency fees for election-related purposes.

An even broader regulation was struck down in *Pocatello Education Ass'n v. Heideman*,[20] where an Idaho statute banned all political payroll deductions for public employees and for private employees not covered by federal labor acts. Several unions challenged the law which the district court found unconstitutional, except to the extent that it applied to deduction programs for state employees where the state incurred costs of setting up and maintaining the program.[21]

---

[18]Michigan State AFL-CIO v. Miller, 103 F.3d 1240, 154 LRRM 2073 (6th Cir. 1997); see also Main Edition at p. 2201; *Washington v. Washington Educ. Ass'n*, 130 P.3d at 361–62, 179 LRRM at 2526.

[19]127 S. Ct. 2372, 181 LRRM 3281 (2007).

[20]No. CV-03-0256-E-BLW, 2005 WL 3241745, 178 LRRM 2554 (D. Idaho Nov. 23, 2005).

[21]*Id.* at 2559. *See also* Utah Educ. Ass'n v. Shurtleff, No.2:03-CV-1100 TC, 2006 WL 1184946, 179 LRRM 2800 (D. Utah May 3, 2006) (district court applied strict scrutiny to hold that restriction making it unlawful for any public employer to grant an employee's request to make voluntary contributions through payroll deductions to political funds sponsored by labor organizations was unconstitutional).

PART VIII

ADMINISTRATION OF THE ACT

Chapter 27

JURISDICTION: COVERAGE OF THE ACT

II. STATUTORY JURISDICTION

B. Foreign Operations

In *California Gas Transport, Inc.*,[1] the Board asserted jurisdiction over unfair labor practices committed in Mexico by an American employer. The Board's interpretation of Supreme Court precedent is that conduct is "extraterritorial," and therefore presumptively not covered by U.S. law, only if it "both occurs outside of the U.S. and causes no effects within the U.S."[2] The Board found that the conduct of the employer caused unlawful effects within the United States by interfering with the employees' ability to freely exercise their Section 7 rights in the United States. The Board rejected the Third Circuit's decision in *Asplundh Tree Expert Co. v. NLRB*,[3] in which the court had denied enforcement to a similar Board decision. According to the Board, the Third Circuit took too broad a view of what constitutes "extraterritorial" activity by failing to recognize the "effects test" as part of the defining standard.[4]

---

[1]347 NLRB No. 118, 181 LRRM 1114 (2006).
[2]*Id.*
[3]365 F.3d 168, 174 LRRM 2929 (3d Cir. 2004), *denying enforcement to* Asplundh Tree Expert Co., 336 NLRB 1106, 168 LRRM 1465 (2001).
[4]*California Gas*, 181 LRRM at 1118 n.11.

III. DEFINITIONS AND LIMITATIONS ON COVERAGE

B. Employer

1. Single-Employer Status

The Board has continued to apply its four-factor test for single-employer status.[5]

4. Exclusions From Coverage of the Act

b. Indian Tribes

In *San Manuel Indian Bingo & Casino v. NLRB*,[6] the District of Columbia Circuit upheld the Board's assertion of jurisdiction over a gaming facility owned and operated by a Native American Tribal government.

c. Political Subdivisions

(1) Departmental or Administrative Arm of Government

In *State Bar of New Mexico*,[7] the Board determined that "the State Bar was created directly by the New Mexico Supreme Court as an administrative arm of the judicial branch of government, and, thus, is an exempt political subdivision under Section 2(2) of the Act."[8]

---

[5]Flat Dog Prods., Inc., 347 NLRB No. 104, 180 LRRM 1383, 1385–86 (2006). *See also* Cadillac Asphalt Paving Co., 349 NLRB No. 5, 181 LRRM 1105, 1109 (2007) ("A single-employer analysis is appropriate only where two ongoing businesses are coordinated by a common master," not where the businesses exist at different times.).

[6]475 F.3d 1306, 181 LRRM 2352 (D.C. Cir. 2007), *enforcing* 341 NLRB 1055, 174 LRRM 1489 (2004).

[7]346 NLRB No. 64, 179 LRRM 1089 (2006).

[8]*Id.* at 1091. The State Bar of New Mexico is an "integrated bar," rather than a "voluntary bar," meaning that membership is a condition for the practice of law in the state. The Board noted that a case involving a voluntary bar would raise different issues. *Id.*, 179 LRRM at 1090 n.4.

C. Employee

1. In General

The Board has continued to recognize that undocumented workers are, despite that status, still "employees" covered by the Act.[9]

2. Excluded Categories of Employees

a. Supervisors

In *Oakwood Healthcare, Inc.*,[10] and companion cases,[11] the Board "refined the analysis to be applied in assessing supervisory status."[12] In particular, the Board interpreted the statutory terms "assign," "responsibly to direct," and "independent judgment" in Section 2(11).

The Board in *Oakwood Healthcare*, construed the term assign as "the act of designating an employee to a place (such as a location, department, or wing), appointing an employee to a time (such as a shift or overtime period), or giving significant overall duties, i.e., tasks, to an employee."[13] By contrast, "choosing the order in which the employee will perform discrete tasks within those assignments," or giving an "ad hoc instruction that the employee perform a discrete task," does not amount to "assigning" for purposes of supervisory status.[14] In a companion case, *Golden Crest Healthcare Center*, the Board held that a person is not a supervisor if he or she has only the power to request that an employee accept an assignment (such as additional hours); the power to require compliance, with the imposition of actual consequences in case of refusal, is prerequisite for a finding of supervisory authority to "assign."[15]

By contrast, under *Oakwood Healthcare*, the phrase "responsibly to direct," does encompass ad hoc decisions as to "what job shall

---

[9]Concrete Form Walls, Inc., 346 NLRB No. 80, 179 LRRM 1193 (2006).
[10]348 NLRB No. 37, 180 LRRM 1257 (2006).
[11]Croft Metals, Inc., 348 NLRB No. 38, 180 LRRM 1293 (2006); Golden Crest Healthcare Ctr., 348 NLRB No. 39, 180 LRRM 1288 (2006).
[12]*Oakwood*, 348 NLRB No. 37, 180 LRRM at 1259.
[13]*Id.* at 1262.
[14]*Id.* See also *Croft Metals*, 348 NLRB No. 38, 180 LRRM at 1298–99 (further elucidating the dividing line between "assigning" and giving ad hoc instructions regarding tasks).
[15]348 NLRB No. 39, 180 LRRM 1288, 1291 (2006).

be undertaken next or who shall do it."[16] But, by virtue of the word "responsibly," the making of such decisions is a supervisory power only if the person giving the direction is "accountable for the performance of the task by the other, such that some adverse consequence may befall the one providing the oversight if the tasks performed by the employee are not performed properly."[17] In order to prove supervisory status, therefore, "it must be shown that the employer delegated to the putative supervisor the authority to direct the work and the authority to take corrective action, if necessary. It also must be shown that there is a prospect of adverse consequences for the putative supervisor if he/she does not take these steps."[18] The Board further indicated that, under this test, an employee would be deemed a supervisor only if the employee's "fundamental alignment is with management" and not with fellow workers.[19] In other words, one is a supervisor under this portion of the statutory test only if the workplace yields "the dynamics of hierarchical authority," such that "the directing employee will have, if and to the extent necessary, an adversarial relationship with those he is directing."[20]

Furthermore, *Oakwood Healthcare* confirms that the power to "assign" and the power "responsibly to direct," like all other parts of the statutory test, amount to supervisory authority only if they are performed with "independent judgment."[21] Under the *Oakwood Healthcare* interpretation, the use of professional or technical judg-

---

[16]Oakwood Healthcare, Inc., 348 NLRB No. 37, 180 LRRM 1257, 1264 n.28 (2006). The Board indicated, however, that a "de minimus principle obviously applies," meaning for instance that the giving of a single ad hoc direction would not be enough to prove supervisory status.

[17]*Id.* at 1264.

[18]*Id.* at 1265. *See also id.* at 1268 (direction held not "responsible" where the putative supervisors were "accountable only for their *own* performance or lack thereof, not the performance of *others*") (emphasis in original); *Golden Crest*, 180 LRRM at 1292–93 (direction held not "responsible" where, although putative supervisors were evaluated on their performance in directing others, there was no evidence that positive or negative material consequences resulted from such evaluations); Croft Metals, 348 NLRB No. 38, 180 LRRM 1293, 1299 (2006) (direction held "responsible" where putative supervisors had received "written warnings . . . because of the failure of their crews to meet production goals or because of other shortcomings of their crews").

[19]*Oakwood*, 180 LRRM at 1265.

[20]*Id.*

[21]*Id.* at 1261.

ment can constitute "independent judgment." "Independent judgment" necessarily implies the use of discretion.[22]

The Board further held in *Oakwood Healthcare* that a person who "spends a regular and substantial portion of his/her work time performing supervisory functions" is a supervisor even if he or she occupies a nonsupervisory role during other periods.[23] Under this formulation, "regular" means "according to a pattern or schedule, as opposed to sporadic substitution."[24] And, while eschewing a strict numerical standard as to what portion of work time is "substantial" under this test, the Board indicated that employees who occupy a supervisory role "for at least 10–15 percent of their total work time" have been deemed supervisors.[25]

Under *Oakwood Healthcare*, as under prior case law, the burden of proof rests with the party contending that individuals are supervisors.[26] The post-*Oakwood* decision in *Avante at Wilson, Inc.*[27] underscores this point. There, the Board emphasized that "particularized" evidence is required, to show with "specificity" the existence of supervisory authority.[28] The Board also noted that the evidence must be specific as to time frame, in that evidence of supervisory authority held at some point in the past is not proof of supervisory authority held at present.[29] Furthermore, the Board noted that indications of supervisory authority in "paper" evidence (such as job descriptions) will not necessarily suffice to demonstrate supervisory authority in actual practice.[30]

---

[22] *Id.* at 1265–67 and at 1268–71 (demonstrating at length, on the facts of the particular case, the Board's approach to the required amount of "discretion" involved in "independent judgment"); *Croft Metals*, 180 LRRM at 1299 (holding that the employer had failed to prove that the putative supervisors used independent judgment in their direction of others).

[23] 348 NLRB No. 37, 180 LRRM 1257, 1267 (2006).

[24] *Id.*

[25] *Id. See also* Golden Crest Healthcare Ctr., 348 NLRB No. 39, 180 LRRM 1288, 1291 n.9 (2006) (individuals will not be deemed supervisors "based on alleged authority that they were never notified they possessed, where its exercise is sporadic and infrequent").

[26] *Oakwood*, 180 LRRM at 1260.

[27] 348 NLRB No. 71, 180 LRRM 1425 (2006).

[28] *Id.*, 180 LRRM at 1426.

[29] *Id.*

[30] *Id.*

b. Managerial Employees

The District of Columbia Circuit held that the Board did not give ample explanation for its fact-intensive decision as to whether faculty of a particular university are managerial employees.[31]

j. Retired Employees

In *Letter Carriers Branch 1227 (United States Postal Service),*[32] the Board noted, but did not decide, the issue of whether a union owes a duty of fair representation to retired employees. The case involved a challenge by retired employees to a union's distribution of proceeds from settlement of a grievance. The Board held that even if the union owed a duty of fair representation to the retirees, it did not breach that duty.

IV. DISCRETIONARY ADMINISTRATIVE JURISDICTIONAL STANDARDS

B. Specific Assertions or Denials of Coverage

In *Firstline Transportation Security,*[33] the Board asserted jurisdiction over an employer that provided airport passenger and baggage screening services under a contract with the Transportation Security Administration. The Board rejected the employer's request that it decline jurisdiction on the grounds of national security. The Board noted that for decades, "in times of both war and peace, the Board has asserted jurisdiction over employers and employees that have been involved in national security and defense," without any evidence that the Board's protection of Section 7 rights had impaired national security.[34]

---

[31]Point Park Univ. v. NLRB, 457 F.3d 42, 180 LRRM 2072 (D.C. Cir. 2006).
[32]347 NLRB No. 27, 179 LRRM 1261 (2006).
[33]347 NLRB No. 40, 179 LRRM 1348 (2006).
[34]*Id.,* 179 LRRM at 1355.

CHAPTER 28

FEDERAL PREEMPTION OF STATE REGULATION

235

II. EVOLUTION OF PREEMPTION DOCTRINE

G. A Foundation: *Garmon* Preempts State Regulation of Conduct Arguably Protected or Prohibited by the Act

A California statute prohibiting the use of state funds to promote or deter union organizing was upheld in *Chamber of Commerce v. Lockyer.*[1] The statute prohibits private employers who receive in excess of $10,000 in state grant or program funds in a calendar year from using such monies to "assist, promote, or deter union organizing." Sitting en banc, the Ninth Circuit held the statute was not subject to *Garmon* preemption, rejecting the contention that the funds restriction interferes with the free speech of employers. Section 8(c), the court held, merely prohibits noncoercive employer speech from being used as evidence of an unfair labor practice and does not affirmatively grant any speech right. In any case, the court further held, the state's strong interest in control of its purse strings brought the statute within a recognized *Garmon* exception. The Second Circuit has reached a contrary view, holding that Section 8(c) does protect employer speech in the union organizing context.[2]

ERISA[3] claims brought by employee-participants asserting that the employer's summary plan descriptions and employee benefit books were misleading were not preempted by *Garmon.*[4]

---

[1]463 F.3d 1076, 180 LRRM 2641 (9th Cir. 2006).
[2]Healthcare Ass'n of N.Y. State, Inc. v. Pataki, 471 F.3d 87, 180 LRRM 3265 (2d Cir. 2006) (finding disputed factual issues precluded summary judgment on *Garmon* preemption issue).
[3]Employee Retirement Income Security Act of 1974, 29 U.S.C. §1001 et seq.
[4]Lupiani v. Wal-Mart Stores, Inc., 435 F.3d 842, 178 LRRM 2940 (8th Cir. 2006).

H. *Briggs & Stratton* Overruled: States May Not Regulate Economic Weapons Furnished by Congress

The Ninth Circuit held that California's statute that prohibits the use of state funds to promote or deter union organizing is not preempted by the *Machinists* doctrine.[5] Although the statute was found to be "regulatory," and thus not protected by the market-participant exception, it does not interfere with an employer's ability to engage in self-help by using its own funds in connection with union organizing.

Courts continue to recognize that the *Machinists* doctrine does not preempt states and local governments from establishing minimum labor standards.[6] Thus, a public utilities commission's determination that prevailing wages must be paid on energy utility construction projects was not preempted.[7] A state law that permits federally recognized joint labor-management committees[8] to access certified payroll records of contractors on public works projects for prevailing wage law enforcement purposes also was not preempted.[9]

Efforts to criminalize the hiring of strike replacements run afoul of *Machinists'* protection of economic weapons of self-help left unregulated by the Act.[10]

---

[5]*Lockyer*, 463 F.3d 1076, 180 LRRM 2641; *see also Healthcare Ass'n of N.Y.*, 471 F.3d 87, 180 LRRM 3265 (finding disputed factual issues precluded summary judgment on *Machinists* preemption issue).

[6]Metropolitan Life Ins. Co. v. Massachusetts, 471 U.S. 724, 754–55, 119 LRRM 2569, 2581–82 (1985).

[7]Southern Cal. Edison Co. v. Public Utils. Comm'n, 140 Cal. App. 4th 1085, 179 LRRM 3215 (Cal. Ct. App. 2d Dist.), *review denied*, (Cal. 2006) ("[t]he prevailing wage requirement at issue here governs a substantial employment term but does not affect the process of collective bargaining or self organization"); *see also* Woodfin Suite Hotels v. City of Emeryville, No. 06-1254 SBA, 2006 WL 2739309, 180 LRRM 2614 (N.D. Cal. Aug. 23, 2006) (minimum wage ordinance applicable to large hotels was not preempted, despite contention that measure impermissibly interjected municipality into labor negotiations and interfered with hotels' use of economic weapons).

[8]*See* 29 U.S.C. §175a.

[9]Helix Elec., Inc. v. Division of Labor Standards Enforcement, No. CIV. 05-2303 FCD KJM, 2006 WL 464083, 179 LRRM 2138 (E.D. Cal. Feb. 27, 2006), *aff'd*, 203 Fed. Appx. 813, 180 LRRM 2960 (9th Cir. 2006).

[10]520 S. Mich. Ave. Assocs. Ltd. v. Devine, 433 F.3d 961, 178 LRRM 2833 (7th Cir. 2006).

III. *Garmon* Preemption in Specific Situations

A. Picketing in General

Garmon preempted a state-law claim to enjoin a union from having its members bang on buckets or make similar noise while leafleting and handbilling outside the Empire State Building, despite the trial court's finding that the volume was sufficient to cause stress and psychological harm to building tenants after prolonged exposure.[11]

D. Other Intentional Torts

1. *Defamation:* Linn v. Plant Guard Workers

Under *Linn*,[12] defamation claims arising out of labor disputes must demonstrate "actual malice," such that the defamatory statement was made "with knowledge that it was false or with reckless disregard of whether it was false or not." Thus, a construction company's claim for defamation failed where the defendant union's charge that the employer had "cheated" its employees in allegedly underpaying health and retirement contributions was, at worst, a matter of dispute by the parties' respective expert auditors.[13] Conversely, however, actual malice was pled sufficiently to survive a motion to dismiss where the defendant employer and co-workers allegedly made numerous statements knowing them to be false concerning violent and intimidating behavior, illegal drug use, and property destruction by the plaintiff union steward.[14]

2. *Inflicting Emotional Distress:* Farmer v. Carpenters

A claim for intentional infliction of emotional distress brought by a union steward against his employer and co-workers was not preempted where the alleged conduct, although stemming from a labor dispute, was assertedly committed in a "particularly abusive

---

[11]Helmsley-Spear, Inc. v. Fishman, 2007 N.Y. slip op. 03340, 2007 WL 1149379 (1st Dep't Apr. 5, 2007), *reversing* 12 Misc. 3d 1151(A), 179 LRRM 2888 (N.Y. Sup. Ct. 2006).

[12]383 U.S. 53, 61 LRRM 2345 (1966).

[13]Chicago Dist. Council of Carpenters Pension Fund v. Reinke Insulation Co., 464 F.3d 651, 180 LRRM 2584 (7th Cir. 2006).

[14]Chung v. McCabe Hamilton & Renny Co., 109 Haw. 520, 179 LRRM 2431 (Haw. 2006).

manner."[15] The court held that the alleged campaign of initiating multiple legal proceedings and spreading false accusations, including witness intimidation, property destruction, and drug use, were "outside the purview of preemption."[16]

3. Fraud, Misrepresentation, and Other Intentional Torts

An employer's claims for tortious interference and statutory fraud were found preempted where the defendant union's handbills alleged the employer had "cheated" its employees in underpaying health and retirement contributions; conflicting opinions by the parties' expert auditors demonstrated a good faith dispute, rather than the "actual malice" required to come within a *Garmon* exception.[17] *Garmon* also preempted tortious interference claims by nonunion employers challenging a union's directing job target and industry advancement fund contributions to other nonunion employers that hired union members to the exclusion of the plaintiffs' employees. The court found the complaint's gravamen was that the union used economic weapons to coerce nonunion employers to hire its members.[18]

A union steward's claims against his employer and co-workers for abuse of process, malicious prosecution, conspiracy, and aiding and abetting were held subject to *Garmon* preemption.[19] The Hawaii Supreme Court found the state-law claims presented a "realistic risk of interference" with the Board's primary jurisdiction to remedy unfair labor practices because the plaintiff's claims included allegations that the defendants' actions were intended to retaliate against plaintiff for his exercise of union activities and to interfere with his employment.

---

[15] *Id.*
[16] *Id.* at 534, 179 LRRM at 2441–42.
[17] *Chicago Dist. Council*, 464 F.3d 651, 180 LRRM 2584.
[18] American Steel Erectors, Inc. v. Iron Workers Local 7, No. 04-12536-RGS, 2006 WL 300422, 178 LRRM 3190 (D. Mass. Feb. 6, 2006).
[19] *Chung*, 109 Haw. 520, 179 LRRM 2431.

IV. PREEMPTION UNDER SECTION 301

B. The Preemptive Effect of Section 301

The principles discussed in the main volume continue to be applied to a variety of state-law claims: breach of contract,[20] tortious interference with business relations,[21] fraudulent misrepresentation,[22] intentional infliction of emotional distress,[23] and negligent infliction of emotional distress.[24]

---

[20]Rose v. Beverly Health & Rehab. Servs., Inc., No. 1:06cv0067 AWI DLB, 2006 WL 2067060, 180 LRRM 2259 (E.D. Cal. July 22, 2006) (discharged employee's state-law claim for breach of individual employment contract was preempted by §301, where her employment was governed by terms of collective bargaining agreement); Fuchs v. Cristal Concrete Corp., No. CV 04-1555 (ETB), 2006 WL 2548169, 180 LRRM 2426 (E.D.N.Y. July 18, 2006) (multi-employer funds' contract claims against signatory employer founded on provision that prohibited subcontracting with nonsignatory employers were preempted by §301); Rentz v. Carsia, No. 3:05-cv-1081, 2006 WL 208799, 178 LRRM 3163 (M.D. Pa. Jan. 24, 2006) (§301 preempted discharged employee's state-law breach-of-contract claim based on employer's alleged denial of contractually prescribed training period because resolution of claim was substantially dependent upon analysis of collective bargaining agreement).

[21]T.H. Eifert, Inc. v. Plumbers & Pipe Fitters, 422 F. Supp. 2d 818, 179 LRRM 2354 (W.D. Mich. 2006) (claim that unions tortiously interfered with employer's business relationship with its workers by inducing them to leave their employment was preempted by §301, where malice or per se wrongful conduct was not alleged and underlying basis of claim was parties' collective bargaining agreement).

[22]Trustees of the Twin City Bricklayers Fringe Benefit Funds v. Superior Waterproofing, Inc., 450 F.3d 324, 179 LRRM 2947 (8th Cir. 2006), rehearing denied, 2006 U.S. App. LEXIS 19820 (8th Cir. Aug. 3, 2006) (contractor's third-party claim that union fraudulently induced it to enter into labor agreement and attendant multi-employer fringe benefit plans was preempted under §301 where analysis of tort claim depended on alleged ambiguity of labor contract); but see Armstrong v. United States Steel Corp., No. 05-1749, 2006 WL 952184, 179 LRRM 2697 (W.D. Pa. Apr. 12, 2006) (retirees' claim that employer misrepresented terms of early retirement package and fraudulently induced its acceptance was not preempted under §301 where alleged misrepresentations concerned information regarding their choice between packages, not terms of labor contract).

[23]George v. AT&T Corp., No. 05-11079-DPW, 2006 WL 1766498, 179 LRRM 3205 (D. Mass. June 23, 2006) (retired employee's claim of intentional infliction of emotional distress was preempted by §301 where claim arose from labor contract).

[24]Id.

Employment discrimination claims are not preempted if premised on rights conferred by state law rather than the underlying collective bargaining agreement.[25]

Likewise, claims under state-law wage payment statutes are not preempted by Section 301 if not founded directly on rights created by, or substantially dependent on analysis of, an underlying collective bargaining agreement.[26]

C. Relationship to NLRB

2. Jurisdiction in Representation Matters

While the Board and the courts have concurrent jurisdiction over Section 301 suits that involve representation issues, cases that are "primarily representational" are reserved to the primary jurisdiction of the Board[27] and those that are "primarily contractual" may be resolved by the courts.[28]

---

[25]Peters v. Sikorsky Aircraft Corp., No. 3:04cv1066(PCD), 2006 WL 2331077, 180 LRRM 2414 (D. Conn. Aug. 10, 2006) (disability discrimination); Williams v. Lockheed Martin Space Operations Co., No. C-05-05210 RMW, 2006 WL 1329889, 179 LRRM 3183 (N.D. Cal. May 16, 2006) (disability discrimination); Adkins v. M&G Polymers USA, LLC, No. 3:05-0052, 2006 WL 659501, 179 LRRM 2321 (S.D. W. Va. Mar. 13, 2006) (age discrimination).

[26]Bluford v. Safeway Stores, No. 2:06cv0523GEBPANJFM, 2006 WL 2131310, 180 LRRM 2243 (E.D. Cal. July 27, 2006); Adams v. Indiana Newspapers, Inc., No. 1:05-cv-1395-DFN-TAB, 2006 WL 2135211, 180 LRRM 2150 (S.D. Ind. July 7, 2006); Doglietto v. AT Sys. West, Inc., No. CIV.S-05-2269LKK/DAD, 2006 WL 194447, 179 LRRM 2061 (E.D. Cal. Jan. 24, 2006).

[27]JBM Inc. v. Production Workers Local 707, 454 F. Supp. 2d 680, 179 LRRM 2757 (S.D. Ohio 2006) (district court deferred issues arising out of employer's declaratory judgment action to Board's primary jurisdiction where dispute involved representational issues and unfair labor practice charges and representation petitions were pending before Board).

[28]MacLellan Indus. Servs. v. Painters Local 1176, No. C 06-04021-MJJ, 2006 WL 2884410, 180 LRRM 3026 (N.D. Cal. Oct. 10, 2006) (district court had jurisdiction over employer's §301 suit for declaratory and injunctive relief against painters union that disclaimed representation after AFL-CIO umpire awarded disputed work to auto workers union, notwithstanding "representational overtones" of dispute); Food & Commercial Workers Local 400 v. West Virginia-Am. Water Co., No. CIV.A2:02-0034, 2006 WL 2822262, 180 LRRM 2901 (S.D. W. Va. Sept. 29, 2006) (action to compel arbitration was properly before district court where underlying dispute involved job eliminations and arbitrator may decide contractual scope of unit question).

V. Preemptive Effect of Other Statutory Provisions

E. Fair Representation

2. *Federal Law Governs*

A union member's state-law claims of fraud and breach of contract were preempted where the alleged knowingly false statements of the union president at a contract ratification meeting were actionable, if at all, only under the duty of the fair representation doctrine.[29]

---

[29]Summerville v. State, County & Mun. Employees Local 77, No. 1:05cv00101, 2006 WL 1932657, 180 LRRM 2105 (M.D.N.C. July 11, 2006).

ACCOMMODATIONS TO OTHER FEDERAL ENACTMENTS

I. THE NLRA AND THE ANTITRUST LAW

F. Application of the Statutory and Nonstatutory Exemption After *Connell*

The plaintiff contractor in *United Rentals Highway Technologies, Inc. v. Indiana Constructors, Inc.*[1] sued an employers' association and its construction unions, alleging that the subcontracting clause in their collective bargaining agreements violated Section 1 of the Sherman Act[2] and state antitrust laws. The subcontracting clause required the association contractors not to contract work under the agreement to

---

[1] No. 1:05-cv-0571-SEB-VSS, 2006 WL 3391350 (S.D. Ind. Nov. 22, 2006).
[2] 15 U.S.C. §1.

firms that did not have a labor agreement or would not sign a labor agreement with the unions.

The court found that the subcontracting clause was permitted under the construction proviso to Section 8(e) of the Act.[3] Based on that finding, the court rejected plaintiff's claim that the clause violated the Sherman Act. The court distinguished the Supreme Court's decision in *Connell Construction Co.*[4] on the basis that the subcontracting clause existed within the context of a collective bargaining relationship. The court found that any anticompetitive effect arising from the clause was mitigated by the policy in favor of collective bargaining, and therefore the agreement was entitled to the nonstatutory exemption from federal antitrust scrutiny.

In *Reed v. Advocate Health Care*,[5] a group of registered nurses sued eight hospitals alleging that the hospitals had conspired to depress the wages of their RN employees, including exchanging public and private wage information. One hospital, whose RNs were represented by a union, filed for summary judgment on the ground that the wages of its RNs were collectively bargained and the complaint was therefore barred by the nonstatutory exemption to federal antitrust laws.

The court denied the motion for summary judgment, finding that the nonstatutory labor exemption did not apply. The court found that the fact that an employer was party to a collective bargaining agreement did not by itself immunize it from suit under the antitrust laws, particularly where none of its alleged co-conspirator employers was a party to the agreement. The court found that the alleged multi-employer conduct occurred outside the context of any collective bargaining scenario.

In *Painters Local 1974 v. Bovis Lend Lease Interiors, Inc.*,[6] the court denied a claim that a multi-employer subcontracting agreement giving exclusive jurisdiction to one union local violated antitrust laws and Section 8(e). The court found that the agreement fell within the nonstatutory exceptions because it was the result of bona fide, arms-length bargaining and because another union had been enjoined from participating in the disputed work.

---

[3]29 U.S.C. §8(e).
[4]Connell Construction Co. v. Plumbers & Pipe Fitters Local 100, 421 U.S. 616, 89 LRRM 2401 (1975).
[5]No. 06 CV 3337, 06 C 3569, 2007 WL 967932 (N.D. Ill. Mar. 28, 2007).
[6]No. 05 cv 2746 (JG), 2005 WL 2205836 (E.D.N.Y. Sept. 9, 2005).

G. Employer Antitrust Suits as Illegal Retaliation for Protected Activity

No Board or court cases have applied *BE&K Construction Co. v. NLRB*[7] in the last year. However, the Division of Advice has issued several memoranda authorizing dismissal of charges that alleged that reasonably based, but unsuccessful, lawsuits violated the Act.[8]

II. THE NLRA AND THE BANKRUPTCY CODE

A. Power of Bankruptcy Court to Reject Collective Bargaining Agreement

1. Requirements for Rejection of a Collective Bargaining Agreement

In their interpretation of Section 1113 of the Bankruptcy Code, courts have continued to apply the analysis set forth by the bankruptcy court in *In re American Provision Co.*[9]

Three cases that concerned the reorganization of Comair, a subsidiary of Delta Airlines, presented several interesting issues growing out of the application of Section 1113. Two of the cases arose out of the proposed rejection of the collective bargaining agreement covering the employer's flight attendants.

In the first case,[10] the court denied Comair's motion to reject the agreement. The court's opinion is instructive on two points. In addressing the requirement for "necessary" modifications, it accepted Comair's position that its labor costs were not competitive with other similarly situated carriers and rejected the union's theory that the modifications were unnecessary because the costs for the flight attendants were relatively small compared to the other employee groups and in relationship to so-called "output costs." The union's "last man standing" argument, i.e., that one relatively minor holdout cost constituency is not economically necessary, could not be sustained in the face of the requirement that all affected parties be treated fairly and equitably. However, the court denied Comair's

---

[7]536 U.S. 516, 170 LRRM 2225 (2002).

[8]Competitive Interiors, Inc., 8-CA-36410, 2006 WL 2040103 (Apr. 26, 2007); ER Advance Ceramics, 8-CA-36318, 2006 WL 2040102 (Mar. 21, 2006); First Student, Inc.,18-CA-18030, 2006 WL 2647541 (Aug. 4, 2006); Mainline Masonry, 4-CA-33391, 2006 WL 1584886 (Feb. 8, 2006).

[9]44 B.R. 907, 118 LRRM 2059 (Bankr. D. Minn. 1984).

[10]*In re* Delta Airlines, Inc., 342 B.R. 685 (S.D.N.Y. 2006).

motion on grounds that the employer had not conferred in good faith because it had taken a position that the wage concessions necessary to achieve its cost reductions were non-negotiable. The court ordered the parties back to the bargaining table.

After the parties resumed bargaining, and were unsuccessful in reaching agreement, Comair renewed its motion to reject the agreement. Based in large part on the parties conduct in this second round of negotiations, the court granted the motion.[11] In the second round of negotiations, Comair focused on changes in work rules to achieve the cost reductions, while proposing to maintain existing pay and benefits. The union refused to negotiate over the proposed changes in work rules. The court granted the motion based on its conclusion that the proposed changes in work rules were necessary for the reorganization, Comair's professed willingness to continue negotiating, and the union's declaration that its earlier proposal was final.

In the third case arising from the Comair bankruptcy,[12] the bankruptcy court granted Comair's motion to reject its agreement with the Air Line Pilots Association. The court based its order on its findings that the economies sought by the employer were necessary for its reorganization, the proposed modifications treated the parties fairly and equitably, the employer had conferred in good faith with the union, the union did not have good cause to reject the proposal, and the balance of the equities clearly favored rejection.

In *Flight Attendants v. Mesaba Aviation, Inc.*,[13] the district court reversed a bankruptcy court's order that had granted a motion to reject. The district court noted that the Eighth Circuit had not decided on the correct standard to determine "necessity" under Section 1113. It proceeded to apply the standard adopted by the Second Circuit in *Teamsters Local 807 v. Carey Transportation, Inc.*,[14] rather than the less flexible standard set forth in *Wheeling-Pittsburgh Steel Corp. v. Steelworkers.*[15] The court concluded that the employer's refusal to negotiate a snap-back provision, and its failure to demonstrate that its proposal fairly and equitably spread the burden of reorganization among all relevant affected parties, particularly its parent corporation, justified reversal.

---

[11] *Id.*
[12] *Id.*
[13] 350 B.R. 435, 180 LRRM 2734 (D. Minn. 2006).
[14] 816 F.2d 82, 125 LRRM 2093 (2d Cir. 1987).
[15] 791 F.2d 1074, 122 LRRM 2425 (3d Cir. 1986).

In *In re Northwest Airlines Corp.*,[16] the bankruptcy court granted the employer's motion to reject its collective bargaining agreement with the Professional Flight Attendants Association. The court concluded that rejection of the agreement was necessary to the employer's reorganization, the employer engaged in good faith bargaining, there was no showing that the employer's proposals treated the union unfairly compared to others affected by the bankruptcy, the proposal was rejected by the union without good cause, and the equities clearly favored rejection. In concluding that the union rejected the proposal without good cause, the court focused on two factors: (1) the union leadership agreed to the proposal subject to ratification, and thereafter may have not given the agreement support during the ratification process; and (2) after the union agreed on the amount of the concessions, it failed to come forward with any alternative proposal that would have reached the target. The court stayed its order for 14 days to give the parties the opportunity to conduct further negotiations, but if no agreement was reached, authorized the employer to implement new terms and conditions of employment consistent with those set forth in the unratified agreement with the union.

Following rejection of the agreement with the union, and Northwest Airlines' implementation of the proposed agreement, the union served the employer with a notice of intent to engage in strike activity. When the employer sought a preliminary injunction in the bankruptcy court, relief was denied based on the court's determination that it was deprived of jurisdiction under the Norris-LaGuardia Act.[17] The district court concluded that the Norris-LaGuardia Act did not preclude the exercise of jurisdiction, reversed the bankruptcy court, and granted a preliminary injunction against the strike.[18] The Second Circuit affirmed,[19] reasoning that an injunction was appropriate because: (1) Northwest's rejection of its collective bargaining agreement after obtaining authorization to do so under Section 1113 abrogated, without breaching, the existing agreement, which thereafter ceased to exist; (2) Northwest's abrogation of the agreement necessarily terminated the status quo created by that agreement, after which both the RLA's explicit status quo provisions and the implicit status quo requirements of Section 2 (First) of the RLA

---

[16]346 B.R. 333, 180 LRRM 2335 (Bankr. S.D.N.Y. 2006).
[17]*Id.*
[18]349 B.R. 338 (S.D.N.Y. 2006).
[19]483 F.3d 160, 181 LRRM 2752 (2d Cir. 2007).

ceased to apply; and (3) the union's proposed strike would violate its independent duty under the RLA to "exert every reasonable effort to make... [an] agreement." In dicta, the court suggested that a union subject to the NLRA would be free to strike, after abrogation of the agreement under Section 1113.

In *In re Allied Holdings, Inc.*,[20] the court addressed whether an order for interim relief under Section 1113(e) was appealable. The union appealed the bankruptcy court's order granting the employer's application for interim relief consisting of a wage reduction and deferral of a wage increase. The union argued that because the employer had not filed an application for rejection of the agreement, the interim order of relief was, for all practical purposes, final and, therefore, appealable because unless a motion for rejection is considered, there would be no way for the order granting interim relief to be appealed. Relying in part on *In re Landmark Hotel & Casino*,[21] the district court concluded that the interim order was not appealable as a final order because (1) Section 1113(e) allows for changes to be made to the order in the future; and (2) Section 1113 permits a debtor to continue to seek authority to reject a collective bargaining agreement even after the bankruptcy court has granted interim relief. The court also rejected the union's motion to grant an interlocutory appeal under 28 U.S.C. §158(a). The court concluded that the bankruptcy's court decision did not involve a controlling question of law, because controlling case law did not prohibit an interim order under Section 1113(e) absent an application for rejection, and because the case turned upon specific facts.

2. *Modification of Post-Retirement Health Benefits*

In *In re Oremet Corp.*,[22] the employer filed a motion for modification under Section 1114 after a plan of reorganization had already been confirmed. The union objected to the modification on grounds that Section 1114 relief was not available post-confirmation. The court rejected the union's argument, noting that the legislative history did not support the union's claim and that Section 1129, also relied on by the union, simply requires that a plan provide for the same level of retiree benefits that Section 1114 protects after the petition is filed, but does not foreclose the debtor from seeking modifi-

---

[20] 2007 WL 474731 (N.D. Ga. Feb. 9, 2007).
[21] 872 F.2d 857, 131 LRRM 2093 (9th Cir. 1989).
[22] 355 BR 37, 179 LRRM 2632 (S.D. Ohio 2006).

cations after confirmation. The court rejected the union's argument that the necessity for Section 1114 relief was to be determined under *Wheeling-Pittsburgh Steel Corp. v. Steelworkers*[23] (requiring that a proposed modification to a collective bargaining agreement must be necessary to prevent liquidation). The court observed that the plain language of Section 1114 requires that modification be "necessary to permit the reorganization of the debtor." The court also rejected the employer's argument that, under the facts, the union was barred by the doctrine of equitable mootness from objecting to Section 1114 relief.

In *In re Towers Automotive, Inc.*,[24] the employer entered into a settlement with the union under which retiree medical benefits, and other retirement benefits, were waived in exchange for a guaranteed sum equal to 20 percent of the employees' unsecured claims. The unsecured creditors committee objected to the settlement on the ground that it impermissibly favored retirees over other unsecured creditors, and constituted a sub rosa plan of reorganization. The court rejected the first argument because the intent of Section 1114 was to ensure that debtors did not seek to effect reorganization on the back of retirees for the benefit of other parties in interest. It rejected the second argument because the settlement did not dispose of virtually all of the assets, did not dispose of all claims against the debtors, and the right of unsecured creditors to vote was not impaired.

3. Bargaining After Rejection Is Authorized

There have been two recent decisions of significance in the airline industry, in which courts have enjoined strikes after the rejection of a collective bargaining agreement.[25] These cases arise under the Railway Labor Act, and the courts specifically distinguished cases decided under the NLRA.

In *Northwest Airlines*,[26] the district court held that, under the RLA, the bankruptcy court had jurisdiction to enjoin the union's threatened strike in response to the company's authorized rejection of the existing collective bargaining agreement. The court noted that parallels to precedent under the NLRA should be "drawn with care"

---

[23]791 F.2d 1074, 122 LRRM 2425 (3d Cir. 1986).
[24]241 F.R.D. 162 (S.D.N.Y. 2006).
[25]*In re Northwest Airlines* 349 B.R. 338 (S.D.N.Y. 2006); *In re* Mesaba Aviation, Inc., 350 B.R. 112 (Bankr. D. Minn. 2006).
[26]*In re Northwest Airlines* at 383.

because of "fundamental differences in the purposes and schemes of these statutes."[27] Specifically, the court found that the NLRA expressly protects the right to strike and there is "no general federal anti-strike policy" under the NLRA.[28] By contrast, the court found that "the RLA contains no such express provisions and, while not removing a union's right to strike once its procedures are exhausted, imposes an elaborate, almost interminable process before such right to strike accrues."[29]

The bankruptcy court, in *Mesaba Aviation*[30] followed the decision in *Northwest Airlines* and enjoined the unions from striking after the court authorized the company to reject the existing collective bargaining agreements. In response to the union's argument based on case law under the NLRA, the court noted that such cases "are not good authority on the issues presented here."[31]

B. Priority of Wage and Employee Benefit Plan Contributions

1. Pre-Petition Claims

The split among the circuits regarding unpaid pre-petition workers' compensation premiums has now been resolved. In *Howard Delivery Service, Inc. v. Zurich American Insurance Co.*,[32] the Supreme Court reversed the Fourth Circuit and held that a claim for pre-petition workers' compensation premiums was not entitled to priority status under Section 507(a)(5) because such premiums are not "contributions to an employee benefit plan...arising from services rendered."

The Court in *Howard* did not address the separate question of whether insurance companies or insurance brokers are among the class of persons entitled to receive priority under Section 507(a)(5) for contributions to employee benefit plans. Courts continue to disagree over this issue.[33]

---

[27] *Id.* at 370.
[28] *Id.* at 371.
[29] *Id.*
[30] 350 B.R. 112.
[31] *Id.* at 127 n.16.
[32] 126 S. Ct. 2105 (2006).
[33] *Cf. In re* Build Tech Sys., Inc., 339 B.R. 328 (Bankr. D. Vt. 2006) (insurers entitled to priority) *with In re* Edward W. Minte Co., Inc., 286 B.R. 1 (Bankr. D.D.C. 2002) (insurers not entitled to priority).

2. Post-Petition Claims for Wages and Benefits Due Under an Unrejected Agreement

Post-petition wage and benefit contribution claims are now generally second priority claims, behind certain domestic support obligations, but may take first priority if a trustee has been appointed or elected.[34]

The Tenth Circuit has joined the Second and Third Circuits in holding that Section 1113(f) does not accord "superpriority" status to wage and benefit claims arising under a collective bargaining agreement unless they are post-petition administrative claims.[35] *Shipwrights Local 2071 v. Uniflite, Inc.*,[36] cited in the Main Edition, was later vacated as moot.[37]

3. Priority of Claims for Wages and Benefits Due Under Rejected Agreement

The Tenth Circuit refused to follow the "minority position" that adopts a "superpriority" for claims implicated by Section 1113, even when the requirements of Section 503 have not been met.[38]

III. THE NLRA AND IMMIGRATION LAW

In *Concrete Form Walls, Inc.*,[39] the Board issued a *Gissel* bargaining order where the employer threatened Hispanic employees with termination and, following the election, discharged four of the employees. The employer asserted that it fired the employees because they were undocumented aliens. At the hearing, the employer sought to rely on an Internet data base search that showed that the social security numbers did not match the names of the employees. The proffered evidence was found to be deficient because it did not identify to whom the social security numbers were properly assigned and because the employer's eleventh-hour concern with IRCA compliance was merely a pretext in light of the fact that the employer had

---

[34]11 U.S.C. §507(a)(1), (2) (2005).
[35]Peters v. Pikes Peak Musicians Ass'n, 462 F.3d 1265, 180 LRRM 2456 (10th Cir. 2006).
[36]110 B.R. 585 (Bankr. M.D. Fla. 1990).
[37]140 B.R. 298 (M.D. Fla. 1992). In addition, *In re Spirit Holding Co.*, cited in the Main Edition, is reported at 157 B.R. 879 (Bankr. E.D. Mo. 1993).
[38]*Peters v. Pikes Peak Musicians*, 462 F.3d 1265, 1269–71.
[39]346 NLRB No. 80, 179 LRRM 1193 (2006).

long held suspicions that the employees were undocumented. Citing *Sure-Tan v. NLRB*[40] and explaining *Hoffman Plastic Compounds, Inc. v. NLRB*,[41] the Board further ruled that there was no basis for the employer's claim that the four Hispanic employees were not statutory employees within the meaning of the Act and ruled they were eligible to vote in an election.

In a class action sex discrimination case, *EEOC v. City of Joliet*,[42] a court entered a protective order prohibiting the employer from requiring plaintiffs to complete I-9 employment eligibility verification forms during the pendency of the litigation. The court based its ruling on the fact that the employer had not previously required employees to complete I-9s and because of "the *in terrorem* effect of inquiring into the immigration status of employees suing their employers."[43]

In 2006, a significant amount of litigation arose from a number of organized protests, including a "Day Without Latinos," in which employees were encouraged by protest organizers to leave or avoid work in order to participate in demonstrations against stricter immigration laws and enforcement. In a number of instances, employers terminated employees who failed to appear for work and the employees or unions filed charges alleging that the terminations violated the Act because the employees were engaged in activity protected by Section 7. In a memorandum issued by the NLRB's Division of Advice in *Applebee's Neighborhood Bar & Grill*,[44] the Division advised the region handling the case to dismiss the charge because, regardless of whether the employee's activity was protected, the employer explicitly terminated the employees only because they walked off the job—not because they attended a demonstration. In reaching its conclusion, the Division pointed out that "Leaving work early is not protected activity even when the object of leaving is to engage in protected activity."[45] The Division assumed without deciding that attendance at the demonstrations was protected and also noted that the case did not involve allegations of animus towards the employees or discriminatory treatment.

---

[40]467 U.S. 883, 116 LRRM 2857 (1984).
[41]535 U.S. 137, 169 LRRM 2769 (2002).
[42]239 F.R.D. 490 (N.D. Ill. 2006).
[43]*Id.* at 492–93.
[44]Case No. 30-CA-17444 (Oct. 17, 2006).
[45]*Id.* (quoting Quantum Elec., 341 NLRB 1270, 1279 (2004)).

RICO AND LABOR LAW

III. Overview of the Statute

A. Key Elements

1. Racketeering Activity

If the alleged predicate act for a RICO claim is fraud, then pursuant to Federal Rule of Civil Procedure 9(b), the facts supporting the alleged claim must be pleaded with particularity.[1]

4. Pattern

The Supreme Court in *H.J. Inc. v. Northwestern Bell Telephone Co.*[2] examined what conduct meets RICO's pattern requirement. A pattern requires at least two predicate acts that are related and that pose a threat of continuing criminal activity.[3]

Because closed-ended continuity is centrally a temporal concept, the lower courts generally have ruled that predicate acts do

---

[1]Stanley v. Electrical Workers (IBEW), 207 Fed. Appx. 185, 180 LRRM 2996 (3d Cir. 2006).

[2]492 U.S. 229 (1989).

[3]Marcoux v. American Airlines, Inc., No. 4CV1376, 2006 WL 842888, 179 LRRM 2546 (E.D.N.Y. Mar. 28, 2006) (court found that plaintiff artificially characterized one alleged criminal purpose as constituting multiple schemes).

not satisfy closed-ended continuity if they occurred over a limited period, although there is no bright-line rule.[4]

B. Three Substantive Violations

2. 18 U.S.C. §1962(b) (Acquiring or Maintaining an Interest in an Enterprise)

b. Control

There is no exact standard for determining the level of authority that must exist for a defendant to have control over an enterprise. Courts have found that the holding of majority stock or actual designation as an officer or director, as well as decision making, can be control.[5]

IV. Predicate Acts Commonly Alleged in Labor Cases

C. 29 U.S.C. §186: Restrictions on Payments and Loans to Labor Organizations

If a payment is made at the request of a person subject to Section 186 (better known as Section 302), the payment, loan, or delivery from an employer to a third party not subject to Section 186 still violates the section, even if the soliciting person did not benefit from it.[6] The offense is triggered by a payment, loan, or delivery of any thing of value, or agreement to do so. A beneficial arrangement such

---

[4]Moon v. Harrison Piping Supply, 465 F.3d 719, 725 (6th Cir. 2006), *cert. denied*, 127 S. Ct. 1832 (2007) (9½-month period of predicate acts, including letter terminating benefits and letter from a doctor stating plaintiff no longer disabled not sufficient); *Marcoux v. American Airlines*, No. 04CV1376, 2006 WL 842888, 179 LRRM 2546 (alleged activity over 11½-month period insufficient and also finding no open-ended continuity).

[5]In *Marceau v. Electrical Workers (IBEW) Local 1269*, No. 05-02874-PHX-MHM, 2006 WL 1889600, 180 LRRM 2088 (D. Ariz. July 7, 2006), the court found that possessing influence over an organization's decision making was sufficient.

[6]United States v. Novak, 443 F.3d 150, 155–56 (2d Cir. 2006) (mutuality of guilt not required to find payor in violation of RICO for payments made to payee that eventually were submitted to union representative), *subsequent appeal at, remanded by* 188 Fed. Appx. 9 (2d Cir.), *cert. denied*, 127 S. Ct. 525 (2006).

as a collective bargaining agreement does not constitute a "thing of value."[7]

E. 18 U.S.C. §1951: "Racketeering" Prohibited by the Hobbs Act

4. *Application of the Hobbs Act to RICO Cases After* Scheidler II

b. The Supreme Court's Interpretation of the Hobbs Act in *Scheidler II* and *Scheidler III*[8] [Revised Heading Title]

In *Link v. Rhodes*[9] the court found that the plaintiff failed to establish that defendants acquired property from him as a result of allegedly ordering his termination, throwing out his complaint, denying the existence of an oral agreement and/or physically attacking him, and intimidating him for criticizing union leadership. The Supreme Court has yet to issue a decision on whether intangible rights constitute property under the Hobbs Act.

c. Courts' Interpretation of the Hobbs Act Post-*Scheidler II*

In *United States v. Bellomo*,[10] defendants were charged with, inter alia, extorting union members' property, that is, their right to democratic participation in the union's affairs as well as their right to the loyal and responsible representation of the union officers, agents, employees, and representatives.[11]

The *Bellomo* decision and the decision in *United States v. Coffey*[12] were essentially, though not explicitly, overruled in *United States v. Gotti*.[13] In *Gotti*, the defendants appealed their convictions, arguing, among other things, that because LMRDA rights cannot be legally

---

[7]Adcock v. Auto Workers, No. 3: 06CV32, 2006 WL 3257044, 180 LRRM 3291 (W.D.N.C. Nov. 9, 2006) (dismissing claim based upon allegation that card-check agreement between union and employer constituted a "thing of value" that was improperly exchanged).

[8]National Org. for Women v. Scheidler, 537 U.S. 393 (2003).

[9]No. C 06-0356 MHP, 2006 WL 3050859 (N.D. Ca. Oct. 25, 2006); *see also* United States v. Gotti, 459 F.3d 296, 180 LRRM 2199 (2d Cir. 2006) (acknowledging that *Scheidler II* did not overrule *Tropiano's* holding that intangible rights constitute property under the Hobbs Act).

[10]263 F. Supp. 2d 561, 575 (E.D.N.Y. 2003).

[11]*Id.* at 569.

[12]361 F. Supp. 2d 102 (E.D.N.Y. 2005).

[13]459 F.3d 296, 180 LRRM 2199 (2d Cir. 2006) (involving intangible rights guaranteed by the LMRDA including: the right to fully and freely participate in the internal affairs and governance of a union; to run for union office; to assemble and express opinions regarding unions; to support and campaign on behalf of a candidate of their choice; as well as right to fair and loyal representation).

exercised by third parties, they cannot support a RICO conviction.[14] The Second Circuit rejected this claim, pointing out that this approach "gives rise to the untenable implication that one can never 'extort,' under the Hobbs Act, illegal property (such as narcotics) because such property cannot be legally used, sold, or transferred."[15] The Second Circuit agreed with the majority of district courts in that Circuit that concluded that intangible property can qualify as extortable property under the Hobbs Act, regardless of whether its exercise, transfer, or sale would be legal.[16] In doing so, the Second Circuit solidified the position that "intangible" property rights can support a Hobbs Act claim.[17]

F. Immigration Violations

In *Garmon*, the Supreme Court established the general rule that federal courts do not have jurisdiction over activity which is "arguably subject to §7 and §8" of the National Labor Relations Act and that the courts must defer in such instances "to the exclusive competence of the National Labor Relations Board."[18]

After remand from the Sixth Circuit, in *Trollinger v. Tyson Foods, Inc.*,[19] the district court denied the defendants' motion to permit an interlocutory appeal of the district court's order denying the defendants' motion for judgment on the pleadings based on the argument that the Supreme Court's decision, regarding proximate cause in *Anza Steel Supply Corp. v. Ideal Steel Supply Corp.*,[20] precluded the plaintiffs' claims.[21] Additionally, the district court certified a class consisting of "all persons legally authorized to be employed in the United States who have been employed" at eight specific Tyson

---

[14] *Id.*

[15] *Id.* at 326.

[16] *Id.* at 325–26.

[17] *Id.* In reaching this decision, the Second Circuit explicitly recognized the split in that circuit regarding whether the rights at issue must be capable of being legally exercised by third parties. Relying on *Scheidler II*, it rejected the decisions in *United States v. Bellomo*, 263 F. Supp. 2d 561 (E.D.N.Y. 2003) and *United States v. Coffey*, 361 F. Supp. 2d 102 (E.D.N.Y. 2005).

[18] 359 U.S. 236, 236, 245 (1959).

[19] 370 F.3d 602 (6th Cir. 2004).

[20] 126 S. Ct. 1991 (2006).

[21] No. 4:02-CV-23, 2006 WL 2868980, 180 LRRM 3012 (E.D. Tenn. Sept. 29, 2006).

facilities "since April of 1998 through the present."[22] The court also rejected Tyson's argument that the plaintiffs would be unable to prove damages and injury on a classwide basis, finding that at the class certification stage, the court "need not determine whether or not the expert's...damage calculation model can survive a Daubert challenge...or whether Plaintiffs' wage suppression evidence as a whole will be sufficient to withstand a Rule 56 motion."[23] The court held that the plaintiffs are only "required to establish a 'colorable' basis for establishing damages."[24]

On December 12, 2005, the Supreme Court granted certiorari in *Mohawk Industries, Inc. v. Williams* on the question of "[w]hether a defendant corporation and its agents can constitute an 'enterprise' under the Racketeer Influenced and Corrupt Organizations Act, 18 U.S.C. §§1961–1968 (RICO), in light of the settled rule that a RICO defendant must 'conduct' or 'participate in' the affairs of some larger enterprise and not just its own affairs."[25] After oral argument, the Supreme Court dismissed the writ as improvidently granted but vacated the judgment of the Eleventh Circuit.[26] The Court remanded the case for further consideration in light of the Court's decision in *Anza Steel Supply Corp. v. Ideal Steel Supply Corp.*[27] On remand, the Eleventh Circuit not only ordered supplemental briefing on the issues raised by the Supreme Court's decision in *Anza*, but also on whether a corporation could be sued under the Georgia RICO statute in light of the Georgia Supreme Court's decision in *Williams General Corp. v. Stone.*[28]

On remand the Eleventh Circuit reinstated its prior opinion in part and modified it in part. The court, citing with approval the Ninth Circuit's decision in *Mendoza v. Zirkle Fruit Co.*,[29] held that the plaintiffs had sufficiently alleged an injury to their business or property, i.e., "a legal entitlement to business relations unhampered by schemes prohibited by the RICO predicate statutes."[30]

---

[22]No. 4:02-CV-23, 2006 WL 2924938, 180 LRRM 3016 (E.D. Tenn. Oct. 10, 2006).

[23]*Id.*, 2006 WL 2924938, at *11.

[24]*Id.* (citing J.B.D.L. Corp. v. Wyeth-Ayerst Labs., Inc., 225 F.R.D. 208, 219 (S.D. Ohio 2003)).

[25]126 S. Ct. 830 (2005).

[26]126 S. Ct. 2016 (2006).

[27]126 S. Ct. 1991 (2006).

[28]280 Ga. 631, 632 S.E.2d 376 (2006).

[29]301 F.3d 1163, 1168 (9th Cir. 2002).

[30]465 F.3d 1277, 1286–87, 180 LRRM 2710 (11th Cir. 2006) (citing *Mendoza*, 301 F.3d at 1168 n.4).

The Eleventh Circuit also concluded that even in light of the Supreme Court's decision in *Anza*, the plaintiffs had sufficiently alleged proximate cause to withstand Mohawk's motion to dismiss. The court found that the plaintiffs' allegations that Mohawk's widespread scheme of "knowingly hiring and harboring illegal workers [had] the purpose and direct result of depressing wages paid to the plaintiffs. Simply put, wholesale illegal hiring depresses wages for legal workers in north Georgia where Mohawk is located."[31] The court rejected Mohawk's argument that other economic factors contributed to the plaintiffs' wages, agreeing with the plaintiffs' claim that Mohawk's conduct "grossly distorted those normal market forces by employing literally thousands of illegal, undocumented aliens."[32]

The court also held that the plaintiffs had satisfied RICO's statutory standing requirement that the alleged injury was "directly caused by the RICO violation."[33] The court, again following the Ninth Circuit's decision in *Mendoza*, held that the plaintiffs' allegations that the racketeering activity had the "express purpose and direct result of lowering" their wages were sufficiently direct to permit the plaintiffs standing to sue, since "Mohawk's conduct was aimed primarily at them."[34] The court also held that based on the Georgia Supreme Court's decision in *Williams General Corp.*, a corporation was a "person" under the Georgia RICO Act and subject to liability.[35]

After the plaintiffs filed a second amended complaint, the court in *Zavala v. Wal-Mart Stores, Inc.*[36] once again dismissed the complaint, this time with prejudice, finding numerous infirmities in the plaintiffs' RICO allegations. The court found that the plaintiffs had failed to plead an enterprise distinct from the person, finding that the enterprise consisting of Wal-Mart and its contractors was also pled as the RICO person throughout the complaint, indeed, "woven into the fabric" of the second amended complaint such that it could not be removed without "restructuring the entire RICO theory."[37]

The court, relying on the Supreme Court's decision in *Anza*,[38] also held that the plaintiffs had not alleged a sufficiently direct injury to meet the proximate cause requirement under RICO. The court

---

[31] *Id.* at 1289.
[32] *Id.*
[33] *Id.* at 1291.
[34] *Id.* at 1292.
[35] *Id.* at 1293–94.
[36] 447 F. Supp. 2d 379 (D.N.J. 2006).
[37] *Id.* at 384.
[38] Anza Steel Supply Corp. v. Ideal Steel Supply Corp., 126 S. Ct. 1991 (2006).

found that the plaintiffs' theories of injury did not allege that the immigration violations directly injured the plaintiffs. Instead, the immigration violations caused the plaintiffs to have a certain immigration status that put them in a position of vulnerability that caused an increased possibility of economic exploitation through the underpayment of wages. The court found that "the injury at the end is an indirect result of the acts at the beginning."[39] The court also found that the presence of several independent and intervening causes, such as the decision of the employer to pay a particular wage and the employee to accept and work at that wage, further weakened the plaintiffs' argument of direct injury. The court found that "[s]uch decisions may be related to irregular immigration status, but are largely independent and intervening."[40] The court also found that like the injury alleged in *Anza*, the immigration violations alleged as predicate acts were entirely distinct "from the immediate cause of Plaintiffs' injuries (underpayment of wages)."[41] Likewise, the court found that determining damages "would be unmanageably complex due to the two-step, indirect theory of causation."[42] Finally, the court rejected the plaintiffs' attempts to rely on the courts of appeals' decisions in *Commercial Cleaning, Mendoza, Trollinger,* and *Mohawk,* finding that in those cases the plaintiffs had alleged that the hiring of illegal immigrants proximately caused injury by depressing wages, while in *Zavala,* the plaintiffs had not alleged hiring as a predicate act.[43]

In *Flores v. Limehouse,*[44] the defendants moved for summary judgment arguing that the Supreme Court's decision in *Hoffman Plastics Compounds, Inc. v. NLRB*[45] barred the plaintiffs' RICO claims because they were admitted undocumented aliens. The district court rejected that argument and held that *Hoffman* was not controlling because IRCA did not prohibit an unauthorized alien from bringing a claim under RICO and that any person who "is capable of holding a legal or beneficial interest in property" could bring an action under RICO pursuant to 18 USC §§1961(3) and 1964(c).[46] In *Flores,* the plaintiffs alleged that their injuries were lost wages and since unauthorized aliens are entitled to minimum and overtime wages under the FLSA,

---

[39] *Zavala,* 447 F. Supp. 2d at 386.
[40] *Id.*
[41] *Id.* at 387.
[42] *Id.*
[43] *Id.* at 388.
[44] No.2:04-1295 CWH, 2006 WL 1328762 (D.S.C. May 11, 2006).
[45] 535 U.S. 137 (2002).
[46] No.2:04-1295 CWH, 2006 WL 1328762, at *3 (D.S.C. May 11, 2006).

the plaintiffs had a legal interest in those wages sufficient to bring an action under RICO.[47]

In *Choimbol v. Fairfield Resorts, Inc.*,[48] the plaintiffs were immigrant workers who performed laundry, housekeeping and grounds maintenance services at Fairfield's properties in Williamsburg, Virginia. The plaintiffs were supplied to Fairfield through a network of contractors who contracted with Fairfield to provide immigrant labor for its hotel and resort services.[49] The plaintiffs brought a RICO suit as well as state-law claims and alleged, inter alia, that Fairfield and its contractors conspired to have them work more than 40 hours in a week, not pay them overtime, and to label them as contractors or subcontractors instead of employees in order to avoid paying overtime.[50] The RICO predicate acts alleged by the plaintiffs were mail fraud, wire fraud, and money laundering. Fairfield moved to dismiss the complaint arguing that the plaintiffs had failed to establish the underlying elements needed to state a claim for the predicate acts alleged in the amended complaint. The court disagreed and held that the plaintiffs had "clearly pled that the payroll checks were 'false and deceptive,' by misleading the plaintiffs about their status and rights under the FLSA."[51] The court concluded that the allegations that Fairfield utilized the mails and telephone transmissions in furtherance of the scheme was sufficient to plead mail and wire fraud and the fact that the payroll checks and time cards were mailed in the ordinary course of business was irrelevant because "[t]he mailing and transmittal of payroll checks and timecards were 'step[s] in [the] plot,' and were incident to the essential part of the scheme."[52] The court also found that the plaintiffs had sufficiently pled an open-ended pattern of racketeering under Section 1962(c) by alleging that the defendants' fraudulent scheme involved over 40 individuals, at least five perpetrators and thousands of payroll checks over a three-year period.[53]

Despite having survived an initial motion to dismiss, the plaintiffs in *Choimbol* several months later had their RICO claims dismissed on a motion for judgment on the pleadings. The court found that the FLSA preempted the RICO claims because the FLSA provided

---

[47] *Id.*
[48] 428 F. Supp. 2d 437 (E.D. Va. 2006).
[49] *Id.* at 439–40.
[50] *Id.* at 441.
[51] *Id.* at 444.
[52] *Id.* (citing Badders v. United States, 240 U.S. 391, 394 (1916)).
[53] *Id.* at 447.

the plaintiffs with comprehensive remedies, and that "[b]ut for the proscription of the FLSA, the defendants' conduct would not constitute the fraudulent scheme plaintiffs allege."[54]

The Fifth Circuit in *Abraham v. Singh*[55] reversed the district court's dismissal of the plaintiffs' RICO claims. In *Abraham*, the plaintiffs were citizens of India who were alleged to have been "recruited under false pretenses to become steelworkers in Louisiana" at a steel manufacturing facility. The defendants obtained visas for the plaintiffs that in turn they alleged bound them to work for one of the defendants, Falcon Steel. The plaintiffs alleged that they paid one of the other defendants between $7,000 and $20,000 for these services, often financing these payments by obtaining high interest loans in India.[56] When the plaintiffs arrived in the United States, there were no jobs for them because there was no manufacturing facility, the defendants confiscated their passports, housed them in poor conditions with little food, and threatened the plaintiffs with imprisonment and deportation when they complained about the poor living conditions and lack of work.[57] Additionally, the plaintiffs alleged that the plaintiffs who were able to obtain work did so by being "farmed out" by one of the defendants, were assessed arbitrary fees, and had their wages skimmed. The plaintiffs also alleged that one of the defendants demanded an additional $5,000 to secure the promised permanent resident status.[58] The alleged racketeering acts were Hobbs Act extortion, visa fraud, immigration violations, Travel Act violations, money laundering, and peonage. The district court granted the defendants' motion to dismiss, finding that while the plaintiffs had adequately alleged that the predicate acts were related, their claims failed the continuity prong of the open-ended pattern of racketeering analysis because the predicate acts did not pose a threat of continuing racketeering activity.[59] The district court concluded that because the defendants' actions were part of a single transaction and took place in the past, "the predicate acts neither threatened long-term criminal activity nor constituted defendants' regular way of conducting their business."[60] The Fifth Circuit held that the district court "erred in turning the Supreme Court's expla-

---

[54]No.2:05cv463, 2006 WL 2631791 (E.D. Va. Sept. 11, 2006).
[55]480 F.3d 351 (5th Cir. 2007).
[56]*Id.* at 353–54.
[57]*Id.* at 354.
[58]*Id.*
[59]*Id.*
[60]*Id.* at 355.

nation of the continuity prong into a stringent pleading require-ment."[61] Rather, the Fifth Circuit held that the plaintiffs had satisfied the continuity prong by alleging that the defendants had "engaged in at least a two year scheme involving repeated international travel to convince up to 200 or more Indian citizens to borrow thousands of dollars to travel to the United States only to find upon their arrival that things were not as they had been promised."[62] The court further found that the allegations included not just the plaintiffs' recruit-ment in India but also their treatment in the United States, included multiple victims and that there was no reason to "suppose that the systematic victimization allegedly begun in November of 2000 would not have continued indefinitely had the plaintiffs not filed this law-suit."[63] Accordingly, the court of appeals held that the plaintiffs had satisfied the liberal pleading standard and had adequately alleged continuity of the racketeering activity.

V. Issues in Civil Litigation

A. Standing

3. *"By Reason of"*

In some cases, plaintiffs have failed to satisfy the proximate cause requirement because the alleged damages were either too specula-tive or incidental to the racketeering activity.[64]

E. Statute of Limitations

In addition to the various accrual rules, there is an issue as to whether there is a separate accrual period for new and independent injuries. Plaintiffs invoke this rule when a portion of their injuries is time-barred under the applicable accrual rule. Under this rule, a

---

[61]Abraham v. Singh, 480 F.3d 351, 355–56 (5th Cir. 2007).

[62]*Id.* at 356.

[63]*Id.*

[64]*See, e.g.,* Johnson v. Hoffa, 196 Fed. Appx. 88, 90–91, 180 LRRM 2375 (3d Cir. 2006) (plaintiff failed to establish proximate causation between the racketeering activity, physical assault, extortion, and mail fraud, and the injury, specifically job loss, because the acts occurred after his job loss, thus he also lacked standing); *see also* Moon v. Harrison Piping Supply, 375 F. Supp. 2d 577 (E.D. Mich. 2005), *aff'd in part and reversed in part, remanded by* 465 F.3d 719 (6th Cir. 2006), *cert. denied,* No. 06-891, 2007 WL 789100 (Mar. 19, 2007).

plaintiff may recover for injury discovered within four years of the lawsuit's filing, although the rule is generally limited to new injuries from independent wrongdoing. As noted in the Main Edition, most circuits have recognized this rule of "separate accrual."[65]

VI. REMEDIES

A. Criminal Sentences

Section 1963 provides that any person found to have violated RICO (i.e., Section 1962) "shall be fined...or imprisoned not more than 20 years (or for life if the violation is based on a racketeering activity for which the maximum penalty includes life imprisonment), or both...."[66]

C. Trusteeships and Other Injunctive Relief

As noted by the Third Circuit, the breadth of civil remedies available to the government makes Section 1964, in many ways, "a more powerful provision than its criminal counterpart, section 1963."[67]

---

[65]Marceau v. Electrical Workers (IBEW) Local 1269, No. 05-02874-PHX-MHM, 2006 WL 1889600, 180 LRRM 2088 (D. Ariz. July 7, 2006) (setting forth elements of separate accrual rule: (1) it must be a new and independent act that is not merely a reaffirmation of a previous act; and (2) it must inflict new and accumulating injury on the plaintiff).

[66]18 U.S.C. §§1963(a) (1994); United States v. Boidi, No. CRIM.A.05-10025-GAO, 2006 WL 456004 (D. Mass. Feb. 24, 2006) (convicted party facing up to 20 years in prison for conviction on RICO charges stemming from money laundering scheme).

[67]United States v. Teamsters Local 560, 780 F.2d 267, 295 (3d Cir. 1985), cert. denied, 476 U.S. 1140, 122 LRRM 2368 (1986). In a similar vein, supervision of a roofers' local by a court-appointed independent monitor was part of a plea agreement under New York's Organized Crime Control Act with respect to extortion charges against several officials of the local in New York v. Roofers Local 8, N.Y. Sup. Ct., Indictment No. 3194, guilty plea 9/19/06.

NLRB PROCEDURES

II. Procedures in Representation Cases

A. The Petition

The Board granted review of the regional director's decision in *Marriott Hartford Downtown Hotel.*[1] In that case, the union sought a neutrality and card-check agreement. The employer filed a petition for an election under Section 9(c)(1)(B). The regional director dismissed the petition based on *New Otani Hotel & Garden*,[2] holding that informational picketing and repeated requests for neutrality and a card-check agreement do not constitute a present demand for recognition. In granting review the Board indicated a willingness to reexamine what sort of activities by a union constitute a "demand for recognition" and whether a card check or an election "is the better way to ascertain employee free choice." [3]

B. Timeliness of Petitions

For the purpose of a unit clarification, the petition must be filed "shortly after" the contract is executed. In *Sunoco Inc.,* [4] the Board measured the time from the date unit employees ratified a memorandum of agreement regarding the parties' collective bargaining contract, not the date of execution of the contract. The period for measuring timeliness was tolled by the parties' decision to engage in further negotiations.

C. Investigation of Petitions

The Board, in *TruServ Corp.,*[5] overruled *Supershuttle of Orange County,*[6] *Douglas-Randall,*[7] and *Liberty Fabrics.*[8] Although the union and the employer entered into a collective bargaining agreement resolving the pending unfair labor practice charge, the Board concluded that dismissing the pending decertification petition under the rationale of *Douglas-Randall* would unjustly deprive employees

---

[1] 347 NLRB No. 87, 180 LRRM 1057 (2006).
[2] 331 NLRB 1078, 167 LRRM 1039 (2001).
[3] *Marriott Hartford*, 180 LRRM at 1057.
[4] 347 NLRB No. 38, 179 LRRM 1366 (2006).
[5] 349 NLRB No. 23, 181 LRRM 1193 (2007).
[6] 330 NLRB 1016, 163 LRRM 1273 (2000).
[7] 320 NLRB 431, 151 LRRM 1281 (1995).
[8] 327 NLRB 38, 159 LRRM 1330 (1998).

of their Section 7 rights. The Board resurrected the precedent that existed prior to *Douglas-Randall*, holding that, "absent a finding of a violation of the Act, or an admission by the employer of such a violation, there is no basis for dismissing a petition based on a settlement of alleged but unproven unfair labor practices."[9] A settlement agreement cannot be construed as such an admission, unless such an admission is an express part of the agreement.[10] Absent such an express admission, there is no basis upon which to conclude that a petition has been "tainted" by unlawful conduct and, thus, no justification for dismissing a timely petition.

An employer is not estopped from filing a unit-clarification petition, even where the employer and union arbitrated the unit-clarification issue, if the employer's agreement with the union lacked language that would limit the employer's statutory right to file a petition with the Board following arbitration.[11]

G. The Election

2. Eligibility of Voters

The Board continues to follow the rule in *Red Arrow Freight Lines*,[12] that an employee who is on disability leave but who has neither resigned nor been affirmatively discharged as of the time of the election, is eligible to vote. The Board found that abandoning this bright-line rule would require it to evaluate medical evidence and potentially open new avenues of litigation beyond its traditional expertise.[13]

Employees who do not work sufficient hours (at least four hours per week) to qualify as regular part-time employees are not eligible to

---

[9] *TruServ*, 181 LRRM at 1193.

[10] TruServ Corp., 349 NLRB No. 23, 181 LRRM 1193 (2007) (citing Passavant Health Ctr., 278 NLRB 483, 121 LRRM 1230 (1986)); Island Spring, 278 NLRB 913, 121 LRRM 1280 (1986); Nu-Aimco, Inc., 306 NLRB 987, 139 LRRM 1393 (1992); Jefferson Hotel, 309 NLRB 705, 142 LRRM 1101 (1992).

[11] United States Postal Serv., 348 NLRB No. 3, 180 LRRM 1227 (2006).

[12] 278 NLRB 965, 121 LRRM 1257 (1986).

[13] Home Care Network, Inc., 347 NLRB No. 80, 180 LRRM 1044 (2006); Abbott Ambulance of Ill., 347 NLRB No. 82, 180 LRRM 1092 (2006); South Coast Hospice, Inc., 347 NLRB No. 81, 180 LRRM 1091 (2006).

vote.[14] But an employee who regularly worked three hours per week doing unit work was eligible to vote as a dual-function employee.[15]

Immigration status is not, however, relevant to an employee's voter eligibility.[16]

An employee who has been hired to work but decides not to work is, nevertheless, eligible to vote where it is not clear when he or she decided not to work.[17]

The Board found that a training "supervisor" who merely verified job application information, but lacked hiring authority, was not a statutory supervisor and, therefore, was eligible to vote.[18]

A delay of 17 hours in transmission of the *Excelsior* list that does not prejudice a party is not grounds to overrule an election.[19]

III. Pʀᴏᴄᴇᴅᴜʀᴇs ɪɴ Uɴꜰᴀɪʀ Lᴀʙᴏʀ Pʀᴀᴄᴛɪᴄᴇ Cᴀsᴇs

B. The Unfair Labor Practice Charge

1. Time for Filing

Section 10(b) provides that "no complaint shall issue based upon any unfair labor practice occurring more than six months prior to the filing of the charge *and the service of a copy thereof upon the person against whom such charge is made.*" The Board continues to interpret the italicized language as requiring service on the person charged, or that person's agent.[20] In *United Electrical Contractors Ass'n,*[21] the Board held that service of a charge upon a multi-employer association constituted timely service on all of its employer-members. The charge allegations directly related to the multi-employer association's express duties as the bargaining agent for its members. Under basic agency principles, recognized under federal law and the Fed-

---

[14]Angotti HealthCare Sys. Inc. dba St. Joseph Ambulance Serv., 346 NLRB No. 110, 180 LRRM 1015 (2006).

[15]Columbia Coll., 346 NLRB No. 69, 179 LRRM 1129 (2006).

[16]Concrete Form Walls, Inc., 346 NLRB No. 80, 179 LRRM 1193 (2006).

[17]*Columbia Coll.,* 346 NLRB No. 69, 179 LRRM 1129; *Home Care,* 347 NLRB No. 80, 180 LRRM 1044; *Abbott,* 347 NLRB No. 82, 180 LRRM 1092 ; *South Coast,* 347 NLRB No. 81, 180 LRRM 1091.

[18]J.C. Penney Corp., 347 NLRB No. 11, 179 LRRM 1372 (2006).

[19]Teamsters Local 705, 347 NLRB No. 42, 180 LRRM 1256 (2006).

[20]United Elec. Contractors Ass'n, 347 NLRB No. 1, slip op. at 2, 180 LRRM 1336 (2006).

[21]*Id.*

eral Rules of Civil Procedure, service on an authorized agent is effective service.[22]

The Board and courts continue to hold that the Section 10(b) period does not begin running until the aggrieved party receives actual or constructive notice of the conduct or action that constitutes an alleged unfair labor practice.[23] Such notice must be "clear and unequivocal."[24] The burden of showing such notice is on the party raising the Section 10(b) affirmative defense.[25] The Board continues to toll the Section 10(b) period in cases of intentional or fraudulent concealment of facts that would create sufficient notice of an unfair labor practice.[26]

The Board continues to apply the three-prong analysis of the *Redd-I*[27] "closely related" test to determine whether amendments to a complaint are time-barred under Section 10(b).[28] The Board considers: (1) whether the untimely allegations involve the same legal theory as the timely charges; (2) whether the untimely allegations arise from the same factual situation or sequence of events alleged in the timely charge; and (3) whether similar defenses would be raised.[29] In *Regency Grande Nursing & Rehabilitation Center*,[30] the Board found

---

[22]*Id.*

[23]Regency Grande Nursing & Rehab. Ctr., 347 NLRB No. 106 (2006); Masco Contractor Serv., Inc., 346 NLRB No. 40, 179 LRRM 1072 (2006); NLRB v. Crossroads Elec., Inc., 178 Fed. Appx. 528, 179 LRRM 2835 (6th Cir. 2006) (notice of incorporation of nonunion, alter ego corporation was insufficient to trigger notice to the union that this new company was committing unfair labor practice or violating the parties' contract by hiring workers not from union hiring hall).

[24]Vallow Floor Coverings, 335 NLRB 20, 169 LRRM 1306 (2001).

[25]Masco Contractor Serv., Inc., 346 NLRB No. 40, 179 LRRM 1072 (2006) (citing Leach Corp., 312 NLRB 990, 991, 145 LRRM 1080 (1993), *enforced*, 54 F.3d 802, 149 LRRM 2285 (D.C. Cir. 1995)).

[26]*Regency Grande.*, slip op. at 2 (rejecting respondent's §10(b) affirmative defense when the respondent "intentionally concealed its recognition" of the union). *See also* General Counsel Memo. GC 07-02, "Report on Case Developments April through August 2006" (concluding that deliberate secrecy on the part of an employer to keep its involvement in a decertification effort hidden from the union made it impossible for the union to have actual or constructive knowledge of the alleged unfair labor practices and tolled the §10(b) period).

[27]290 NLRB 1115, 129 LRRM 1229 (1988).

[28]*Regency Grande*, 347 NLRB No. 106 (untimely denial-of-wage-increase claim was not "closely related" to timely charge of improper recognition in the absence of majority support); Success Vill. Apartments, Inc., 347 NLRB No. 100 (2006); WGE Fed. Credit Union, 346 NLRB No. 87, 179 LRRM 1314 (2006) (supervisory threats of job reduction during union organizing campaign not "closely related" to timely §8(a)(3) discrimination allegation).

[29]*WGE Fed. Credit Union*, 346 NLRB No. 87, 179 LRRM 1314.

[30]347 NLRB No. 106 (2006).

merit in a Section 10(b) defense to an allegation which the General Counsel added at the hearing. The original, timely filed charge, alleged that the employer had unlawfully granted recognition to another union. The Board determined that the amended charge, alleging that the employer conditioned certain employees' receipt of wages and bonuses on employees' signing forms in support of another union, was not "closely related" to the original charge. The addition of a Section 8(a)(3) allegation based on the employer's entering into a contract containing a union-security clause was, however, "closely related" to the original charge and not barred by Section 10(b).

4. Settlement of Unfair Labor Practice Charges

During FY 2006, the office of the general counsel achieved a settlement rate of 96.7 percent in meritorious unfair labor practice cases.[31] The lead case outlining the factors that the Board will consider in accepting a settlement remains *Independent Stave*.[32] Although the Board gives consideration to the general counsel's position regarding a settlement agreement, the general counsel does not have veto power over settlements once the trial has begun. Rather, it is exclusively the Board's duty to decide whether to honor a settlement.[33] Where the parties' different understandings of the language of a settlement agreement warrants the conclusion that there was no meeting of the minds, the agreement will be set aside.[34]

In *TruServ Corp.*,[35] the Board held that a timely decertification petition can be processed despite a settlement agreement resolving alleged Section 8(a)(5) unfair labor practices when the petition was filed following the alleged unlawful act, but prior to the parties reaching a settlement agreement. The Board overruled its prior decisions in *Douglas-Randall Inc.*,[36] *Liberty Fabrics, Inc.*,[37] and *Supershut-*

---

[31]General Counsel Memo. GG 07-03, "Summary of Operations (Fiscal Year 2006)."

[32]287 NLRB 740, 127 LRRM 1204 (1987).

[33]Septix Waste, Inc., 346 NLRB No. 50, 179 LRRM 1073 (2006).

[34]Doubletree Guest Suites Santa Monica, 347 NLRB No. 72, 180 LRRM 1444 (2006) (citing Howard Elec. & Mech., 293 NLRB 472, 472 n.2, 490, 131 LRRM 1743 (1989), *enforced mem.*, 931 F.2d 63 (10th Cir. 1991)).

[35]349 NLRB No. 23, 181 LRRM 1193 (2007).

[36]320 NLRB 431, 151 LRRM 1281 (1995).

[37]327 NLRB 38, 159 LRRM 1330 (1998).

tle of Orange County,[38] restoring the doctrine enunciated in *Passavant Health Center*[39] and its progeny.

The union filed an unfair labor practice charge, alleging that TruServ had unilaterally changed employee healthcare and pension benefits and failed to make required payments. The region deferred the charge to arbitration under the *Collyer*[40] doctrine. Eight months later, a driver filed a petition to decertify the union. The regional director concluded that the decertification petition was blocked by the pending charges. The employer and the union commenced bargaining for a new contract two months after the decertification petition had been filed. The parties executed a new agreement shortly thereafter, and simultaneously executed a settlement under which the union agreed to withdraw the pending unfair labor practice charge and related grievance. The regional director then dismissed the decertification petition, relying on the Board's decision in *Douglas-Randall*.[41] The Board, however, reversed, concluding that there was no basis for finding that the decertification petition had been tainted by unlawful conduct and that the driver who filed the petition did not consent to its withdrawal.[42]

The Board ruled that "absent a finding of a violation of the Act, or an admission by the employer of such a violation, there is no basis for dismissing a petition based on a settlement of alleged but unproven unfair labor practices. To do so would unfairly give determinative weight to allegations of unlawful conduct and be in derogation of employee rights under Section 7 of the Act."[43] A decertification petition may not, however, be processed if: (a) the settlement precedes the filing of the petition; (b) the regional director finds that the employer instigated the petition or solicited the showing of interest; or (c) the settlement of the charge includes an agreement by the decertification petition to withdraw the petition.[44]

---

[38]330 NLRB 1016, 163 LRRM 1273 (2000).

[39]278 NLRB 483, 121 LRRM 1230 (1986).

[40]Collyer Insulated Wire, 192 NLRB 837, 77 LRRM 1931 (1971).

[41]320 NLRB 431, 151 LRRM 1281 (1995).

[42]TruServ Corp., 349 NLRB No. 23, 181 LRRM 1193 (2007).

[43]*Id.*, slip op. at 2.

[44]*Id.*, slip op. at 1.

a. Informal Settlements

The Board acknowledges the importance of finality when examining settlement agreements,[45] and continues to find that a party may violate the Act by making illusory settlement promises or executing an informal settlement agreement with no intention to comply with its terms.[46] Post-settlement conduct may support setting aside a settlement agreement.[47]

b. Formal Settlements

The Board will scrutinize the terms of the parties' formal settlement stipulation, and may reject the stipulation or remand it to the regional director when it finds a stipulation deficient or unclear.[48]

c. Non-Board Settlement Agreements

In *Dilling Mechanical Contractors,*[49] the Board overturned an administrative law judge's (ALJ's) sua sponte ruling that the general counsel had breached a non-Board settlement agreement and was, therefore, estopped from alleging that the employer had committed an unfair labor practice by entering into the agreement in bad faith. The Board ruled that, despite the general counsel's participation in the settlement negotiations, the general counsel was not a party to the non-Board settlement agreement. As a non-party, the general counsel could not breach the agreement. It followed, therefore, that the general counsel could not be estopped from pursuing an unfair labor practice charge based on the employer's alleged bad faith in entering into the settlement agreement.[50]

---

[45]Septix Waste, Inc., 346 NLRB No. 50, 179 LRRM 1073 (2006) (concluding that a settlement agreement barred subsequent unfair labor practice charges based on pre-settlement conduct even when the current allegations of unlawful pre-settlement conduct were not the subject of a charge at the time of the prior settlement).

[46]Dilling Mech. Contractors, 348 NLRB No. 6 (2006); Scripps Health, 347 NLRB No. 4, 179 LRRM 1253 (2006) (settlement agreement set aside based on party's post-settlement breach and unfair labor practice).

[47]*Id.; see also* Diamond Elec. Mfg. Corp., 346 NLRB No. 83, 179 LRRM 1262 (2006) (settlement agreement containing nonadmission clause may not, however, be used to shed light on parties' post-settlement conduct).

[48]Plumbers & Pipe Fitters Local 290 (Kinectic Sys., Inc.), 348 NLRB No. 61 (2006) (Board majority rejected formal settlement stipulation because agreement was deficient and unclear on procedures for challenging noncompliance).

[49]348 NLRB No. 6 (2006).

[50]*Id.*

5. The Complaint and the Answer

The Board continues to apply the three-prong analysis of the "closely related" test to determine whether amendments to a complaint are time-barred under Section 10(b).[51] The Board also continues to allow the general counsel broad discretion to determine whether to consolidate proceedings.[52]

The Board continues to enforce the requirement that answering parties responding to back-pay specifications must provide specific answers under Section 102.56 of the Board's Rules and Regulations. A general denial is not sufficient. Failure to provide specific answers will result in a finding that the allegations are deemed admitted under Section 102.56(c). For example, in *ELC Electric, Inc.*,[53] the Board granted partial summary judgment in favor of the general counsel when a respondent's answer did not set forth specific alternative figures or support for its assertions that the general counsel's figures were incorrect.

In *Heartland Industrial Partners*,[54] the Board reaffirmed that the allegations of a complaint must be related to the unfair labor practice charge.[55] In that case, a side letter agreement between the employer and the union governed union organizing at companies subsequently acquired by the employer. The agreement required the newly acquired companies to execute similar agreements with the union. The general counsel maintained that several provisions of the parties' alleged "hot cargo" agreement violated Section 8(e) of the Act.

The employer acquired two companies and caused each to execute an agreement with the union. The first acquired company executed an agreement with the union in January 2003, and the second in July 2003. The initial unfair labor practice charge was filed

---

[51]Regency Grande Nursing & Rehab. Ctr., 347 NLRB No. 106 (2006) (untimely denial-of-wage-increase claim was not "closely related" to timely charge of improper recognition in the absence of majority support); Success Vill. Apartments, Inc., 347 NLRB No. 100 (2006); WGE Fed. Credit Union, 346 NLRB No. 87, 179 LRRM 1314 (2006) (supervisory threats of job reduction during union organizing campaign not "closely related" to timely §8(a)(3) discrimination allegation).

[52]Sprain Brook Manor Nursing Home, LLC, 348 NLRB No. 84 (2006).

[53]348 NLRB No. 17 (2006).

[54]348 NLRB No. 72, 180 LRRM 1473 (2006).

[55]*Id.* (quoting NLRB v. Fan Milling Co., 360 U.S. 301, 44 LRRM 2236 (1959) ("[A] complaint alleging violations not specifically alleged in the charge is proper if the matters asserted in the complaint 'are related to those alleged in the charge and...grow out of them...' ")).

on August 6, 2003, alleging that the original agreement between the employer and the union had been reaffirmed by the January 2003 agreement. An amended charge filed in September 2004 generally asserted that the agreement between the employer and the union was reaffirmed each time a newly acquired company was required to execute a similar agreement. The Board rejected the argument that the complaint was time-barred under Section 10(b).

The Board held that "the original charge [was] timely with respect to the [second company's] agreement entered into in July 2003, even though the charge [did] not allege that [the] agreement was unlawful."[56] The Board explained that the second company's agreement, referenced in the complaint, was "sufficiently related" to the first company's agreement alleged in the original charge. It reasoned that: (1) the original charge agreement clearly informed the respondents that the original agreement between the employer and the union was being challenged under Section 8(e); (2) there was no allegation or evidence of prejudice; and (3) the employer and the union would raise the same defenses.[57]

9. Compliance Procedures

In September 2006, the general counsel announced procedural changes in compliance procedures for election cases involving technical violations of Section 8(a)(5) following the certification of an exclusive bargaining representative.[58] The revisions are designed to expedite the processing of these cases. Historically, voluntary compliance with Board orders finding Section 8(a)(5) violations in these cases has been extremely rare.

Under the new procedures, the regional director will immediately contact the employer's representative by phone or email to determine whether there will be compliance after receiving the Board's technical Section 8(a)(5) decision. Absent compliance, the region will immediately refer the case to the Board's appellate court branch for court enforcement. The regional office is expected to make this referral within seven calendar days following receipt of the Board's order. This marks a significant shortening of the 30-day period that the regions customarily use.

---

[56] *Id.*, slip op. at 2.
[57] *Id.* at 2–3.
[58] General Counsel Memo. GC 06-07, "Procedural Initiatives in Election Cases."

10. Applicability of the Equal Access to Justice Act

In *Raley's and Independent Drug Clerks Ass'n,*[59] the Board held that the Equal Access to Justice Act (EAJA) provides the sole mechanism for asserting claims for attorney fees against the general counsel. Following the ALJ's dismissal of most of the complaint allegations (i.e., prior to a final Board decision), the respondents asserted a claim for attorney fees against the general counsel. Respondents relied upon the Board's "inherent authority," citing *Tiidee Products,*[60] and asserted that the general counsel had abused the trial process and pursued frivolous theories of liability.

The ALJ rejected the request for fees in *Raley's,* and the Board affirmed. In *Tiidee Products,* the Board cited its inherent authority to control its proceedings, awarding attorney fees to a union where an employer had engaged in "frivolous" litigation. Under the *Tiidee Products* doctrine, the Board exercises its inherent authority to order one private party to pay sanctions to another private party. This is readily distinguishable from requiring the United States to pay attorney fees to a private party. The sovereign immunity of the United States deprives the Board of any "inherent authority" to issue sanctions against the general counsel. Although the EAJA constitutes an express waiver of U.S. sovereign immunity, it provides "the only available avenue for Respondents to assert claims for attorney fees against the General Counsel" and must be construed strictly in favor of the government.[61] Both the EAJA and the Board's implementing rules provide that an eligible party may not apply for attorney fees until the Board has issued a final decision.[62] Accordingly, parties may not seek attorney fees until the Board issues its final decision in a case, and then only pursuant to EAJA's other conditions.

---

[59]348 NLRB No. 25 (2006).

[60]194 NLRB 1234, 79 LRRM 1175 (1972), *enforced,* 502 F.2d 349, 87 LRRM 2255 (D.C. Cir. 1974).

[61]*Raley's,* 348 NLRB No. 25, slip op. at 8 (2006); *see also* Irwin Indus., 325 NLRB 796, 158 LRRM 1218 (1998) (the Board rejected a respondent employer's claim for attorney fees against charging party union, finding that §10(c) of the Act did not authorize an award of attorney fees against any party not named in the complaint as a respondent); *Cf.* Lake Holiday Manor, 325 NLRB 469, 157 LRRM 1209 (1998) (the Board relied on inherent power to award attorney fees against respondent employer for engaging in "bad faith" litigation in favor of union).

[62]*Id.* (citing 5 U.S.C. §504(a)(2) and NLRB Rules and Regulations §§102.143–155).

IV. Procedures Applicable to All Cases

C. Subpoenas

In *Wal-Mart Stores, Inc.*,[63] the Board held that the respondent had waived any attorney-client privilege with respect to the production of certain documents and files that had been subpoenaed by the general counsel. During the underlying unfair labor practice hearing, the general counsel had served a subpoena duces tecum for certain documents and files, which the respondent moved to quash on grounds of attorney-client privilege. The ALJ granted the motion to quash. While the case was pending at the Board, the respondent filed a motion to supplement the record, advising that it had subsequently produced the previously subpoenaed documents pursuant to a court order in an unrelated state court proceeding. The Board remanded the proceeding to the ALJ to reopen the record and receive relevant evidence, to make findings, and to take further appropriate action, noting that, "[o]nce waived, the attorney-client privilege is lost in all forums for proceedings running concurrent with or after the waiver occurs."[64]

---

[63]348 NLRB No. 46 (2006).
[64]*Id.*, slip op. at 6.

Chapter 32

NLRB ORDERS AND REMEDIES

III. Orders and Remedies in Complaint Cases (Section 10)

A. Provisional Remedies

1. General Principles

a. Discretionary Injunctions Under Section 10(j)

(2) The Board's Utilization of Section 10(j)

In FY 2006, the Board authorized 10(j) relief in 25 cases, and 22 cases were filed in various courts.[1] In the end-of-term report on utilization of Section 10(j) released in January 2006, the general counsel reviewed the Agency's Section 10(j) activity between June 1, 2001 and December 31, 2005.[2]

(3) Judicial Standards

Recently, in *Gold v. State Plaza, Inc.*,[3] the district court analyzed the differences between injunctions requested under Section 10(j) and 10(*l*) and refused to apply the reasonable cause standard to Section 10(j) injunctions. The district court was persuaded by both the plain reading of the statute as well as the analysis of other courts that the application of the traditional four-pronged test for injunctive relief was the appropriate standard to follow.

---

[1] *See* Summary of Operations for Fiscal Year 2006, NLRB Gen. Counsel Memo. No. 07-03, and Submission of Section 10(j) Cases to the Division of Advice, NLRB Gen. Counsel Memo. No. 07-01, *available at www.nlrb.gov.*

[2] NLRB Gen. Counsel Memo. No. 06-02, *available at www.nlrb.gov.*

[3] 435 F. Supp. 2d 110, 179 LRRM 3240 (D.D.C. 2006).

(5) Delay in Filing Petition

The courts continue to consider the issue of delay in evaluating the appropriateness of injunctive relief under Section 10(j).[4]

B. Final Orders and Remedies

1. Final Orders and Remedies for Employer Misconduct

a. Section 8(a) (1) Violations

In remedying the effects of an unlawful no-solicitation policy, the Board has not only ordered an employer to remove the unlawful rule from its employee handbook, but also to distribute new handbooks without the unlawful rule as well as distribute a notice explicitly informing employees of their right to solicit in nonwork areas and during nonwork time.[5]

The Board has yet to expand the standard notice posting requirement to include Internet posting.[6] It has noted, however, that electronic posting may be appropriate if a "concrete fact pattern" warrants this otherwise "unprecedented step."[7]

c. Sections 8(a)(3) and (4) Violations

(1) In General

In *Nordstrom, Inc.*,[8] the Board found it unnecessary to consider a charging party's request that the employer explicitly be ordered to expunge references of unlawful Section 8(a)(3) activity from its electronic records and litigation files because the "Respondent does not contest the application of the order to its electronic records."

---

[4]Overstreet v. El Paso Elec. Co., 176 Fed. Appx. 607, No. 05-51544 (5th Cir. 2006). *See also* GoNannies, Inc. v. GoAuPair.com, Inc., 464 F. Supp. 2d 603 (N.D. Tex. 2006).

[5]Winkle Bus Co., 347 NLRB No. 108, 180 LRRM 1369 (2006).

[6]National Grid USA Serv. Co., 348 NLRB No. 88, 181 LRRM 1254 (2006) (Board declined sua sponte to order posting of notice on employer's Internet website because no record evidence that respondent "customarily communicates" with its employees electronically); Nordstrom, Inc., 347 NLRB No. 28, 180 LRRM 1028 (2006) (no supporting evidence presented at the hearing that respondent "customarily communicates" with its employees via the intranet).

[7]Nordstrom, Inc., 347 NLRB No. 28, slip op. at 1 (2006).

[8]*Id.*

d.   Section 8(a)(5) Violations

(1) In General

In *Agri Processor Co.*,[9] the Board issued a bargaining order in this test of certification case where the employer contended that certain of its employees had not been eligible to vote because they were undocumented aliens. The Board noted that "unless and until the employees are declared to be illegal and are discharged and/or deported, they remain employees" lawfully entitled to vote.

(2) Duration of Bargaining Order

In determining whether to extend the certification year, the Board continues to consider factors such as the nature of the violations and their impact on the bargaining process, the extent of bargaining, and the union's conduct during the negotiations.[10]

(5) Remedies for Particular Kinds of Section 8(a)(5) Violations

(b) Supplying Information. In *United Electrical Contractors Ass'n*,[11] where a multi-employer association and its members failed and delayed to provide necessary information requested by the union, the Board extended the certification year for a "reasonable period of time" instead of a full year because of delay in processing the case. In refusing to order that the notices be sent to all unit employees employed by each employer-member over an 11-year period, the Board took into account the "practical considerations relating to the parties involved" concluding that such a requirement would be "unduly burdensome."

In *Pan American Grain Co.*,[12] the Board issued a broad remedial order based, in part, on the employer's repeated disregard for its obligation to provide relevant information requested by the union.

(c) Bargaining Orders Without Certification. (i) Where the union can show a majority. The Board continues to recognize the extraordinary nature of a *Gissel* bargaining order and that it is "to be used only in circumstances where it is unlikely that the atmosphere can

---

[9]347 NLRB No. 107, 180 LRRM 1222 (2006).

[10]Mercy, Inc. dba Am. Med. Response, 346 NLRB No. 88, 179 LRRM 1205 (2006) (only three-month extension ordered as record failed to establish that 10-month delay in beginning bargaining was attributable to employer).

[11]347 NLRB No. 1, 180 LRRM 1336 (2006).

[12]346 NLRB No. 21, 179 LRRM 1085 (2005).

be cleansed by traditional remedies."[13] Accordingly, the Board continues to issue category II *Gissel* bargaining orders where the employer's conduct, while less pervasive, still undermines majority support and impedes the election process.[14] However, the Board recognizes that delays in the processing of cases may render a *Gissel* bargaining order unenforceable so instead it may order a second election as an alternative remedy.[15]

In *Concrete Form Walls, Inc.*,[16] the Board issued a *Gissel* bargaining order where the employer made unsupported claims that certain of its employees were not entitled to vote and could be properly discharged because they were undocumented aliens with no legal right to work. In dismissing its defense, the Board noted that the employer's reliance on *Hoffman Plastics*[17] was misplaced, and that undocumented workers are nonetheless employees within the statutory definition of Section 2(3) of the Act.

(h) Remedies Against Successor to Bargaining Obligation. In *Cadillac Asphalt Paving* and its alter ego or successor, *Cadillac Asphalt LLC*,[18] the Board declined to find an alter ego relationship, and instead found the successor employer to be a "perfectly clear" successor who was not privileged to establish the initial terms and conditions of employment without first bargaining with the union.

Similarly, the Board continues to find that a successor employer's privilege to set the initial terms and conditions of employment can also be lost through its own unlawful conduct.[19]

---

[13]Diamond Elec. Mfg. Co., 346 NLRB No. 83, slip op. at 9, 179 LRRM 1262 (2006) (single post-settlement violation insufficient to warrant *Gissel* order). *See also* Dairyland USA Corp., 347 NLRB No. 30, 180 LRRM 1074 (2006) (no *Gissel* order where employer engaged in pattern of unlawful assistance to union sufficient to taint union's majority).

[14]Evergreen Am. Corp., 348 NLRB No. 12, 181 LRRM 1288 (2006).

[15]Smithfield Foods, Inc., 347 NLRB No. 109 (2006) (despite repeated and pervasive unfair labor practices, second election ordered because of Board's long and unjustified delay). *See also* Cogburn Health Ctr. v. NLRB, 437 F.3d 1266, 179 LRRM 2065 (D.C. Cir. 2006) (District of Columbia Circuit refused to enforce the Board's *Gissel* bargaining order because of "changed circumstances" including significant employee and management turnover over a 10-year period).

[16]346 NLRB No. 80, 179 LRRM 1193 (2006) (employer discharged four employees because they voted in election).

[17]Hoffman Plastic Compounds, Inc. v. NLRB, 535 U.S. 137, 169 LRRM 2769 (2002).

[18]349 NLRB No. 5, 181 LRRM 1105 (2007).

[19]JLL Rest., Inc. dba Smoke House Rest., 347 NLRB No. 16, 180 LRRM 1537 (2006).

(i) Withdrawal of Recognition. In addition to ordering an affirmative bargaining order for an unlawful withdrawal of recognition, the Board has found it appropriate to order an employer to permit a union to post union notices on employee bulletin boards, and to provide the union with up-to-date lists of bargaining unit members' names and addresses.[20] However, the Board has declined to order a multi-employer association to mail the notice to all former unit employees when the requirement would be unduly burdensome.[21]

2. Special Remedial Problems Involving Employers

a. Flagrant Violations

Where an employer has been found to have committed repeated and pervasive unfair labor practices, the Board continues to resort to "extraordinary" remedies to effectuate the remedial purposes of the act including reading the notice to employees in their native language if necessary.[22] In *Pan American Grain Co.,*[23] where the employer demonstrated a "proclivity to violate the Act," the Board issued a broad remedial order requiring the employer to not only cease and desist from refusing to provide information, but from violating the Act "in any other manner."

In *Beverly Health & Rehabilitation Services, Inc. (Beverly V),*[24] the Board issued a broad corporate-wide cease-and-desist order based on the prominent roles of corporate officials in committing the unfair labor practices. The Board also ordered two versions of the notices to employees: One to be posted at the facility where the unlawful conduct occurred and at the managerial offices involved, and the other to be posted nationwide at all of the employer's remaining facilities. Noting four previous cases involving this employer, the

---

[20]Highlands Hosp. Corp., Inc. dba Highlands Reg'l Med. Ctr., 347 NLRB No. 120, 180 LRRM 1414 (2006).

[21]Expert Elec., Inc., 347 NLRB No. 2, 180 LRRM 1341 (2006) (first unfair labor practice occurred more than seven years earlier).

[22]*See, e.g.,* Smithfield Foods, Inc., 347 NLRB No. 109, 181 LRRM 1069 (2006) (ordering that notice be posted, mailed to employees, and read to employees in both English and Spanish); *but see* Chinese Daily News, 346 NLRB No. 81, 179 LRRM 1182 (2006) (finding no need to read notice to employees or translate administrative decision into Chinese language).

[23]346 NLRB No. 21, 179 LRRM 1085 (2005).

[24]346 NLRB No. 111, 179 LRRM 1284 (2006). *See also* Beverly Health & Rehab. Servs., Inc., (Beverly IV), 335 NLRB 635, 171 LRRM 1472 (2001), *enforced in pertinent part,* 317 F.3d 316 (D.C. Cir. 2003) (broad corporate-wide cease-and-desist order).

Board remarked that the "repetition of this now-familiar pattern of unlawful actions on the part of corporate officials warrants a finding that the Respondent continues to have a proclivity to violate the Act, and that its widespread misconduct demonstrates a general disregard for its employees' Section 7 rights."[25]

b. Litigation Costs, Attorneys' Fees, and Union Expenses

In assessing defenses, the Board continues to adhere to a general rule that only "truly frivolous litigation" warrants the extraordinary remedy of shifting the costs of litigation to the employer.[26] However in *Beverly Health & Rehabilitation Services, Inc. (Beverly V)*,[27] the Board declined to award litigation expenses incurred to establish that the respondent was a single employer even though the employer's defense had been rejected by the Board in four other cases. While the Board had put the employer on notice in *Beverly IV* that further litigation on this defense would not be warranted, *Beverly IV* had not yet issued at the time *Beverly V* was being litigated.[28]

The Board continues to hold an employer responsible for the reimbursement of bargaining expenses to a union brought about because of an employer's bad faith in negotiations.[29]

c. Imposing Remedial Order on Successor to Wrongdoer

Under long standing precedent, a *Golden State*[30] successor can be ordered to remedy the unfair labor practices of a predecessor employer.[31] However, the Board continues to decline finding *Golden State* successorship when a successor cannot effectively protect itself

---

[25] *Beverly Health (Beverly V)*, 346 NLRB No. 111, slip op. at 14.

[26] John Kopp and Natalie Kopp dba N&J Constr., 348 NLRB No. 7, 180 LRRM 1222 (2006) (no expenses awarded as employer had no history of violations, nor bad faith in its actions leading to litigation or in the conduct of litigation); Agri Processor Co., Inc., 347 NLRB No. 107, 180 LRRM 1222 (2006) (Board affirms without comment ALJ's finding that award of legal expenses not justified as expenses were nominal).

[27] 346 NLRB No. 111, 179 LRRM 1284 (2006).

[28] *Id.*, slip op. at 14, (referring to "Beverly IV," 335 NLRB 635, 171 LRRM 1472 (2001), *enforced in part*, 317 F.3d 316 (D.C. Cir. 2003)).

[29] Dish Network Serv. Corp., 347 NLRB No. 69, 180 LRRM 1496 (2006) (union expenses include lost wages to employees who attended the negotiations).

[30] Golden State Bottling Co. v. NLRB, 414 U.S. 168, 84 LRRM 2839 (1973).

[31] *See, e.g.*, Dearborn Gage Co., 346 NLRB No. 71, 179 LRRM 1250 (2006) (successor employer held jointly and severally liable for failure of predecessor to notify employees of plant closing and failure to bargain over effects of plant closing; successor employer found not to be a "perfectly clear" successor).

during the transactional process from its predecessor's potential unfair labor practice liability.[32]

e. Imposing Remedial Order by Piercing the Corporate Veil [New Topic]

In *Carpenters Local 2471 v. NLRB*,[33] the District of Columbia Circuit remanded that portion of the case involving the Board's failure to pierce the corporate veil of the employer as had been recommended by the administrative law judge. The court chastised the Board for failing to cite evidence sufficient to support its findings as well as failing to explain why it disregarded conflicting record evidence.

3. Final Orders and Remedies for Union Misconduct

a. Sections 8(b)(1)(A) and (B) Violations

The Board continues to issue cease-and-desist-orders in cases involving threats of physical violence directed at union members.[34]

b. Section 8(b)(2) Violations

(1) General Principles

In *Plumbers & Pipe Fitters Local 420 (Carrier Corp.)*,[35] the Board found that the union had violated Section 8(b)(2) when its agent gave a negative employment reference concerning a member, in response to an inquiry from a signatory employer with whom it did not have an exclusive hiring hall arrangement. At the time, the member was appealing his expulsion and fines from the union for previously working for a nonsignatory employer. Finding that the union had caused the employer not to hire the individual, the Board ordered the union to notify the employer that it had no objections

---

[32]Lebanite Corp., 346 NLRB No. 72, 179 LRRM 1166 (2006) (successor could not have structured lease from predecessor to protect itself in a meaningful way as predecessor's unfair labor practice liability was substantially greater than amount of rental payments). *Cf.* JLL Rest., Inc. dba Smoke House Rest., 347 NLRB No. 16, 180 LRRM 1537 (2006) (finding successor liable for predecessor's unlawful conduct where notice posting and mailing would not impose an undue hardship).

[33]Nos. 05-1416, 06-1098, 2007 WL 776859, 181 LRRM 2609 (D.C. Cir. Mar. 16, 2007), *enforcing in part and remanding in relevant part*, A.J. Mech., Inc., 345 NLRB No. 22, 178 LRRM 1093 (2005).

[34]Food & Commercial Workers Local 7R (Conagra Foods, Inc., dba Longmont Foods), 347 NLRB No. 97, 180 LRRM 1466 (2006) (union organizer's threat to physically assault member because of her intraunion activities found coercive).

[35]347 NLRB No. 53, 180 LRRM 1015 (2006).

to the individual's hiring and to make the individual whole for the employer's failure to hire.

e. Section 8(b)(4) Violations

The standard remedy in Section 8(b)(4) cases continues to be a cease-and-desist order, a requirement to post notices at union offices and meeting halls, and a requirement to provide extra copies of signed notices for voluntary postings by the employers involved.[36] Additionally, the Board can require that copies of the notice be mailed at the union's expense to all of its members.[37]

---

[36]Sheet Metal Workers Local 7 (Andy J. Egan Co.), 345 NLRB No. 119, 178 LRRM 1321 (2006).

[37]Laborers E. Region Org. Fund (Ranches at Mt. Sinai), 346 NLRB No. 105, 180 LRRM 1109 (2006).

Chapter 33

JUDICIAL REVIEW AND ENFORCEMENT

I. INTRODUCTION

The district courts continue to exercise *Leedom* jurisdiction in very limited circumstances,[1] and are reluctant to review decisions by the general counsel to not issue an unfair labor practice complaint.[2]

II. APPELLATE REVIEW AND ENFORCEMENT

A. Board's Rulings Subject to Review

1. Parties Entitled to Enforcement and Review

The district courts continue to hold that a party's appeal must be based upon an adverse effect or cognizable injury.[3]

B. Scope of Review

1. Questions of Fact

The First,[4] Second,[5] Sixth,[6] and District of Columbia[7] Circuits continue to grant substantial deference to an administrative law judge's (ALJ's) credibility findings.

---

[1]Amerco v. NLRB, 458 F.3d 883, 888–90, 180 LRRM 2165 (9th Cir. 2006) (holding that *Leedom* jurisdiction does not apply "outside the context of Section 9 actions or other situations in which meaningful judicial review is unavailable"); Government Employees Local 2150 (AFGE), 453 F.3d 500, 501, 179 LRRM 3147 (D.C. Cir. 2006).

[2]New England Health Care Employees Dist. 1199 v. NLRB, 448 F.3d 189, 179 LRRM 2577 (2d Cir. 2006).

[3]Food & Commercial Workers Local 204 v. NLRB, 447 F.3d 821, 826–27, 179 LRRM 2708 (D.C. Cir. 2006) (holding that employer's attorneys were not aggrieved parties and, therefore, lacked standing to pursue appeal).

[4]NLRB v. Hotel Employees & Rest. Employees, 446 F.3d 200 (1st Cir. 2006).

[5]Gaetano & Assocs., Inc. v. NLRB, 183 Fed. Appx. 17 (2d Cir. May 16, 2006) (stating that the court will accept an ALJ's credibility determinations unless the testimony is "incredible or flatly contradicted by undisputed documentary testimony").

[6]Neoprene Craftsmen Local 788 v. NLRB, 187 Fed. Appx. 477 (6th Cir. June 27, 2006).

[7]Cogburn Health Ctr., Inc. v. NLRB, 437 F.3d 1266 (D.C. Cir. 2006).

III. DIRECT REVIEW AND ENFORCEMENT

B. Review of Unfair Labor Practice Proceedings

The circuit courts continue to follow *Myers* in determining whether review of a Board decision may occur prior to issuance of a final Board order.[8]

---

[8]Amerco v. NLRB, 458 F.3d 883, 890 (9th Cir. 2006) ("Each of our sister circuits that has considered this question has answered it as we do, holding that [*Kyne*] and [*Fay v. Douds*] are inapplicable to Section 10 unfair labor practice hearings.").

TABLE OF CASES

Cases are referenced to Supplement chapter and footnote number(s): e.g., *13:* 13, 17 indicates the case is cited in Supplement Chapter 13, at footnotes 13 and 17. Union locals and other subdivisions are included with the parent unions, which are sorted by popular name (e.g., Teamsters, not International Brotherhood of Teamsters). Entries beginning with numerals are alphabetized as if spelled out. Alphabetization is letter-by-letter (e.g., "Novak" precedes "Nova Plumbing").

301